D1600554

AMERICAN DESERTER

GENERAL EISENHOWER AND THE EXECUTION OF SLOVIK CASE.

CHARLES WHITING

ESKDALE   PUBLISHING

British Library Cataloguing in Publication Data:

A catalogue record for this book is available
from the British Library

Copyright © Charles Whiting 2005

ISBN   0-9538677-3-0

First published in the UK in 2005 by

Eskdale   Publishing
Eskdale House
46 St Olaves Rd
York
England
YO30 7AL

BOOKS PUBLISHED BY ESKDALE PUBLISHING

CHARLES WHITING - AMERICAN HERO
The Life and Death of Audie Murphy
Isbn 0953867706
CHARLES WHITING - AMERICAN EAGLES
The 101st Airborne's Assault on Fortress Europe 1944/45
Isbn 0953867722
CARL SHILLETO - THE FIGHTING FIFTY-SECOND RECCE.
The 52nd (Lowland) Divisional Reconnaissance Regiment RAC in
North-west Europe, September 1944 - March 1946
Isbn 0953867714

FORTHCOMING IN 2005

CHARLES WHITING - HITLER'S DEFEAT
The War in Europe. April-May 1945.
Isbn 0953867773
CHARLES WHITING - HITLER'S WARRIORS
The Final Battle of Hitler's Private Bodyguard, 1944-45
Isbn 0953867765

ACKNOWLEDGMENTS

I would like to thank in the US - Mr. Tom Dickinson, Mr S Trickler III, Barney Calka, Mr Kehetan (The Macombe Daily), UK - Mr Carl Shilleto, Hunter Downs, Julian Whiting, Germany - Herr Gerhard Kristan and Herr Prohuber and Dr Paul Maquet from Belgium for their kind assistance with this book

Charles Whiting
York, England

CONTENTS

BOOK ONE: 17
ONE: Eddie and Ike 18
TWO: Hard Luck Division 49
THREE: The Death Factory 75
FOUR: Under Sentence of Death 91
FIVE: Fall Guy 113
BOOK TWO 137
ONE: The Battle 137
TWO: The Decision 161
THREE: Execution 179
Afterword 195
Envoi 219
Footnotes 225
Bibliography 229
Index 231

INTRODUCTION

The Coward

"I could not look on Death, which being known

Men led me to him, blindfold and alone."

Rudyard Kipling

By the evening of Thursday, 9th July 1987, it was clear that they had lost the body.

The remains in reality, for the body had long since perished and withered to bones in the forty years or so since it had been buried, had been dug up on the previous Wednesday in Eastern France, been transported to Paris-Orly and had been scheduled to arrive at Detroit Metropolitan Airport on Thursday evening. It had been agreed that a change would take place at New York's Kennedy and then onto Detroit by TWA's Flight 769. But, it had not arrived.

Now as the nation's press and the handful of mourners waited anxiously, ready to receive America's best known soldier of WWII, the harassed officials of Transworld checked the flight computer manifest time and time again. After all it wasn't every day that they lost a body.

The display indicated that the remains had been certainly placed on the plane. French customs' formalities and the like had ensured that every detail had been registered on the computer. But thereafter they had disappeared, seemingly without trace. As a worried Richard Huff, TWA's flight agent, told the reporter from the *Washington Post*: ' We've gone through pretty much all the options,' adding', if the body had been unloaded from the plane at Kennedy by some chance, it might be in New York. 'He had frowned and concluded, while the newspaperman scribbled away and the cameras clicked, 'But unfortunately New York is a large place ... there are lots of places to check there. 'And that for the time being was all that worried Huff was prepared to say.

Huff was not the only worried man at Detroit Metropolitan last Thursday evening. Bernard B. Calka, another Polish-American like the missing dead man, was, too.

After all he had been waiting for this day for over six years. The retired WWII veteran and firefighter had spent over five thousand dollars of his own cash and a lot of time and heartache, fighting US officialdom to have the body released and returned to a homeland that he had last seen in the summer of 1944. As Calka, a humble decent man, told the waiting reporters, eager for a human interest story. 'I realise this is history, and that. But, he is an American and I'm an American; he's Catholic and I'm a Catholic and, of course, he was Polish and I'm Polish. 'As the ex-fire fighter from Michigan informed the reporter of the *Boston Globe*.' All I wanted was to bring home the remains of a Polish kid and to see he was buried with human dignity, the kind he never experienced in his troubled life and in death. 'He added somewhat surprisingly for an ex-military policeman, who had once guarded military murderers, rapists, deserters and the like, he deserved punishment, but not the firing squad...a strong America must never be afraid to forgive.'

Here and there were nods from the assembled camera crews and journalists. After all, all of them directly or indirectly, had been involved in the Vietnam War.

They knew that their America had fought a new kind of war for the USA: One that could not be seen in terms of black white like World War Two-good against evil. The 20th century had grown up. America and Americans were becoming more tolerant of those who had not been able to live up to the standards of conduct and bravery shown by American men in the old wars.

Bernard Calka seemed able to read the younger men's minds. He related that he himself had written to President Regan for a pardon for the missing man only the week before. He'd asked the President, if in the present wave of pardons for deserters, draft dodgers connected with Vietnam, it wasn't too much to ask for this blot against a Polish kid, who from his teenage days had been in trouble, to be given its final rest.

But then the strange syntax was forgotten as the good news began to come in. Dwayne Swindle TWA, station manager in Detroit, suddenly informed the press the remains had been found. They had been loaded on TWA flight 803 and had wound up in San Francisco. The airport workers had assumed the remains would be in a coffin, not a box. 'He smiled, added, as if this was just another case of a passenger's misplaced valise? It's just a matter of lost luggage. We've misplaced the thing somewhere.'

At Six thirty that night the 'thing', now draped in 'Old Glory', was on its way to Detroit. The long awaited ceremony could finally go ahead....

Eddie and Antoinette on their wedding day 1943

On the following Saturday, watched by more newspaper people than mourners, perspiring under a burning hot July sun, the casket was interred. Due to protests, understandable protests under the circumstances, by the local chapter of Veterans of Foreign

Wars, the Stars and Stripes flag had been removed from the casket. Now it was adorned with mini-flags, which could give no offence, and red and white and blue flowers. Solemnly, after a service in Polish and English, the casket was lowered next to the body of the dead man's wife Antoinette, at Woodmere Cemetery in Dearborn, where he had once worked in a plumbing shop in the mid-40's.

The handful of mourners were mostly in tears. His sister Margaret Sobolewski, aged 70, who laid a wreath on the casket, said sadly, I'm glad my brother is here. It's been on my mind for a long time. I'm happy it's finally over with. The other sister, Anna Kadlubowski sobbed.

Others were angry as well as sad. The dead man's old buddy of 1944, John Tankey, now pushing 70, wearing his Purple Heart medal, told the press, 'They wanted to make an example out of somebody, and Eddie was it.'

Mrs Slovik, living under assumed name, refused war widower's pensions by the US Government

Another World War II veteran, who had never known the dead man in life, but had become a passionate advocate for him since then, Italo-American, Robert 'Rocky' Definis, snorted to the newspapermen, 'His *crime* was that he couldn't kill anyone and that is one of the Ten Commandments.' After campaigning for the dead man for thirteen years, he still felt he was getting a 'raw deal'.

Then it was over. Soon a headstone, modest of course, for these people were humble, poor folk, would be placed over his grave. Ironically it would read: *'HONOR AND JUSTICE PREVAILED'.*

One man, who was not present that day, though he had done more than anyone to bring about this supposedly successful conclusion, would have undoubtedly have laughed cynically at that statement. Thirty of so years before, he had mused aloud, 'why had I bothered to travel so far, to ask so many questions, all to know one dishonoured Polack private from Detroit?.... Nobody knew about the tragedy, he had been a secret....And I knew that his experience is the most unusual of any citizen who had borne arms for the United States within my lifetime....(He) was killed by the United States for the crime of refusing to serve the United States with a rifle and a bayonet, for desertion to avoid the hazardous duty of close combat, and the only American to be executed for such an offence.

But, although the man, William Bradford Huie, who had written that, had died the year before, still believing it was his duty to 'write and upset and proud of it because they (i.e. the establishment) needed it', the secret he had first brought to light in 1954 still rumbled on. Honour and Justice had not yet prevailed....

Slovik before desertion

But who was he, this dead Polish-American, whose secret Huie had been the first to discover and which had aroused so much passion, debate and fury four decades before? Even today, fifty-seven years after the event, it is still no different. The Polish-

American's case can still arouse public anger on both side of the fence: between those who feel a great injustice was done in 1945 and those who maintain the contrary.

He was a Polish-American kid born on the wrong side of the tracks. Raised during the depression he had a weakness for running with the wrong crowd. His mother was an alcoholic; his father violent. One brother went to jail early. If that wasn't bad enough the pale, skinny sandy-haired kid was born with badly bowed legs. Several times his legs were broken in unsuccessful attempts to straighten them and for most of his youth he walked with pain. At that time, with that background, his parents failing to integrate and speaking a mixture of Polish and English, one could say the prognosis for Eddie Slovik, for that was the kid's name, was bad. But, then again, there were many like him who didn't go wrong and became law-abiding upstanding citizens.

Not Eddie. According to Huie, his apologist as well as biographer, Eddie always maintained that he had, had his first brush with the law at the age of 12 when he stole a loaf of bread.

Barney Calka (Left) and Mitch Kehetian (Right)

In August 1944, private Slovik landed on the now quiet 'Bloody Omaha'.
Two month earlier, his future commanding officer General 'Dutch' Cota had urged his stalled men forward with the cry that only 'dead men are staying on this beach'. But that was over now. Cota's 28th Division, to which Slovik was heading as a reluctant replacement, was already fighting on the River Seine. In the event Slovik reached the Seine and made contact with his 'outfit'. According to his own statement he came under some shelling and that was the end of his fighting career.
It was then that Eddie Slovik decided to make his separate peace with Hitler's third Reich. As he recorded that night at Elbeuf on the Seine, I was so scared, nerves (sic)

and trembling that at the time the other replacements moved out I couldn't move. I stayed there (sic) in my foxhole till it was quite (sic) and I was able to move.'

But Eddie didn't move forward, but backwards. He deserted for the first time. On October 8th, Slovik and the man who had welcomed his body back to Dearborn, Tankey, his fellow deserter, turned up again at the 28th Infantry Division, now on the Belgo-German border. Here they reported and instead of being thrust into the divisional stockade, they were assigned to company G,109th Infantry Regiment. Now not too many questions were being asked. General Cota needed 'bodies'. He was running out of riflemen. The 28th Division had turned out to be an unlucky division. The men were calling it the 'Bloody Bucket' , after it's blood-red bucket-shaped divisional patch. Its losses were high.

Tankey went off and became a good soldier, being wounded and invalided home in the process. Not Eddie. The ex-con had a plan which he believed would keep him out of combat and allow him to survive the war. Just after reporting to his company commander, he approached him again and said he was 'too scared', ' too nervous' to be a rifleman in the line .Then he asked ,' If I leave now, will it be desertion?'

It would. But Slovik didn't mind. He walked away and next day turned up again to hand in a note which stated 'I'll run away again if I have to go out their (sic).'

Slovik was taking a calculated risk. He didn't believe the army would shoot deserters. Not the US army. The army authorities had not shot an American deserter since the civil war and even then President Abraham Lincoln, the commander-in - chief, had had to give his authority to do so. Even if he were sentenced to death for desertion 'in the face of the enemy', as had so many before him, his sentence would be commuted to imprisonment - and Eddie Slovik knew how to handle 'time'.

But Slovik miscalculated. The circumstances of that winter in the 'Death Factory', the slaughter of the 28th division in the Hurtgen Forest, were against him. The 28th fought hard. But the going was just too tough and the German defenders too hard. First companies fell apart, then battalions. The 'Bloody Buckets' casualties mounted until in the end after a mere two weeks in combat, the 28th had suffered over 6,000 casualties, a third of its strength. In the end it seemed even regiments and their commanders were refusing to fight. Something had to be done. An example had to be set. Eddie Slovik was that example.

On a snowy morning in the French Vosges, the last day of January 1945, Eddie Slovik, lost his bet with death. He was shot by twelve comrades for desertion, the first American soldier to be executed on that count since 1864. An obscure weakling all his life, though probably quite calculating, he became the most famous private soldier (or would 'infamous' be a better description?) to come out of World War Two. And the officer who had signed Eddie's death warrant was 'Ike', that democratic Supreme Commander with the ear-to-ear smile, who had become the darling of the media throughout the Free World in that same war. That fact lent an added piquancy to the affair.

By 1954 when William Huie published his account of Eddie Slovik 'one of the most dramatic and controversial books of our day' (as one reviewer gushed), 'Ike' was President of the United States and no longer so popular as he had once been half a decade of so before. Times were changing in the United States. There had been the three-year war in Korea, the first one that the USA had neither lost nor won. Hundreds of American soldiers in enemy captivity had gone over to the communists. The old black-and-white rules of military conduct and honour no longer seemed to apply. People started to question the military establishment.

It was no different back home.

Now it was the age of the young, the *'Rebel Without a Cause,'* the *'Wild Ones'*. The old values were being questioned. The Establishment, too, even the United States of America and all those military traditions harking back to General Washington and the Founding Fathers that went with that Establishment. It was an ideal time for that arch-establishment figure, eighth generation Southerner William Huie to publish his book. By the time he had died he would risk a prison sentence twice himself for his views and attitude, but in his whole long writing career, he'd never find a better subject that Polack ex-con Eddie Slovik.

The ex-general who had once described his role in WWII as a *'Crusade in Europe'* and had been portrayed in his 1952 presidential campaign as the boy from the wrong side of the tracks who would grow up to be a great figure on his way to the presidency was now shown to be a typical hard-nosed member of the West Point military establishment: one who would condemn another kid from the wrong side of the tracks to death just for the sake of an example. As Huie saw it and, perhaps five million of his readers, too,, Slovik was shot because he was an ex-con, a worthless criminal, who would serve *'pour encourager les autres'*. In other words, Eddie Slovik had been executed as part of a calculated plan, worked out in detail in advance and at the top to stop the rot in the front line, where American soldiers were surrendering and running away by their scores, soon their hundreds, every day that dawned.

As author Huie summed it up over half a century ago now in his book: 'Now, Eddie, they can all know you-everybody from the privates in the firing squad up to the President...if you are that Conscious Being, you can know them....And quite a few thoughtful Americans, in whose name you were shot to death, can now sit in judgement on Private Slovik-*and on the United States* ' (author's italics).

But was it that simple? Had the 'Slovik Case' just been a confrontation between a humble private soldier with a minor criminal record and a harsh military establishment? Had Eddie Slovik been so naively single-minded as Mr Huie had made him out to be? Could Eddie have really believed that when he stated to the authorities that he couldn't-wouldn't fight-he would get away with it? We have seen that the 'Bloody Bucket' to which he had been sent, had suffered 6,000-odd casualties in the two weeks leading up to Eddie's court martial. Did he really think that its commander, General Cota, would show much mercy after that? After all, Cota's own reputation was on the line too. Wasn't the truth of the matter that Eddie Slovik had gambled deliberately when he had deserted and then later refused to fight-and failed?

There were, too, other pieces of the Eddie Slovik puzzle which Mr Huie and others had not taken into account in 1953 when they had concluded that Eddie Slovik had been a victim of a cruel military establishment because 'I stole a loaf of bread when I was 12'.

It is true when they maintained that President Roosevelt ought to have had a word in the final outcome. After all the President was the Commander-in-Chief of the Armed Forces just as Abraham Lincoln had been in 1864. What they didn't know half a century ago was that Roosevelt could be quite as ruthless with his soldiers as Huie made Eisenhower out to be in the Slovik case. In that same December when Slovik was sentenced to death by Eisenhower, Roosevelt was informed of the infamous 'Malmedy Massacre' of some 150 GI's by the 1st SS Panzer Division.[1] His response was a cynical 'Well, it will only serve to make our troops feel towards the Germans as they have already learned to feel about the Japs.' Not one word of regret.

Besides Roosevelt was a dying man. He wasn't much interested in the fighting war either. He left all that to a General Marshall, Eisenhowers's mentor and boss. Both of those generals felt they were fighting 'America's Gettysburg of the 20th Century' in the Bulge. They weren't one bit concerned by the feelings of the ordinary GI at that particular moment. With an estimated 40,000 US deserters on the run, a twenty-five percent deficiency in the rifle divisions, and an increasing tendency of US soldiers to surrender when confronted by the enemy at close-quarters, the two senior commanders felt there was an urgent need for drastic measures. It couldn't be left to the 'legal eagles' and 'bleeding hearts' back in Washington. Action was needed *now*. The rot had to be stopped at the front and, if it took the immediate shooting of one ex-con named Eddie Slovik, so be it.

But there was something else that Huie knew nothing at all about in 1953: something that might well have motivated General Eisenhower, rattled and nervous, when he, alone, signed Eddie Slovik's death warrant on December 23,1944. It is a factor that has never been considered in this context. Indeed it is one that has hardly ever caught the attention of historians of World War Two in Europe.

It was this. As |Eddie Slovik waited for execution in the Paris Stockade that Black Christmas of 1944, twenty miles away on the other side of the French capital, General Dwight D.Eisenhower, the allied Supreme Commander, felt that he, too was under sentence of death... On that Saturday, the last before Christmas, just like 'Eddie' ,'Ike', too prepared for a violent end.

BOOK ONE

ONE: EDDIE AND IKE

"A Thousand shall fall at my right hand and ten thousand at my left, but the arrow that flies by day shall not come near me."

The Bible

On the evening of Friday 28th June, 1940, a long queue of lorries, vans and horse-drawn carts lined up along the White Rock Quay, Guernsey in the British Channel Islands. The farmers and market-gardeners were preparing to unload their 'chips', twelve pound baskets of tomatoes, into the holds of the waiting British freighters. It was a fine evening. The locals chatted amongst themselves in their local French patois. Over the sea on the continent, the war was raging, but on this sunny June evening, the fighting seemed a long way off.

Then, abruptly, startlingly, at five to seven, six planes flashed into sight. They came from the east, gathering speed by the second. The locals stopped their idle chatter. They shielded their eyes against the slanting rays of the dying sun. Above them three of the planes raced right across the island from east to west. The other three lost height. They were coming down quickly. Someone spotted the cross and swastika on the lead plane's wing. '*Jerries*' he yelled, using the English word. A moment later the machine guns started to chatter. The locals panicked. Some threw themselves under their vehicles. Others dropped under the pier and pressed their faces to the wet shingle. A few were terrified enough to jump into the sea.

Ike's HQ. in Paris. Skorzeny's Target

Almost before they were aware of what had happened, the German planes had vanished, roaring into the high blue of the June sky. But behind they left a confused, sorry mess of dead and dying civilians, their blood mingling with the squashed red pulp of Guernsey's pride, their tomatoes. The Germans had arrived in the Channel Islands, the only part of the British empire which the Nazis were going to occupy in World War Two.

Four years of occupation followed. They were hard ones. In this one-time holiday island, which had always been a place of plenty, foodstuffs became hard to obtain. By 1944 that British stable, tea, cost £28 a pound and a bar of soap, ten shillings. But the islanders had their cricket and football matches, as of old, complete with 'fixtures' against their enemies, the Germans. There were dances too, behind locked doors to the music of the forbidden BBC. And it wasn't only the male islanders who attended; the Germans did too. There were now plenty of 'Jerry bags', who would dance with them - and more. By 1942 the German authorities had to issue an order stating that 'Sexual relations with either German soldiers or civilians are strictly forbidden during the next three months'. Still the VD rate continued to rise.

By June 6th, 1944, the food situation of the islanders had become bad. That of the 30,000 odd Germans, who called themselves now *'Division Kanada'* (for that is where they thought they'd end up finally) was little better. Their rations were cut to 1,125 calories a day. TB was epidemic. Military doctors estimated that only five percent of the men were fit for combat.

Skorzeny 1943. Rescue of Mussolini

So when on June 6th, the Allies invaded the Continent and virtually cut the islands off, the hungry German occupiers thought the end was nigh. It wasn't. Their commanders were determined to fight on, even if their troops were starving. As a result the mutinous troops formed secret societies which were prepared to even assassinate their officers if they didn't give in to the Allied demands to surrender.

But there was one seemingly insurmountable problem facing these would-be mutineers. It was the 'Madman of the Channel Islands', as they called him. He was 46 year old Admiral Huffmeier, one-time commandant of the battleship *Scharnhorst*, and now commander of all German forces on the occupied British Islands. Tall, hard-boiled, the Admiral was a fervent Nazi, who didn't believe that he and the forces under his command should just remain passive and wait until they were all transported off to the Allied POW camps in Canada. Once the Bailiff of Jersey, Alexander Coutanche, had remarked to the Nazi Admiral, 'In truth, both *you* and I are prisoners of the British Royal Navy. His answer had been , 'that is what you think.' For Huffmeier was determined, even if the Channel Islands were now cut off from the mainland, to do his best for the Fatherland, even if it meant sending his ragged hungry troops to attack the enemy's rear in France.

Thus it was that Huffmeier started to attempt to collect information of what was going on the now American-occupied French coast with an eye to using it to his advantage at some later day.

But as the Allies captured one port after another in Normandy and Brittany, the pressure on Huffmeier mounted. Churchill, who was not prepared to waste valuable troops on the recapturing of the Islands, ordered that no German should be allowed to escape from them and no food got in. The Americans, on the other hand, wanted to see an end to the German occupation just across the water from their positions in Normandy and Brittany. So on September 9th, 1944 a plane flew over Guernsey, dropping flares instead of bombs, to advise the defenders of its presence.

By now the ruddy lights of these flares, called 'Christmas trees', by the Germans, the flak gunners could see a solitary parachute floating down before the twin-engined plane disappeared. Hastily they ran out into the fields to secure it and found attached to the chute a metal cylinder marked 'not explosive'. Mystified the gunners carried it to the headquarters of one of the senior German commanders, Count von Schmettow, whose name had been written on the device as well.

Gingerly, the Germans removed a series of envelopes inside the cylinder. They feared it might be a trick. Were there high explosive devices within, aimed at killing the islands' top German commanders? There weren't. Instead they found the last envelope, wrapped in oiled silk, was addressed personally to Count von Schmettow. It contained a request from 'Eisenhower's HQ'. It was to reconnect the cable link between the Channel Islands and France so that the Germans could talk over the phone with a senior member of Eisenhower's staff.

Under the circumstances-there was the fanatical Huffmeier and the Gestapo to reckon with-the Count was forced to refuse. Indeed a few days later, Schmettow, knowing that the British had agents on the Islands, published a message intended for the *Reichsminister fur Propaganda*, Dr Goebbels, in the local paper. It stated that: 'The three Island Fortresses will faithfully hold out to the last. With this we salute our Fuhrer and our Fatherland.

That seemed to be the end of the affair. But not for Admiral Huffmeier. The naval fire-eater decided he would carry out some intelligence work from the Islands, using his meagre resources. It might help the embattled Fatherland. Naturally his main concern was to carry out the fight from the Islands to the Continent. At the moment that, of course, was not feasible. In the meantime, therefore he'd let Berlin know what he could.

He knew that back in the Reich, the old German Secret Service, *die Abwehr,* had been incorporated in the SS's own secret service since the German Army generals attempt on Hitler's life. The SS, bolder, more aggressive than the old school *Abwehr* officers, would be grateful for any information that would allow them to act. In particular, now the German Army was fleeing France, the SD, as the SS secret service was called, would need anything he, Huffmeier, could find out about Allied dispositions in newly liberated France. In particular, the SD might find the location of Allied Headquarters very useful as possible targets for clandestine ops.

Unknown to Huffmeier, 'the madman of the islands', the Abwehr had, had the same idea back in 1943. Then a 35 year old French woman of Russian descent, Mathalie Sergueiew, had been used for specifically this task. Her *Abwehr* spy master, a thick-set veteran Emile Kliemann who code named his female agent 'Tramp', told her to apply for a visa to enter England as a nurse.

Hitler had begun to break his own rule that there would be no assassination attempts made on enemy leaders. Already an aeroplane supposedly carrying Churchill had been attacked by German plane over the Bay of Biscay. It had been a case of mistaking the identity of one of the passengers, a businessman who looked very like Churchill. However the attack did cause the death of Leslie Howard, a beloved movie star of that period.

That fall, Hitler's secret agents were already well into the planning of 'Operation Long Jump' the paradrop into Persia. The aim of this bold operation was the assassination of all main allied leaders, Stalin, Churchill and Roosevelt, when they conferred in November 1943 at the Persian capital of Tehran.

Skorzeny and his Adjutand

Now it seems that there were plans being mooted at top level in Berlin that the assassination of major enemy military commanders, Montgomery, Eisenhower and the like might well postpone of the coming invasion of Europe for months, if not years. After all the Germans knew the Allies had been planning this Second Front since 1942 already, and, in essence, the planning had been built round the leaders of the military operations. A new leader would probably demand a radical change of plan to fit in with his personal view of how the invasion should be carried out. When, Montgomery, who would lead the cross channel invasion, arrived back in the UK in '44, he did exactly this.

So 'Tramp's' mission also included a significant task: she was to find out the location of General Eisenhower's SHAEF headquarters.

'Tramp' soon to be code-named 'Treasure' by her British female control, Mary Sherer, proved to be a double agent for the British. MI5, counter-intelligence, already knew she was working for the Germans and that (as her cousin reported from Cambridge) she was 'something of an adventurer'. In particular, she seemed more concerned with the fate of her beloved pet dog 'Frisson' than her duties as an agent, living on the knife-edge of being arrested for treachery and shot as a spy.

**Memorial of the 28th Infantry Division ('The Bloody Bucket')
on the River Sauer, Luxembourgh, today**

In the end 'Frisson' proved to be her downfall. Despite her usefulness to the British as a spy, the bureaucrats wouldn't allow her to bring in her dog. It remained in quarantine in Gibraltar, while she ate her heart out in the home counties. Her work was affected. Then 'Frisson' died and 'Tramp-Treasure' vowed revenge. As Mary Sherer, her control, reported to her boss, 'this exceptionally troublesome and temperamental agent' was upset about her dog and 'has seriously threatened that if the dog doesn't arrive soon she will, not work anymore.' Now, 'Frisson' would never

arrive and 'Treasure' formed a new and secret link to the German Klieman
Not for long. She got cold feet and told Mary Sherer what she had done. Thereafter she was no longer trusted by MI5. Someone else took over her transmissions and 'Treasure' was passed over as an agent to de Gaulle's London based Free French (that transfer was indicative of what British Intelligence thought of their French counterparts!) Thus 'Tramp-Treasure' passed out of the secret history of WWII: and the location of General Eisenhower's HQ in England remained a secret for the rest of his stay in that country. The would-be assassin's hand had been stayed...

Nearly a year later now. Admiral Huffmeier reasoned that the capsule intended for Count von Schmettow revealed something important. Why else have the undersea cable between the Channel Islands and mainland France restored so that the Americans could talk to the Count unless there was someone in France who could negotiate at the highest level? That could mean only that Eisenhower had established his headquarters in France.

Now Huffmeier knew a lot about staff officers and their commanders. He had fretted at being one himself for a while, when he would have dearly loved to have gone back to sea. Hadn't he spent all those long dreary months as the port-bound commandant of the unseaworthy and damaged Scharnhorst. Staff officers loved the comforts and luxury of rear headquarters, where there was little danger.

**Replacements for the 28th Division arriving at the Front
(Luxembourgh), Winter 1944**

Commanding Generals, as Huffmeier well knew, rarely ventured close to the front line. Their headquarters might well be a couple of hundred kilometres behind the firing line. Thus, if Eisenhower was typical, and the enemy were now within striking distance of the Reich's frontier, it was well possible that the Allied Supreme Headquarters was still situated not too far from the enemy's original landing sites in Normandy.

Despite von Schmettow's reaction to the first US attempt to request him to surrender, the Americans tried again. On the afternoon of Friday, 22 September, an American motor patrol boat, FK 56, commanded by 1st Lt. Meyer approached Guernsey under a white flag. The US craft was allowed to reach the outskirts of St Pierre-

Port. Here a German officer met the boat and encountered a 'Major from Eisenhower's Headquarters', as the Germans recorded at the time.

The Major asked the German officer if he knew the latest developments in the West, that France had been liberated; that the Allies had driven through Belgium and Luxembourg and had actually crossed into Germany in the German-Eifel region. Finished with the details of the US conquests, the 'Major from Eisenhower's HQ', asked if Count von Schmettow was now prepared to discuss the matter further with him.

Von Schmettow back in St Peter Port, wasn't. He told the German officer to report to the 'Major' that he was fully aware of the situation in the West (he wasn't of course). He didn't want to discuss it any further.

Presumably with a flea in his ear, the US motor boat and the 'Major from Eisenhower's Headquarters' set sail again. Unfortunately the whole garrison of the Channel Islands hadn't been informed the 'FK 56' was sailing under a flag of truce. Anyway it was a gusty overcast day and the white flag had become wound round the mast of the American craft by the wind. The result was that the German batteries at Alderney opened fire. But the great guns missed and the motorboat ploughed on through the choppy waters to safety. But not before the craft had been observed by no less a person than that Nazi fire eater, Admiral Huffmeier.

The latter observed the ship's closely as it left Alderney and set course for Le Cateret on the continent beyond. Huffmeier, like most of the German Navy's big ship men, knew this stretch of the French coast intimately. He had to. St Nazaire, Lorient and the like had been well used as safe havens for the *Kriegsmarine* during the four years German occupation of France.

Now he concluded that the 'FK 56' was heading for either Cherbourg or Cateret. In the event Admiral Huffmeier was wrong. But he was the first of the 'fortress commandants' on the French coast, now left far behind enemy lines, to realise that Allied Supreme Headquarters were now in France. Thus it was on the same day that Admiral Frisius, the German fortress commandant of Dunkirk, reported to the German High command in Berlin that fresh airborne serials were passing over the Channel coast port heading for Arnhem, Huffmeier made his own report. He knew he personally could do little about Eisenhower's new headquarters, however temptingly close it was now. But he reasoned the people in Berlin could. Thus his report commenced its relatively long journey from the besieged Channel Islands to Admiral Doenitz's naval headquarters at Kiel-Murwik and from there to the German admiralty in a bombed Berlin. Here Huffmeier's report remained for a time while Naval Intelligence pondered what use they could make of Huffmeier's findings.

In the end the elegant naval staff officers decided that they hadn't the resources to carry out some sort of an attack on Eisenhower's HQ, once they had discovered where exactly it was now located. The *Luftwaffe* felt the same. The Airforce planners simply couldn't find the necessary plans for an aerial assault. So the information passed on by the 'Madman of the Channel Islands' drifted through the various ministries in Berlin's *Wilhelmsstrasse* until it finally reached the headquarters of the

Sicherheitsdienst, the newly amalgamated German Secret Service and that of the SS. The man who received that information was perhaps that September the most unlikely high-ranking Nazi who would do anything about it.

For General der SS Walter Schellenberg, who ran his undercover empire from his Berlin HQ desk, (which contained two hidden machine guns ready to open fire at any would-be assassin at the press of a button), was a born survivor. Schellenberg, a sleek ex-lawyer, his face marked with duelling scars from his student days, had already realised the way the wind was blowing. Germany had virtually lost the war and he, for one, was not going down with the sinking ship. Let others make whatever dangerous plans for the Allied Supreme Commander's future - or lack of it. He wanted no part of any scheme which might endanger his own future.

Thus it was that Huffmeier's guess where Allied Supreme Headquarters and its chief Eisenhower might well be located on the Continent, landed on the desk of that scar-faced giant, whose features looked like the work of a demented butcher's apprentice run amok. The information had reached the right man for the job at last. If anyone could make use of it at this eleventh hour in the history of the Nazi Germany it was *Obersturmbannfuhrer* Otto Skorzeny.

On that same Friday that Admiral Huffmeier reported his findings to the Reich, four hundred miles away in the German border village of Nusbaum, a young Eifel villager returned to his hiding place in his barn. A few days before he had met his first American. 'He looked drawn and tired. He wanted something to drink so I gave him milk'. Then the young German, named Hermann Putz, had thought the weary American, armed with a machine pistol, meant the end of the war. If the 'Ami', as the locals called the Americans, had already penetrated the Reich, following the fleeing, beaten German Army, it had to mean that the Third Reich had come to an end and Hitler's days were numbered. Thank God!

But now this Friday with the German guns booming in the distance, Putz realised that he had been wrong. The 'Ami', who occupied his village, a cluster of rundown houses around the church, were pulling out. 'Already they had pulled down the cooks' tent and a cannon had been towed away. People were running back and forth... A truck was running round and round doing something, almost as if the driver were drunk or in a very great careless hurry. One thing was clear. The 'Ami' had had enough. They were clearing out. At nine that morning we crawled out of our hiding place and drew in a deep breath of clear air'.

Naturally in his account, the old Putz didn't mention that he and his fellow villagers looted what the Americans had left behind- and it was a lot. He stated solely that they 'ate a good breakfast'. Some time later a lone German soldier, in camouflage uniform came down the road from Frelingen. Behind him 'came personnel carriers filled with victorious young panzer grenadiers, 'as Putz recorded fifty years on.' Hastily they stopped and looted the vehicles the 'Amis' had left behind. That was probably their reward for a successful attack. Then they went, following up the retreating 'Amis', munching 'Hershey bars and smoking their looted 'cancer sticks' (as they called the 'Ami' cigarettes) like a bunch of happy schoolboys'.

The *Death Factory* 1944

What Putz was viewing as a 15 year old boy was the retreat of the US Army's Fifth Corps, commanded by General Gerow. A week before its three divisions, the 4th, 28th Infantry and the 5th Armoured had made the first Allied attack into Hitler's Germany. Between the Belgian village of Schoenberg and the Luxembourg one of

Bollendorf-Pont, the 50,000 Americans had caught the Germans by surprise.

They had crossed the two border rivers of Our and Sauer (*Sure* in French), penetrated the Siegfried Line in part and advanced in the Wallendorf-Bollendorf sector some six miles into the Reich. It had been a successful operation, carried out on the run with little previous preparation and Gerow had been very pleased with his men. Unfortunately for the Americans, the men of the 5th Armoured and the 112th Regiment of the 28th Infantry Division, had by chance struck the Germans where two German armies met. Aged Field Marshal von Runstedt, the German Commander-in-Chief in the West, saw the dangers inherent in an attack of that kind. Immediately he had thrown the remnants of six German divisions, including armour, against the American bridgehead.

Now under intense German pressure the V Corps were being pressed back against the Our-Sauer river line save in the North, where the GI's of the US Fourth Division were digging their toes in and holding their meagre gains.

Not the fifth and the 112th. Desperately they too were trying to hold onto a water-front for future operations into Germany. Later the Top Brass maintained that they had failed this first time because they had lacked rifle strength and supplies. As soon as they had sufficient fuel, ammunition and above all riflemen to fill the gaps in their ranks, they would attack once more. But that wasn't to be.

The Germans increased their efforts. They pushed the 'Amis' back relentlessly. Village after village, bought with young American blood, was evacuated. Here and there, so the victorious Germans maintained, the 'Amis' panicked. They abandoned their positions at the first sight of the advancing German tanks and fled. In one case, so the Germans said, an American infantry major, presumably from the 28th Division's 112th Infantry regiment, broke into a house, stole civilian clothes, swam the River Sauer and didn't stop until he reached the safety of Luxembourg City far to the rear.

By Saturday, 23rd September the battle was virtually over. As the weather cleared, the old fox, von Runstedt threw in 25 German fighters and a new German division, the 19th Infantry. It advanced along the line of the River Sauer, which divides Germany from Luxembourg. The fresh German Infantry rolled up the American-held bunkers, one by one. They came upon fifteen unsuspecting Sherman tanks of the US Fifth Armoured Division. The enemy knocked out the lot. The last American defences began to crumble.

That day the War diary of Rundstedt's HQ noted with satisfaction: 'The main battle line is now firmly in our hands, in hard-fought battles, LXXX Corps had succeeded in throwing back the enemy.....Thirty -one tanks and ten reconnaissance vehicles have been destroyed, in addition nine enemy planes have been shot down and 52 prisoners taken. The enemy dead numbered 531...'

Thus the first American attack on Germany had ended in failure. Although V Corps retained a narrow foothold in the enemy country, along the Luxembourg sector of the front, they were forced to withdraw to that country. Here the line settled down. From now onwards for three long months this would become the infamous 'Ghost front' where the US Command sent green divisions to be 'blooded' (as the brutal phrase of the time has it) and battle-weary ones to recuperate. Only when that 'Ghost Front'*2 exploded into action in mid-December, 1944 would the 4th and 28th Infantry Divisions fight again in the area. And by then those old divisions would have disappeared into the maelstrom of total war. In the meantime the V Corps divisions, in particular, the 28th Infantry would settle down to assess the cost of their first venture across that unholy frontier. How bad had the 'butcher's bill' been?

It was high, especially in the case of the 28th, a Pennsylvanian National Guard out-fit. Thirty-seven percent killed, wounded and captured, which meant that one third of the division had succumbed to battle. More important, these casualties came from the fighting arm of the 28th, the key rifle companies: The ones which did the fighting. And it must be remembered in WWII that it required in the US Army nearly five men to keep one man in the line, doing the fighting. As the GI's wise-cracked, 'one man in the line and six men to bring up the coke'.

In the fall of 1944, there were still more than enough men to bring up the 'coke'. But those who actually did the fighting, the riflemen, were becoming ever-increasingly in short supply. The Battle for Normandy had taken a tremendous toll on the US Army's rifle companies. There had been nearly 100,000 casualties by the time the Army had reached the German frontier. Naturally there were still new US infantry divisions in the pipeline, already present in the UK or waiting in the States to be shipped to the European Theatre of Operations, but these divisions could not sup-ply the replacements the divisions already in combat needed. The new divisions in the UK or waiting for shipment overseas in the USA had already lost some of their best men - in some cases, several thousands - as replacements for the fighting divisions. So they were out of the question.

So replacements for the E.T.O. infantry divisions had to come from Replacement Training Centres in the United States. Here there was a mixed bunch of men of all ages, who had been transferred to the infantry from other arms, the Army Air Corps, Coastal Artillery etc. etc., or who had lost their parent outfits and had been 'parked' in the RTC's until employment could be found for them.

Unfortunately for the division in Europe crying out for 'bodies', many thousands of these men could not be called upon immediate replacements for overseas. In es-sence, these men came in two classes: soldiers who were not yet 19 and what were called 'pre-Pearl Harbour Fathers'. In addition there were others who suf-fered from mental and physical problems that might well ensure they'd be dis-charged from the US Army altogether (nearly a million men were released during WWII on the score of mental instability).

US Law didn't allow men younger that 19 to go overseas to combat outfits. The same ruling applied to older men, 'the pre-Pearl Harbour Fathers', as the authorities called them in such a quaint manner. These were soldiers who had married and fathered children prior to 1941 and the outbreak of war. They, too, were not allowed to be sent overseas to a combat outfit. Thus it was that individual reinforcements being sent to fill the gaps in the fighting divisions were a mixed bunch.

Unlike British reinforcements, who were all of the A-1 category, i.e. the top of the range of the British Army's various physical categories, and although they included 18-year olds, were within the age range best suited for infantry combat (between 18 and 25), the Americans were of varied physical- and more important mental- categories, often ranging right up to their '30's'. They were the 'Dads' and 'Pops' often encountered in the unit histories of US fighting outfits in the European theatre of operations.

Many formed the backbone of their squads and companies. But some were born shirkers: the men who lost their false teeth (a man who can't eat, can't fight) when the going got tough. Others deserted at the first opportunity, moving in with local whores and living off the military black market in gas, tyres, overcoat, cigarettes and the like.

But even when the 'replacement' (as the US Army originally called 'reinforcements' before it was realised that 'replacement' had unfortunate undertones for the men in question) were good, there were problems. How should the division at the receiving end of these new soldiers integrate them? Should they be allotted as individuals to separate squads? Or should they remain in a larger grouping, in which they knew each other?

Allotting reinforcements as individuals brought with it problems. Who would look after the 'new boys'? The veterans tended to stick together, working on the 'buddy' system. ' I'll look out for you, you look after me'. That wouldn't work with these greenhorns who had no combat experience.

Trying to integrate the reinforcements as a larger group, say as a platoon, even as a company, was problematic as well. Who would train anything from 30 to 180 reinforcements, new to the front, in the survival tricks of combat? Wouldn't these large scale units of 'new boys' simply be used by battalion commanders as an extra platoon or company? Regardless of the probably high casualties these inexperienced soldiers might incur, they'd be thrown into battle whenever there was an emergency and the battalion C.O. needed 'bodies'.

It was a problem that was never solved. Unlike the British Army in Europe, the American Forces never came up with the idea of 'Divisional Battle Schools' where reinforcements would be given extra training under the command of battle-experienced infantry officers and NCO's. As General Jacob Devers, commander of the US Sixth Army Group, wrote that year to Gen. McNair, in charge of these matters, who was killed by 'friendly fire' in France in the summer of 1944, 'Your replacement system is bound to break down as it has done in this theatre'.

Now as September gave way to October and the battered 28th Division was licking its wounds and perhaps wondering what had happened, when the pundits back home were maintaining the 'boys will be home for Christmas', set about finding approximately 2,000 infantry replacements for the men Division had lost in this first battle of the Siegfried Line. For the top brass of V Corps and the 28th had been alerted to prepare for the new battle already raging to the north. Officially it was to be known as the 'Battle of the Hurtgen forest'. But to the GIs who would fight there in that green hell on the German border between Monschau and Aachen, which would swallow up a whole division of US infantry a month, it was called with brutal simplicity *the Death Factory*.

Two months before the US 28th Infantry Division had had its greatest moment of fame in WWII when the news cameras caught it marching through the newly liberated Paris. In June 1940, the German conquerors had paraded their tanks and battle-worn infantry through empty streets as a demonstration of strength, intended strictly for home audiences. Now the US authorities wanted to do the same thing - only in larger format for a world audience. Paris was naturally a symbol for the Free World. After all, as they quipped in Ivy League Colleges, 'When a good American dies he goes to Paris'. As Private First Class Verner Odegard of the 28th remembered: 'We didn't have a damn thing to do with the taking of Paris. We just came in a couple of days later when someone got the bright idea of having a parade and we just happened to be there'.

'As long as I live I don't guess I'll ever see a parade like that. Most of us slept in pup tents in the Bois de Boulogne the night before and it rained like hell and we were pretty dirty, so they picked out the cleanest guys to stand up front and on the outside. I had a bright shiny new patch so they put me on the outside. It was a good place to be, too, because every guy marching on the outside had at least one girl on his arm kissing him and hugging him and marching right alongside him.'

We were marching twenty-four abreast right down the Champs Elysees and we had a helluva time trying to march because the street was jammed with people laughing and yelling and crying and singing. They were throwing flowers at us and bringing up big bottles of wine.'

'The first regiment never did get through. The crowd just gobbled them up. They just broke in and grabbed the guys and lifted some of them on their shoulders and carried them through into the cafes and bars and their homes and wouldn't let them go. I hear it was a helluva job trying to round them up later.'6.

The parade in August 1944, staged by the US Army deliberately to show the French that it was they, *Les Americans,* who had freed France and Paris, not General de Gaulle, as the tall gawky General wanted his people to believe, was, in essence, pure Hollywood. It fitted right in with Tinseltown's concept of what wartime Europe under the 'Nazi heel' was like, and just how the Europeans delighted at the 'liberation' by American 'boys'.

For nearly three years now, those doomed soldiers of the 28th Division, who were marching straight through Paris to battle, had probably been fed on a diet of half-truths and downright lies. Movies, the most popular form of entertainment at the time had depicted wartime Occupied Europe in strictly simplistic, propaganda terms. The bad guys wore the black uniform of the SS. The good ones were dressed in striped 'Apache' sweatshirts and rakish berets. Naturally they had a Gaulloise glued to their bottom lip and the rest of these Europeans, labouring under Nazi repression , were fervent patriots. Man, woman and child, they fought the German enemy wherever they could and more often than not they died in the attempt, usually with some suitably patriotic slogan on their lips.

The reality was different. One month before the 28th had commenced its celebrated march down the Champs Elysses, a million Parisians had cheered the 'Marshal' on that same Champs Elysses. That same Marshal Petain who had worked with the Germans throughout the Occupation and his troops had killed and wounded 1,000 British and American troops when they had landed in North Africa in 1942. Even as late as the first week in August with the Allies already breaking out of Normandy, Pierre Laval, that greasy arch-traitor who had collaborated with the Germans right from the start, had been preparing a provisional government in Paris, which he felt would be able to co-operate in the same manner with the American Supreme Commander Eisenhower.

Naturally Laval was living in cloud cuckooland and both he and Petain were eventually spirited off to Germany with the rest of the important traitors and *collabos*, who had worked hand-in-glove with the Nazis for the last four years. Behind them, however, they left many thousands of Frenchmen and women who were either compromised or who had believed in the German cause, the 'New Order' and that forerunner of the post-war Common Market, 'the European Community', the German-controlled *Europaische Gemeinschaft* of 1942.

They came in all kinds. Fervent anti-communists, who saw the only hope for Europe in the anti-communist 'crusade' led by Germans in Russia. Collaborators and office-seekers. Pimps, whores and black marketers. Fellow traveller artists and writers. Corrupt French cops and members of the fascist paramilitary *Milice* run by Vichy Government. *And spies.*

For both the *Abwehr* and the Gestapo-SD of the SS, had run extensive networks of agents, informers and 'moles', who had not only spied and informed on their own people, the 'patriots', but also on Allied networks located in their country.

Now after the debacle and great retreat of the *Wehrmacht* of August 1944 these networks were in some disarray. Naturally those of the agents who were in most danger of being apprehended 'took a dive', as the parlance of the time had it. Others who had the means bought new identities (not difficult in wartime France) and departed for France's colonies or remoter country regions in the south. But there were others, still prepared to work for the German cause.

These were either the most compromised with blood on their hands, who knew they didn't stand a chance if they were apprehended by the new French authorities in charge (that fall and winter an estimated 100,000 Frenchmen and women were executed by their fellow countrymen in the great *'epuration,'* the purge); or those, as foolish as they may have seemed that summer, who still believed in German cause and final German victory.

Their German spymasters and naturally their Gestapo-SD bosses might well have fled with the beaten *Wehrmacht*, trying frantically to reach the safety of the Siegfried Line before it was too late, but once there the old contacts were picked up once more. Dollars, British pounds, new Francs started to come through to pay these 'sleepers', as they were called, once more. Much of it might well be forged by the Jewish experts incarcerated in the Reich's concentration camps. But they didn't know that. The foreign currency served its purpose well enough. Frenchmen, trained in Germany's spy camps around Berlin, began to be parachuted into 'liberated' France by the top secret German *KG 100*. These renegades, equipped with short wave radios, were to contact the 'sleepers' and inform Berlin of the current situation with their old spy rings. For now Berlin, and, in particular, Obersturmbannfuhrer Otto Skorzeny in his training camp outside the German capital urgently needed information on allied intentions and personalities.

One of the latter was naturally the Supreme Commander Eisenhower himself. Now and again 'Ike', with his familiar ear-to-ear smile, was featured in the Allied newsreels visiting his troops at the front. But the officers who censored those newsreels had specific instructions to cut out anything which might indicate where Eisenhower was permanently located. Thus it was in that last week if August 1944 when 'Ike' came to watch the 28th Division parade through Paris and visit General de Gaulle, German Intelligence still suppose he was in Southern England.

In fact, 'Shellburst', the code-name given to Eisenhower's advanced headquarters, was already in France, as Admiral Huffmeier in the Channel Islands would soon conclude it was. Surprisingly enough it was located virtually in the very spot where nine months later, the firebrand Admiral would carry out his daring raid on the American rear echelon. Granville barely a score of miles as the crow flies from the Channel Islands. [*3] As Kay Summersby, Eisenhowers's mistress, described it: 'In early September, our advance headquarters was in Granville, a fishing port, where Ike had a house with a picture postcard view of Mont-Saint-Michel, the ancient Benedictine abbey that, when the tide was high, rose like a magic island in the bay'. Ironically enough, in view of the problems that Eisenhower was beginning to have with the birdlike British general of the same name, the house overlooking Mont-Saint-Michel, was called *'Villa Montgomery'*.

But on that 29th August, Eisenhower and that 'damned new Joan of Arc', as Roosevelt called General de Gaulle scornfully, met for the first time in the newly liberated French capital. Naturally de Gaulle, who felt -rightly- that President Roosevelt and Prime Minister thought that he was a moaning upstart, had his usual gripe. As de Gaulle wrote later: 'We congratulated each other on the happy outcome of events in Paris. I did not hide from him, however, how dissatisfied I was with Gerow's [*4] attitude as I was entering my own capital and grasping the boiling cauldron in my hands'.

Naturally, Eisenhower, the political general, used to touchy foreign allies - 'a bunch of goddam prima donnas', as 'Ike' called them privately - smoothed over the difficulties and confided in de Gaulle a secret. As de Gaulle described the exchange: 'Eisenhower said that he planned to install his headquarters in Versailles. 'For once de Gaulle didn't complain. He knew that if he had trouble with the French communist or any other political grouping for that matter, the Americans would step in and help. Trouble near the Allied - read, *American* - Supreme Headquarters - would simply be not allowed.

Naturally Eisenhower would move his HQ into Versailles not only for military reasons, but also for political ones. His masters in Washington and London wanted to keep a tight rein on the French maverick. Versailles, just outside Paris, would suit their purpose perfectly.

De Gaulle seemingly didn't realise that. Supreme egotist that he was, he saw the proposed move merely as potential support for his own new regime. Accordingly, as he wrote afterwards in his normal high-handed manner, 'I approved the move, believing it a good idea to have the Allied Commander-in-Chief lodged out of Paris, but useful that he should be near.

And that was. On the off-chance, or so it appears, Eisenhower had revealed to de Gaulle, presiding over half a dozen political factions, all at each other's throats and all totally untrustworthy, a secret for which German Intelligence would have given their eye teeth late that summer.

But German Intelligence and in particular, that hulking, scar-faced giant, Skorzeny, need not have worried. They'd find out soon enough. For if their spies in France didn't discover the coming move, there'd be some Frenchman or other around de Gaulle, who would be only too eager to betray the secret for coin of the realm.

For as Group Captain Freddie Winterbotham, guardian of the '*Ultra*' secret and for a time in WWII, the deputy head of British MI 6, once remarked, 'We, in the 'Old Firm' (Secret Service) never trusted de Gaulle and his French in London during the war or Prince Bernhard of the Netherlands for that matter. They were always nosing about our offices. And if anyone was going to blab a secret to the enemy, it would have been those two and their minions'.

A harsh verdict. But for the time being, Freddie Winterbotham, who was currently in France himself with Patton and then Bradley, need not have worried. It would be over a month before Eisenhower actually moved to Versailles. In the meantime he returned to Granville to nurse his 'football knee', which he had first injured as a cadet at West Point and now again in a minor aeroplane accident. All the same he ordered those involved in the move from Bushy Park, England to Versailles, to ensure a news blackout on all Allied Troop movements.

As his naval aide and PR man, Lt. Commander Butcher noted in his diary for September 9, 1944: 'Ike has ordered operation secrecy for Allies forces pushing toward Germany. The British and Americans are less than twenty miles from the German border... We are going so rapidly that if he (Eisenhower) permits prompt dissemination of news, the hard-pressed Germans, with their communications disrupted, can keep their war maps up to date by listening to the BBC'.

So for the time being, any would-be assassins in Berlin had to wait for any further news about the whereabouts of their future target, General Eisenhower. Beside Germany was already beginning to fight for its very existence on that remote frontier. Division after division was piling up on the western border of the Reich, ready to deliver the death blow to Hitler's vaunted '1,000 Reich', which looked as if it might not survive to the end of 1944.

Life on both sides of the battlefront was becoming decidedly complicated, if not confused.

Four days before the 28th Infantry division made that celebrated march through Paris, the leading elements of the 'Keystone Division', as the National Guard outfit called itself, were engaged in a heavy fire fight at the French town of Elbeuf.

Elbeuf, a small place, was located on the south bank of the river Seine, some eighty miles north west of the French capital. Here the new commander of the German Army group B had ordered his retreating Seventh Army to hold fast. The stocky little Field Marshal Model, who had just taken over command, was only carrying out the Fuhrer's own order. For he had stated to the Field Marshal, who was known throughout the *Wehrmacht* as the 'Fuhrer's Fire Brigade', (for he always seemed able to put out 'the fire', whenever he front was in danger) 'let us hold firm at the Seine'.

But even Model couldn't achieve that. The American were everywhere, the German Seventh Army was in full retreat and wherever German troops massed the feared Allied '*Jabos*' -fighter-bombers-fell out of the summer sky and literally shot the defenders to pieces.

Nevertheless, the German resistance was strong enough . It kept the *Amis* at bay for most of that day and here and there heavy fighting occurred, with the 28th Division being forced to use air and artillery to crush the doomed German defenders of the bridge sites over the Seine.

As General Hans Speidel, Rundstedt's chief-of-staff, described the hopeless German situation later: 'when those fighter-bombers swooped down, raking us not only with bombs but with machine-gun fire as well, any movement of the banks (of the Seine) was impossible...Hundreds and hundreds of barges were destroyed. The left bank was in places a mass of tangled canons, tanks and military vehicles, some of them with their engines still turning or beginning to go up in flames. Panicky wounded horses ran madly about or tried to escape from their harness, with their teeth and the whites of their eyes showing. Poor creatures. I couldn't help feeling sorry for them'.

The General did not seem to feel particularly sorry for the men, however. He acknowledged that 'the troops that superintended the passage were called upon to make a heavy sacrifice and they deserve high praise for it'. But he failed to mention that 40,000 German soldiers who surrendered to the British and Canadians on that and the next day in August and the 18,000 who fell into American hands

Still it was a tremendous blood-letting and those who were there, even the most hard-hearted and unimaginative, were struck by the terrible carnage and slaughter on the roads leading to Elbeuf, where the 28th Division had set up its HQ temporarily. The roads were littered with the bloody, still smoking remains of German columns which had been trying to reach the Seine in time to be evacuated by the waiting barges - and failed. Dead men were sprawled everywhere like bundles of abandoned bloody rags. Tanks and self-propelled guns, which were either shot-up or had run out of fuel had run into the ditches, the dead crew men hanging out of the blackened charred turrets. But those who came that way that terrible, hot August day, with the sun attracting the hordes of big greedy bluebottles to the stinking, already bloating dead, were moved most not by their fellow humans. But by the dead horses. In the accounts of the suffering of the escaping German columns, it is always the dead and dying four-legged creatures which attracted the most compassion on the part of the victors.

Alan Morehead, the Australian war Correspondent, noted that the Canadians who were soon to take over the Elbeuf sector from the 'Yanks', were more concerned with the fate of the horses than that of German dead and dying all around them'. The wounded kept dying, 'he recorded for the British 'Daily Express'. 'They are all jumbled on top of one another and the stench makes it difficult for one to refrain from being sick. Outside a Canadian soldier is mercifully going round shooting wounded horses with a Luger pistol'.

But if the veteran war correspondent, who had reported from ten different battle fronts in the last five years was having difficulty in not being sick, one can guess the effect of this charnel house outside Elbeuf on young soldiers approaching a battlefront for the very first time.

There were fourteen of them. A month before they had been in the States, another world. Then in the last week of July 1944, they had been shipped from Fort Meade to Scotland. Travelling through England to Southampton, they finally embarked for the war zone, following the same route taken by thousands of bewildered young men before being landed on Omaha Beach. By mid-August they were on Omaha Beach, still showing the scars of that terrible battle of D-Day, which had almost defeated the US invaders.

Here they spent five days, while their documentation was processed by the 3rd Replacement Depot at Mortain, the site of the final German attack on the US beach-head only a couple of weeks before. The 3rd Replacement Depot was typical of its kind: a place of boredom, poor food and isolation. For although these replacement depots were packed with young men waiting for their particular date with destiny at the front, they were still lonely. For the men had come from different outfits all over the Sates and they couldn't really make friends while they were waiting for a post-ing. What was the use? They could be separated from their new buddies at any moment, never to see each other again.

As one of the fourteen wrote to his wife on August 20, 1944: 'Darling, there isn't much I can tell you about France. The place is all torn up. The wine is gone. The only thing there is for us is to drink cider and I don't like cider. It tastes like you know what'.

But that particular PFC, Eddie Slovik, of whom we shall hear more- a lot more- was not going to be drinking cider which tasted 'like you know what', much longer.

On August 25th, the fourteen set off, walking about five miles from Omaha Beach. PFC Tankey, who had known Eddie Slovik back in the States, recalled long after-wards, that they stopped 'at some place (where) we were issued with ammunition by a noncom and told that we had been assigned to G Company, 109th Infantry'.

This was the fourteen men's introduction to the 28th Division, busy slaughtering Germans on the River Seine. It was typical of the treatment handed out to replace-ments: cold, unfeeling and with no attempt to make the replacement feel that they were coming to a new outfit that would take care of them to the best it could in combat. They didn't even know that the 110th Regiment was one of the three infan-try regiments which made up the 'Keystone Division', the '28th Pennsylvanian Na-tional Guard'.

Thereafter the new boys got into a truck with the NCO who had issued them with the ammunition and set off for the front. As Tankey recalled, 'We drove to Elbeuf for four or five hours and we saw a lot of destruction and dead bodies. At first it got to us, but after a while we got used to it. Eddie (Slovik) noticed it and acted about like the rest of us'.

So they moved, excited, perhaps a little frightened and definitely shocked as all replacements are when they see that the dead are not only dressed in uniform of the enemy, but in the same one that they are wearing. Perhaps for the first time, it hits them. One of those dead fellows slumped, bloody and abandoned in that ditch, with the flies buzzing about his head in a great black-blue cloud could be *me*!

On the outskirts of the river-bank town the replacements were told to get out of the truck. The driver wasn't going to chance his vehicle in the smoking, shelled French town. So they slung their packs and their rifles, now loaded with live ammo instead of the practice stuff they had been used to in the States.

It was getting dark now. But here and there the evening sky was split startlingly, frighteningly by a sudden burst of cherry-red flame as yet another shell exploded over the Seine. They advanced cautiously, knowing from training that they should move well spaced out. But too nervous to do so. Instead they crowded together in that instinctive human manner, feeling safer when in close proximity to their fellow men.

Another member of the frightened little group was a PFC Thompson. He stated afterwards, ;It took quite a while (to find anyone) because there was a lot of confusion. We moved around some but stayed close together so none of us would get lost.'

Soon some of them would get lost-for quite some while. But not yet. As Tankey remembered: 'When we walked a mile or so we heard shots fired…at us. We all ducked for cover, and shells started to drop around us. What an experience for a rookie!

New fear set in. The shots had separated them. They didn't like that. By now they were fearful of their own shadows. After all they thought they were under fire. They were in a strange city and even their guide, the NCO didn't seem to know where he'd find the company to which they had been assigned.

'More shells started to come over,' Tankey remembered afterwards, 'and I really started digging like I never dug before. Shells started to drop near me, what a feeling and I was really scared'.

Like his short-term buddy Slovik, Tankey was a Catholic. Now he began to pray and as he thought, 'it lifted the shelling and I thanked God. Then the moon was out and I was laying flat on the ground in my hole, looking at the heavens with clouds around'.

So they went to ground at approximately eleven o' clock that August night, with Tankey, suddenly showing a hidden lyric streak in his nature, lying in his hole "watching the moon and the drifting clouds, tinged silver by the light of the moon", until finally he and Slovik, who was similarly dug in not too far away, drifted into sleep.

Two hours later Thompson also saw or at least *heard* Slovik in the immediate vicinity. For he recognised Slovik's voice, as the latter called out to a fellow replacement. That was the last time Thompson and anyone else, (save Tankey), of that little group of frightened men, lost in the middle of a big war, with apparently the whole world falling down about them, ever saw PFC Eddie Slovik.

Next morning when Tankey and Slovik woke up out of a troubled sleep, the NCO and the rest of the replacements had disappeared. Seemingly they had moved on, without notifying Tankey and Slovik, leaving them to slumber on in their pits among the smoking rubble. But that wasn't true, for Slovik, at least, had heard the others move. As he wrote himself on October 9, 1944 in a poorly spelled confession: 'We were shelled again. I was so scared nerves and trembling that as the other Re-placements moved out I couldn't move. I stayed there in my foxhole till it was quiet and I was able to move.' Tankey did the same, though he maintained he had heard nothing during the night. So he rationalised he hadn't abandoned the 'Keystone Division' - no sir. The 'Keystone Division' had abandoned him!

So the two young soldiers, in name at least, were alone. What were they to do? Should they attempt to find the Company to which they had been assigned? Or even any US unit? It wouldn't have been difficult, even if Elbeuf was in the last throes of the battle between the US 1st Army and the retreating German Seventh. There were signs everywhere, nailed to telegraph posts or beneath the French road and direction signs. No other army ever posted as many of these as did the Ameri-can. Headquarters, depots, ammo, even laundries or VD reporting centres were sign-posted. Americans like nationals of no other country had been brought up on advertising signs, commercial and civic. The average American soldier, however lowly his function, wanted his unit to be recognised by a stencilled sign of some kind or other.

But Tankey and Slovik did not do the expected. They didn't try to find 'their' sign. Instead they wandered around Elbeuf until they found a safe billet to keep them off the streets for the rest of that long August day. In the end they found it: a French hospital. How they explained to the French medics, their hospital overflowing with civilian casualties, why they sought refuge there is no longer known. But somehow they did. All that night they hid in the hospital, grateful for the bowls of milky coffee that the staff brought them and hunks of fresh, warm bread until the next morning when the firing over the river had begun to cease. Then they emerged to the new dawn.

The 28th Division had gone and with it the company to which the two of them had been assigned. Men in the same uniform they wore, young frightened, brave men, had died and been wounded that night. But the rest, perhaps, almost shocked out of their minds by the battle and the resulting carnage, had gone on to the next bat-tle. They hadn't run away. They hadn't broken down. They hadn't thrown their weapons away and refused to fight again. Tamely they had accepted their fate and it was almost predetermined that it would be tragic.

The infantry made up a mere seventeen percent of the 'fighting' troops. But they suffered seventy per cent of the total casualties. One didn't need a crystal ball to know that sooner or later, two out of three of those young men of 'Keystone Division' who now prepared to march on Paris that day would not survive it or if they did, they'd bear its scars for the rest of their days.

Not Eddie Slovik. Six months before he had written to his poor crippled wife that he would never fire his rifle in anger. Now on this August dawn he could tell himself he hadn't He never would. But he, wouldn't survive the war. He would die, not at the hands of the enemy, but at those of his fellow countrymen. In shame.

II

HARD LUCK DIVISION

'Run away? Run away? Damm me, sir, of course soldiers run away. Every soldier runs away. But the good ones always come back. They're the fellows.

Duke of Wellington

Up on the German border, the fighting front had slowly but surely bogged down. What fighting there was, was to the north of where the 28th Division had made its first attack on the Siegfried Line. Between the little medieval German town of Monschau and the old Imperial city of Aachen, where once the Holy Roman German emperors had been crowned, in particular, the first, Charlemagne, the rest of Hodges' First Army was attempting to batter down the German defences.

In particular, the great one-time Roman city of Aachen proved a tough nut to crack. Elements of three US divisions, the 1st, the 30th Infantry, and the 3rd Armoured, were involved. They fought their way through the preliminary defences of the Siegfried Line, then into the bomb-shattered city itself. Week after week, the American infantry fought from house to house-to house, street-to-street, winkling the stubborn German defenders, some of them SS, from their fortified cellars. Finally at a cost of nearly two thousand casualties, the Americans forced the surrender of the city at midday on 21 October 1944.

By that time a new battle was raging to the south of Aachen, between the city and Monschau, what later became known as the Battle of the Hurtgen Forest. It was even more savage than that of Aachen, swallowing up US troops by the company, battalion, regiment and in the end by the division. Why it was ever fought, no on in the US command could really ever explain afterwards. But by the time it was over, five months later, it had cost more US casualties than *five years* of fighting in Vietnam.

That October day when Aachen finally surrendered and General Cota continued to prepare his division for the new battlefield to the north in the Hurtgen Forest, the Americans might have taken comfort from the first reports coming from the old Imperial city. It seemed that the local citizens regarded the Americans more as liberators that conquerors

As a war correspondent reported: (The mob) precipitated themselves at me, brandishing their fists. 'Where have you been so long?' they shouted. 'Why didn't you deliver us sooner from these devils'. They meant their Nazi bosses. The war correspondent recorded: 'It was a stunning sight. These were the people of the first German town occupied by the Allies. And they were weeping with joy...we have been praying every day for you to come'.

An American officer who informed a bunker of German civilians that the battle for their shattered city was over, recorded just how much the populace seemed to hate Hitler and his Party bosses. 'Then came the insults, Bloodhound, bandit' gangster. All this was levelled at the beloved Fuhrer....It was the breakdown of a nation after it had played the wrong cards for five years. Maybe it was the rage of a gangster let down by the gang-leader, but it was a hatred you find only in civil wars'.

Temporarily at least, those reactions might have cheered the Top Brass. They had indeed the makings of a breakdown in the Nazi system, if not a civil war, as the impressionable young officer has supposed. At all events it was something that had to be fostered. They needed to show the world and naturally those Germans still 'suffering' under the Nazi yoke that there were 'good' Germans and 'bad' Germans. The 'good' Germans, such as those in Aachen, now under the US command should be given an opportunity (naturally with 'guidance' from the Americans) to rule themselves.

Thus it was that as the fighting died down in Aachen the new US military government selected a prominent citizen of the city, who had been persecuted by the Nazis and was now prepared, if somewhat reluctantly, to take over the civic control of Aachen as its *Oberhurgermeister*. His name was Franz Openhoff and he had exactly six months to live before the Nazi hit squad murdered him.

The Nazi officer who was first offered the task by Reichsfuhrer SS Heinrich Himmler was indeed the man most likely to succeed in such undertaking. He was Otto Skorzeny, the scarfaced Austrian giant, who was the previous year had snatched the deposed Italian dictator Mussolini away from his captors on the top of a remote mountain. It was an act of bold daring that Churchill had even been forced to praise in the House of Commons in 1943.

In that same year, Skorzeny and his killers had attempted and failed to kill not only Churchill, but also Stalin and Roosevelt in 'Operation Long Jump' when the three world leaders had met at the Tehran Conference in November. One year later he had kept Hitler's reluctant ally Hungary in the war on Germanys' side by kidnapping the favourite son of the Hungarian dictator Horthy, plus he had been involved in several long range plots deep into the heart of Soviet Russia to assassinate key Russian industrial and military leaders. If anyone was capable of assassinating the new, and in Nazi eyes, treacherous Senior Lord Mayor of Aachen, Oppenhoff, it was Obersturmbannfuhrer Skorzeny. Currently he was planning a similar op. in 'British' mandated Palestine, which he hoped would turn into a war between Jews and Arabs there.

Thus when the Nazi plotters had finally identified who the new civilian head of the US-controlled administration in Aachen was, Himmler himself summoned Skorzeny to the former's HQ at Hohenlychen outside Berlin to consider what was to be done. The subject was simple and brutal - *murder*!

Himmler got down to business straight away. He introduced his indirect subordinate to the head of a new underground organisation he had just created. This was the Werewolf Group, which was to be headed by a former Police chief and SS general, who had once been a member of the dreaded *Einsatzkommandos*, in the east, General Pruetzmann.

Himmler explained that the Werewolf was an underground organisation composed of 5,000 ex-Hitler Youth and German Maidens, plus a number of SS men. It would be the job of this new resistance organisation to operate in those parts of Germany, already conquered by the enemy in the east and west, and 'liquidate' those traitors who were now working with the Western Allies and the Russians.

To begin with the werewolves would assassinate Oppenhoff. The Amis had made a great deal of Oppenhoff's appointment and how he was supported by the majority of civilians in the newly US-occupied part of Germany. Now he would have to be taught a lesson. He would pay the ultimate penalty. Thus the locals would learn there was no escape from the long hand of Nazi underground justice. 'In the territory where they (the Americans) believe they have conquered, 'the weak-chinned, bespectacled head of the SS, proclaimed 'new resistance will spring up behind their backs time and time again-and the Werewolves, brave as they were, volunteers all, will strike the enemy.'

After this opening the discussion commenced on how and who would carry out the mission to be code-named 'Operation Carnival', named ironically after the traditional Lenten feast of Catholic Aachen.

All knew naturally of previous operations of the kind carried out by the hulking scar faced Austrian and that he possessed rings of agents, many of them so-called 'sleepers', which reached right into the heart of the low Countries and France. Pruetzmann, who perhaps thought the Openhoff mission was too hot a potato for him, suggested in the light of Skorzeny's past experience and expertise, he might be the ideal person to command the proposed 'Operation Carnival'.

Skorzeny looked doubtful.

Himmler stepped in. He peered through those schoolmaster's pince-nez of his, which made the sallow-faced, weak-chinned head of the SS look even more sinister and said, 'I think this would be your kind of work, Skorzeny'.

Skorzeny didn't rise to the bait.

So Himmler added, giving the Austrian a chance to wriggle out if he wished; then Skorzeny *was* one of the Fuhrer's favourites. Perhaps Himmler knew, too, of the other assignment that the Fuhrer had given to his fellow Austrian, only weeks before, 'Or do you have enough on your plate already?'.

Although ambitious as he was, always ready to take on new tasks, as long as they brought him power and fame, Skorzeny answered in the affirmative, 'Reichsfuhrer, I feel I have enough to do already'.

There the matter was settled and the group of high-ranking plotters got on with the rest of the agenda for that day. But that initial meeting, which finally led to the murder by the Werewolves of France Openhoff in his home on Palm Sunday, March 1945 proved one thing. Otto Skorzeny was prepared to stop at nothing if his actions furthered the cause of National Socialist Germany, with which his own future and fate were linked intimately. Even murder wasn't ruled out!

For Skorzeny that autumn so long ago with Nazi Germany fighting for its very existence the assassination of an obscure catholic lawyer who had become the puppet lord mayor of an occupied German border city, which he had never even visited, must have seemed very small fry indeed. Surely, the man who had planned to kill President

Roosevelt himself, told himself, there must be bigger fish to fry...

I Pvt. Eddie D. Slovik #36896415
Confess to the Desertion of the
United States Army. AT the time
of my Desertion we were in
Albuff in France. I come to
Albuff as a Replacement. They
were shilling the town and we
were told to dig in for the night
The Flowing Morning they were
shilling us again. I was so
scared nerves and trembling
that at the time the other
Replacements moved out I
couldn't move. I stayed their
in my Fox hole till it was quite
and I was able to move. I then
walked in town. Not seeing any of
our troops so I stayed over night at
a French hospital. The next morning I
turned myself over to the Canadian
Provost Corp. After being with them six
weeks I was turned over to American
M.P. They turned me Lose. I told my
commanding my story. I said that if
I had to go out their again I'd
Run away. He said their was nothing he
could do for me so I Ran away again
AND I'll RUN AWAY AGAIN IF I
HAVE TO GO OUT THERE 5555
signed Private Eddie D. Slovik
A.S.n 36896415

Prosecution Exhibit #4
11 Nov 44

5555

74

Slovik's written refusal to fight. November 1944

54

Ever since he had joined a student duelling society as an engineering student at the University of Vienna in his youth, Skorzeny had always fought on the principle it was best to 'go for the head'. Here on the *Paukboden* (the duelling square) armed with a heavy sabre, he had learned to intimidate his opponent by wild slashes at his face. And it worked.

In the war since he had taken over the German 'Hunting Commando', modelled on the British SAS, he had worked on the same principle. Unlike the SAS, Skorzeny didn't believe in strictly military missions. Usually they didn't achieve long-term results. On the contrary Skorzeny felt that his commando missions had to influence political events, even the fate of nations. In his three major missions since he had taken over the command of the SS's 'Hunting Commando' - the rescue of Mussolini; the kidnapping of Admiral Horthy's son; and the attack on Marshal Tito's HQ in the Jugoslav mountains -he had done exactly this. He had turned the direction of the war in Germany's favour.

Now he knew that Hitler was already planning a great surprise counter-attack in the West. On it would hang Germany's fate. Indeed the Fuhrer himself had disclosed the daring operation to him personally, a lowly SS colonel. He had told Skorzeny that he, Hitler, had been shocked by the Americans' use of soldiers, clad in German uniforms during the attack on Aachen. He had said that two armies could play that game and had, in due course, authorised the head of SS Hunting Commando to raise a whole brigade, which equipped with US vehicles, arms and wearing US uniforms. This brigade, the 150th Panzer Brigade, would infiltrate the *Ami* lines even before the attack in the West had commenced, sabotaging, spying and guiding the follow-up units of the 6th SS Panzer Army to their objectives.

According to Skorzeny, the Fuhrer had also ordered him to form a special, top-secret unit within this top-secret armoured brigade. It would be made up of some 200-odd fluent English-speakers. These men, again wearing US uniforms and kitted out with means of assassination, including vials of poison, and huge sums of foreign currency, would penetrate deep into the enemy hinterland. As Skorzeny explained their mission after the war to the court which tried him for alleged war crimes. '(They) were to penetrate to the River Meuse, spying and sabotaging on their route, and there to reconnoitre the bridge across that river for the armoured follow-up!

In the light of Skorzeny'statement, a simple assignment, one that was quite legitimate save that these 'jeep teams' as they were called, would be wearing US uniforms. This would mean that they would be shot out of hand if apprehended by the *Amis*. But that was naturally one of the risks of war.

But would Skorzeny have been content with a mission of that limited nature and one that by its very secret and illegal nature would hardly bring him any great kudos if it succeeded? It is hardly likely. So what was Skorzeny's real reason for turning down 'Operation Carnival' in favour of a low-level, secret reconnaissance mission. Had he at that time a hidden agenda: one that after Germany lost the war he was careful to conceal?

We know in that key October interview with Hitler when he was informed of the extent of this new offensive in the West, Hitler told Skorzeny (according to the latter's) statement to Allied intelligence after his capture in 1945): about the tremendous quantity of material which had been accumulated...He then told me that I was to lead a panzer brigade which would be trained to reach the Meuse bridges and capture them intact...He then sent me to see Generaloberst Jodl,*[5] who gave me more details of the plan and the role of the brigade. I then spoke to General Field Marshall Keitel and a colonel and they completed the details of my role'.

By the time that the US military authorities came to check Skorzeny's statement after the war-the war crimes section was naturally up to its eyes in work-all the other major participants in that October top secret briefing were dead. Hitler had committed suicide and Jodl and Keitel had been executed for war crimes. The only survivor was Skorzeny himself and as the old legal adage has it 'one witness is no witness'.

In essence, was something else planned that October day at 'Wolf's Lair', which Skorzeny thought it wiser to forget after Germany lost the war? And was it something so dastardly, at least in the eyes of the Western Alliance, that Hitler and Skorzeny thought it wiser not to commit its details down to paper?

For we know that a military victory that Hitler hoped for soon in the west would undoubtedly weaken the Anglo-American bond for a while. It might even postpone Germany's defeat at the hands of the great coalition into 1945. But what then?

Hitler was realist enough to know that he wouldn't be able to knock the coalition partners out of the war for good. Even if he achieved a military victory, they, especially America, would rally once more and continue the war until his '1,000 Year Empire' was finally defeated. But if a military victory in the west was allied to a decisive blow to the top allied military leadership, the outcome of what was to be known as the 'Battle of the Bulge' might be totally different.

Destroy the Allied military leaders in the West, and while the coalition partners argued who should replace that leadership he, Hitler would have time to complement the military victory with the final development and use of the new generation of terror weapons that would follow the V-I and V-2.

Already the Fuhrer knew that the only person keeping the coalition functioning successfully in the field was Eisenhower. The American Supreme Commander, the ever-smiling, cheerful 'Ike', had weathered many Anglo-American storms in the past two years. What, however, if Eisenhower were removed? Who would hold the shaken, defeated Anglo-American armies together after a serious defeat in the West?

It couldn't be another Britisher. The Americans, were now fielding three soldiers for every British one so it had to be an American. But what American could take

56

over Eisenhower's position as Supreme Commander? Certainly not Bradley. MacArthur was a virtual dictator in the Pacific. He wouldn't give up his fiefdom out there to take over Europe. General Marshall in Washington wouldn't come into question either. He was too old, too out-of-touch with the personalities concerned. Besides, the dying President Roosevelt needed him too desperately to control all his armies throughout the world.

With Eisenhower dead, the Allied armies in the west defeated and in leaderless disarray, Hitler must well have felt he could achieve a better peace for Germany than the Allied one currently on offer- *unconditional surrender'*. Had Eisenhower to die?

Slowly but surely by torturous and intricate paths and byways the future of the obscure private who had deserted on the Seine and the general, who had just taken up his *great* post in Versailles were being linked. How? By the threat of sudden violent death!

Eddie Slovik (or Slovikowski) was born the son of a poor Polish immigrant Josef Slovikowski on February 18, 1920. Like so many Poles of his time and class Josef graduated to the fringes of the automobile industry, in which he worked most of his life. Here young Eddie grew up in what essentially was a kind of 'little Poland', with life centring on the Roman Catholic Church and the 'Plant, and where everyone spoke Polish (of a kind) and ate the same kind of heavy cabbage and pork dishes. Naturally, as was customary in Slav communities where life was hard and there were few pleasures, there was heavy drinking and not a little crime, often committed when the petty criminal was 'under the influence'.

Thin-chested, sandy-haired Eddie Slovik left school at 15. He hadn't been a particularly good student and in the depressed '30's there were few jobs available for Polish kids, who were not fitted for heavy manual work (Eddie's best weight was only about 140 lbs even when the Army had fed him up for a year or so) and had not even finished high school. Predictably, or at least sociologists, who studied people like Eddie, thought it was predictable, Eddie Slovik turned to petty crime to get through.

As was often quoted at the time when the true details of what had happened to Eddie Slovik came out eight years after the events, Eddie stated bravely minutes before a firing squad shot him to death: 'Don't worry about me. I'm okay. They're not shooting me for deserting the United States Army-thousands of guys have done that. They're shooting me for the bread I stole when I was twelve years old'.

It is doubtful that Eddie Slovik was sent to jail for stealing a loaf of bread in Chicago at the age of 12, or even if he ever stole a loaf. But he was put on probation at that age for breaking and entering. Thereafter he was accused of several petty crimes until in 1937 at the age of seventeen he was sent to the Michigan State Reformatory at the small town of Ionia, a hundred miles of so from his hometown of Chicago.

Here he was trained in the electric shop, where he proved to be an obedient prisoner, who kept to himself and avoided trouble. As one of his supervisors remarked afterwards, 'He was a friendly good-hearted kid....never laughed much or played jokes'. Harry Dimmick, the supervisor, added significantly in view of the events leading up to Eddie Slovik's death so violently: 'Weak as dishwater, sure, scared and insecure....but we thought he had a good chance because he didn't hate'.

No one ever came to see Eddie in prison. Perhaps his family had given him up-his father had taken to drink. One brother was in jail too. But it didn't seem to worry the young prisoner. In the phrase of the time, he 'kept his nose clean' and September 1938 he was released on parole. 'On the outside' he lasted exactly four months before he gave himself up for having stolen a care and wrecking it on an icy patch.

For the next two years Eddie Slovik kept out of trouble - he had to. He was inside again for a term for almost three years, until in April 1942 he was paroled to work in a plumbing company in Detroit. This was to be the last time he would see the inside of a prison until he was entered into that makeshift military one on the other side of the Atlantic Ocean. At the age of 22, he was free at last in a transformed America, where industry was booming and Detroit, the biggest manufacturer of military vehicles in the world, was crying out for labour -even Blacks and ex-cons'.

Afterwards, when the true facts of the 'Slovik Case' came out, apologists for Eddie made out the case that he had never had a chance. William Bradford Huie, the ex-reporter, who took up the 'Slovik Case' back in 1950, quotes one of his respondents as saying, 'Eddie Slovik came out of (jail) weak and scared and feeling inferior…a petty thief… a 'con' who knew he'd always be, at best, an 'ex- con'. Huie concluded that Eddie Slovik 'was a depression kid who never had much of a chance'.

But in view of America's booming economy and the acute shortage of young fit male labour, Eddie had every chance. Within the limits of his background , education, intelligence and his modest ambitions, Eddie should have been heading in 1942 for what was termed in that year 'the gravy train'. Everywhere fit young single men of his age group had vanished, swallowed up by the needs of a rapidly expanding US Armed Services. Not Eddie. As an ex-con he was classified as '4-f ' and therefore excused military service. Men like Slovik, 'ex-cons' or not were at a premium, admittedly he had a two-year probation term hanging over him, but all he had to do was to find a new non-criminal environment, report to his probation officer once a month, keep off the drink and, with a job and perhaps a woman (both easily found in the USA in that middle year of the war), he was set to start a new life: one that would lead to a change in his fortunes and a decent, prosperous career, his petty youthful crimes long forgotten.

For the next year things went well for Eddie Slovik. He had a job waiting for him. The pay wasn't much even then -fifty cents an hour - but it was a job. And then he found a woman-the 'Mommy' of his dreams.

He found her in a plumbing shop, where Margaret Slovik, Eddie's older sister worked. She was plump, heavy bosomed Antoinette Wonewski, 27 years old, a Roman Catholic and a Polish-American like himself. She was ideal for him and Eddie seemingly overlooked her two 'defects': she was five years older than he and she was, as unfeeling people put it crudely, a cripple. She had one leg three inches shorter than the other and walked with a pronounced limp. She was often ill, too, but Eddie found out that later and, just like her age and the limp, it didn't seem to worry him particularly. The main thing was that he had found a woman, who would become the substitute for his mother and the rest of his family which had apparently abandoned him when he had started to 'do time'.

As he expressed it himself. She was his 'dream girl', the one 'I had been dreaming of while I was in jail'. Why he even admired not only her figure, but 'your purty legs'.

Despite the fact that she was already engaged to another man and that Eddie was an ex-con, currently employed as a humble ditch-digger, he was someone she could make something of: a man who could succeed. For Antoinette wanted nothing more than her own modest version of the American dream: a small but well furnished home, good food and perhaps one day a family, together with the necessary modest car.

In September 1942, her mind made up about Eddie, the two of them went to his probation officer to ask for permission to marry. The probation officer wasn't too enthusiastic about the proposal. He tried to dissuade them. Eddie, supported by Antoinette, refused to be discouraged and in the end officialdom relented and the probation officer gave his approval. On Saturday 7 September 1942, they were wed, spending all of their savings to make an occasion of it in the Polish fashion. Two days later the Anglo-American invasion force landed in North Africa and the re-conquest of Occupied Europe commenced, not that such things mattered one jot to the happy newly weds. They were strictly concerned with their own petty affairs and the money and job offers that the booming wartime US economy was bringing for them, the children of the Depression.

One year later, however, the war finally caught up with the happy couple. In the meantime they had furnished their little nest. Eddie had found the best job of his whole short working life, doubling his pay in the process to over a dollar an hour. It came on the first anniversary of their wedding.

It was a busy day. Not only were they celebrating the anniversary, Antoinettes' recovery from a series of illnesses, but they were also moving into a new apartment. Thus it was that night, as Antoinette scrambled some eggs in their new kitchen that Eddie got round to opening a letter which had been forwarded to him from the old address by his sister.

His sudden silence caused his wife to limp into the dining room. There sat Eddie, his face frozen, tears in his eyes. Wordlessly he handed the letter to his wife. She read it and began to weep silently too. It was Eddie's draft notice. He had been called up into the Armed Services!

Eddie Slovik must have experienced the same mixed emotions of many another American male had at that moment, especially if he were married and had a family to worry about. But Eddie's reaction was tinged also by a nasty selfish, self-pitying bitterness. According to his wife, Antoinette, he cried at that moment, 'Eighteen months ago when I got out of jail and had nothing, they wanted no part of me! Now, when I'm a married man, with a pregnant wife and all *this*! Now they want me to go to the army. *Wouldn't you know it!*

Predictably Eddie Slovik turned out to be a bad soldier. Not that he didn't obey orders and maintain discipline. His fault was that he was a whiner, determined not to become proficient with his weapons-he boasted he'd never fire his rifle in combat-always hectoring his C.O. to be released from his service His comrades liked him well enough, but most of them, prepared to make the most of life in the infantry, felt he was a 'gold-bricker' determined to find some pretext so he'd be discharged.

But Eddie had failed. Now in the August of 1944, Eddie had, in a way, discharged himself once he and Tankey awoke that morning in shell-battered Elbeuf. Whatever the circumstances, Tankey (who went on to become a good fighting soldier, wounded inaction and awarded the Purple Heart), and Slovik never contacted their division, the 28th Infantry, once the fighting on the River Seine ended.

Instead they made their separate peace with the enemy. As soon as the 'Yanks' had set off on the jaunt to Paris and that celebrated through-march, they waited to see what happened. They didn't have to wait long. The US 1st Army was replaced by the Canadian 1st Army. Without a moment's hesitation they 'volunteered' for 'Maple Leaf Boys', joining the Canadian 13th Provost Corps. For the next sixty day period while their division suffered its thirty-seven percent casualties in the Siegfried Line fighting, and then prepared for the even greater blood-letting in the Hurtgen Forest to come, Slovik and Tankey became temporarily 'Canucks'.

The 13th to which the two deserters - we can't mince words for that was what they were 'deserters in the face of the enemy', as military jargon had it-consisted of eighteen soldiers under the command of a sergeant-major. Theirs was a 'cushy number' as the Canadians would have been first to admit. Their job was basically to follow the fighting troops to post notices in French and English to alert the civilians in the rear combat zone of what Martial Law meant for them.

The former infantrymen, Tankey and Slovik, soon transformed themselves into supply personnel, scavenging and scrounging, trying their best to keep the Canadians happy by supplementing their diet which seemed ,as Tankey confessed later, to consist mainly of corned beef, 'Bully beef for breakfast, dinner and supper'.

Together with the Canadian MPs, who seemingly asked no questions, happy to have a couple of pairs of extra hands, they travelled around a lot as the 1st Canadian Army moved along the coast on the flank of the British 2nd Army. They passed from France and into Belgium, looking expertly, doing a nice bit of black marketing with the civilians and generally enjoying this time out of war. They met girls naturally, but still Eddie tried to correspond with his wife - how is not exactly clear. But the two of them did contact their regiment, the 28th Division's, 109th Infantry, to inform the relevant authorities that they had 'got lost'.

Not for much longer. Their Canadian hosts were now leaving France, getting closer to the dangerous fighting in Holland, where even MPs were being killed. Slovik and Tankey realised that time was running out for them. Besides, it appears that the

Canadians were becoming sick of their American 'guests'. Perhaps their superiors were asking questions, too. After all, they were not just bill-posters, but military policemen and MPs were supposed to arrest deserters. So Tankey decided he'd return to the war. Surprisingly Slovik went with him.

Thus it was that on October 5, 1944, they reported again to the 'Keystone Division'. Perhaps to their surprise, they were not arrested after their long absence, nor were they charged. It appeared that they had been carried as 'missing' or 'absent without leave'. They were free men - for a while....

Pennsylvania has a proud military tradition that goes back to the days of the Founding Fathers. Here in June 1775, George Washington became Commander-in-Chief of the Revolutionary Forces. It was in the same state that the 24 British standards captured at Yorktown were presented to Congress. Here there was-and -is the 'City Troop' which goes back to pre-Revolutionary days. It escorts every US president who visits the Commonwealth of Pennsylvania. It was not surprising, that the 'Keystone Division', named after that keystone wedge of Pennsylvania between the Great Lakes and the Atlantic, felt itself a unique outfit. Back in 1941 when it was reactivated for Federal Service by President Roosevelt, it could boast three artillery batteries which had fought with Washington against the British. It was proud too that the 28th 'Keystone' Infantry Division had been the first militia unit in the United States to adopt the title 'National Guard' from the French revolutionary 'garde nationale'. In due course this old formation would fight in the war of 1812, the Mexican War between the States and that great blood-letting where it did yeoman service, the Great War.

Now in 1941 after Roosevelt had federalised the Division it was not starved of funds as it had been ever since 1918 (in the year 2001, its budget, for example is eight billion dollars). But the division was still riddled with political appointees in a state which was noted for its political corruption, and 'cronyism' was rife.* 6

Thus the interwar years had taken their toll. One of its first new commanders, Omar Bradley (the 'Tentmaker', as Patton called him maliciously-) felt it was poorly led, poorly trained and riddled with 'political appointments'. As the future head of the US 12th Army Group in Europe noted at the time. 'It was ...known as the 'Iron Division' or the 'Keystone'. A less fitting epitaph than 'iron' could not be imagined.

Bradley, the Division's third commanding officer in a space of six months, tried his best to reorganise the division, but he concluded even then that the 28th like most national guard outfits should be shut down and a start made with other types of non-regular army, large-scale units.

That wasn't to be. Still the 'Keystone Division' tried. It trained and it trained, achieving a decent standard more than once only to have its better officers and NCOs poached time and time again for other outfits being sent overseas. Finally, however, in October 1943, it sailed for the United Kingdom, under the command of Major General Lloyd Brown.

Here the training commenced yet once again for the action in Normandy to come in the early summer of 1944. Their first taste of combat shocked the 28th's soldiers. They had been trained long and hard, as we have seen. But that training had not prepared them for the toughness and slaughter of the Norman Bocage country. Here the battle raged from hedgerow to hedgerow, where a handful of Germans could hold up a whole company, even a whole battalion. The National Guard outfit made slow progress, taking heavy casualties and slowly beginning to earn the nickname the Division was saddled with for the rest of the campaign - the 'Bloody Bucket' (the divisional insignia did resemble a red bucket).

Once again heads rolled. After one month in combat, Major-General Brown was replaced by Brigadier General James E Wharton. He lasted a matter of hours. He was shot through the head by a sniper while visiting one of his front-line regiments and died almost instantly.

Now the man who would command the 28th for the rest of the war and set his stamp on the division for the remainder of its fighting career took over. He was General Norman Cota, a craggy, overweight regular army general of forty-seven, who looked older and possessed the reputation of being tough -very tough indeed.

'Dutch' Cota, as he was nicknamed, though he hadn't one drop of German blood in his veins, was like Patton. He came from a relatively rich family and had attended Worcester Academy before being nominated for West Point at the age of 20. There Cota graduated in 1917, but like Eisenhower, Bradley etc. he didn't go overseas. It wasn't until November 1942 when he was already forty-five years old that the future general would hear a shot fired in anger.

Thereafter Cota's promotion was rapid. He served with the 'Big Red One'. The US1st Infantry Division in North Africa. The he was sent to Britain where he played a role in the British Combined Operations centre until finally he became deputy commander of the US 29th Division, 'The Blue and the Gray'.

It seemed that the 29th had become morbidly afraid of action and the resultant casualties. For the division had been too long in the UK-two years to be exact. Its men wisecracked, 'We've been in England so long that our job won't start till the war is over. They're gonna have us wipe the bluebird shit off the White Cliffs of Dover', just you wait and see'.*7

The men of the 'Blue and the Gray' were sadly mistaken. At least those of its 116th Infantry Combat Team were, now led by 'Dutch' Cota. For on D-Day, Cota took the team ashore in company with his old division, 'the Big Red One' to fight and die on 'Bloody Omaha'. The night before the assault landing, Cota told his regimental officers, 'You're going to find confusion. The landing craft aren't going to be on schedule and people are going to be landed in the wrong place. Some won't be landed at all... We must improvise, carry on and not lose our heads.'

Bloody Omaha proved Cota right on every count. There was more than confusion. There was mass slaughter. As one of the two general officers on the beach, Cota saved the day. For instance he saw a Ranger battalion stalled behind a fortified hill. Angrily he bellowed, 'You men are Rangers. I know you won't let me down.' They didn't. They stormed the hill and took it. The advance from the body-littered beach could continue.

Later, Cota's citation for the Silver Star and the British Distinguished Service Order (DSO), the country's second highest honour, presented by the Field Marshal Montgomery personally, stated that 'Norman Cota penetrated inland on this D-Day to a point the American front-line as a whole would not reach until two days later.' One month later, again in the forefront of the assault, Cota won the Purple Heart when he was wounded in the attack on St Lo, plus a second Silver Star.

In short, Dutch Cota appears to have been a brave man. It is sure that he was a general officer who knew what life was like at the 'sharp end' and he had shed his own blood to prove it. But as we will see, he was bitten by the fatal bug that had attacked many American senior officers of his age and type. He would do virtually everything to obtain promotion. For there were too many of them, who lived for their 'standing': their place in the list of seniority which in peacetime ensured promotion.

It was understandable. In the inter war years those American regular officer who had survived the post World War One cuts or had not quit the service due to lack of promotion, let their lives be ruled by the rate they crept up the ladder of promotion. With luck, living on those remote 'forts' on poor pay in poor quarters, they might retire as majors or 'light colonels'. Now in the booming war years they had become, often to their great surprise, general officers.

So in the war they couldn't fail. They'd never get another chance like this. Now they had military servants, army cars with chauffeurs, flunkies and aides: all the trappings of upper income life. They were even mentioned in the newspapers, had their photographs taken for the popular press, gave interviews which were taken seriously, even appeared in the newsreels shown in the movie houses back home. Now instead of commanding half companies, a hundred men or so, they had control of whole divisions, perhaps even corps, 15,000 to 60,000 men. And if the truth were known, these portly overage officers, who had perhaps lived with the same boring wife for thirty years or more, had willing nubile mistresses: foreign women half their age, who admired them and spoiled them in bed. God-dammit it was a second youth of a kind not granted to the average man. A position like that, two star, even three star, general, was worth fighting for-and not only *against the enemy*.

It was not surprising therefore that General Cota and generals of his kind would fight to the utmost in battle, regardless of the cost in human life. It was not that they were inherently unfeeling, cruel men. It was because they couldn't appear to fail for if they did (and the sacking of at least a dozen US generals who had failed in Normandy had proved it) this new world and its glamorous trappings would undoubtedly disappear. There was no denying that.

Now this mid-October 1944 'Dutch' Cota was faced with taking his newly refurbished and reinforced division into the greatest battle it would fight in the whole eleven-month long campaign. Not that he knew that at the time, Still he did know that the troops fighting in the Hurtgen Forest were failing badly. They simply were not taking their objectives. And General 'Dutch' Cota was certain that when the 'Keystone Division' went into those hilly forests that bordered the Siegfried Line, it would not fail. He simply couldn't afford failure *personally*.

It was, therefore, understandable that Slovik caused a stir when he arrived at the 28th's 109th Regimental HQ at Rocherath, Belgium, together with Tankey. On that October 8th, Tankey was prepared to go into the line and fight. Slovik wasn't. He reported to Company Commander Ralph Grotte, of the company to which he had been assigned on the afternoon of the 8th. Without any hesitation Slovik told G Company commander Grotte that he was 'too scared and nervous' to serve with a rifle company in the line. If he, Slovik, were not kept back in the rear as a cook, jeep driver, something of that nature, he'd run away.

There was no equivocation. Slovik made his statement, clearly under stress, but in a determined manner. He obviously meant what he said. Grotte's reaction was controlled. He didn't bluster. He didn't try to persuade. He had a lot of other things on his mind. Instead he told Slovik firmly that he should go to the Company's fourth Platoon with the company sergeant-major and stay there.

As the legal review of the subsequent court-martial explained in more detail afterwards: 'accused (Slovik) was never present with the company for duty except on October 8 for one or two hours...Grotte assigned him to 4th Platoon, turned him over to the platoon leader and forbade him to leave the company area unless he had permission from the company commander. The platoon leader conducted the accused to his platoon and introduced him to his squad leader.'

But the usually weak-willed 'ex-con' wasn't going to give up just like that. Perhaps he felt that the Army had no right to deal with him in this manner, society hadn't bothered much about him in the hungry thirties. Now he was a married man with a crippled wife and they wanted him-the outcast-to put his life on the line in a combat outfit. Why should he fight and perhaps die for an America that had done precious little for him in the past?

So, he slipped away from his new platoon and returned to company headquarters. There he accosted Captain Grotte and asked (as the official statement put it later) 'if he could be tried for being absent without leave'.

Grotte was in no mood to play games with this new member of his company. He told Slovik he would find out, placed him under arrest and had him returned to his platoon.

As Slovik was marched off under a two man escort, Grotte called Tankey, who was waiting for his assignment to the company HQ and exchanged a few words with him about his 'buddy' Slovik. But before the conversation could develop much, Slovik was back yet once again. This time he blurted out, 'If I leave now will it be desertion?

Grotte answered, it would be.

That did it. Without any further discussion, Slovik took off fast, followed by a surprised Grotte. The latter again spotted Tankey, who had just seen Slovik leaving 'in a hurry without his gun'. Grotte said: 'Soldier, you'd better stop your buddy. He's getting himself into serious trouble'.

But as Tankey stated afterwards: 'Eddie walked right past me without looking at me. He started walking down a little hill, fast. I ran after him, fifty or hundred yards, caught up with him, grabbed him by the shoulder and stopped him'.

'Come back Eddie', he said , 'You don't want to do this'. As Tankey remembered after the war, 'He just looked at me, dead serious.' 'Johnny' he answered, 'I know what I'm doing'.

Then, he jerked away and kept going. I figured he would be back. I never saw him again. When he didn't come back, I figured he had been assigned to some other outfit. I never knew he was in trouble.

Eddie Slovik was-very serious trouble indeed. The die was cast. There was no way back now.

Nearly three weeks before, General Eisenhower had moved his headquarters from the remote coastal town of Granville to Versailles outside Paris, just as he had told General de Gaulle he would at the parade of the 28th Infantry Division through the French capital.

Here at Versailles the Supreme Headquarters assembled a huge staff of office workers, planners, servants and the usual flunkeys and visiting 'firemen' who gravitated to such places, if they pulled strings hard enough.

The actual numbers working at Versailles were kept secret for obvious military reasons and, after the war, for probably more personal ones. Some authorities maintain that at least 21,000 soldiers worked at Supreme Headquarters and that each of Eisenhower's key staff members, some 27, had a large personal staff of his own. For example, Scottish general Kenneth Strong, Ike's Chief of Intelligence, had a 1,000 strong staff. However, it is clear that most of those employed there, away from the blood, cold and misery of the front, had found a well-upholstered sinecure. As the peacetime recruiting sergeants might have said ' a home away from home'...a 'cushy number'.

Eisenhower certainly had. He had his mistress- Kay Summersby -and his intimate coterie of friends and staff who shielded him from the dire realities of the winter war now developing at the front. There was General Bedell 'Red' Smith, his Chief-of-Staff (also with mistress) who was as fiery-tempered as his nickname and hair colour. General Everett Hughes, Ike's 'eyes and ears', drinking crony and card-player (another with mistress in tow), who provided him with all the latest tittle-tattle on his fellow general officers.

Then came 'Tex', his booming voiced record-man; Telek, the poodle dog; 'Mickey', his orderly, etc., etc., all commanded in a way by the former PR and radio man, Commander Butcher, who also supervised the running of his 'home'. Home was centred on Marie Antoinette's Petit Trianon, the splendid 18th century baroque structure which had been part of the little estate she had created (before she was so cruelly execute) in order to play a 'simple' milkmaid, dressed naturally in a fabulously expensive 'simple' silken gown.

Up to a couple of months before, the house which Eisenhower's staff had picked for him had been the home of no less a person than Field Marshal Gerd von Runstedt, the supreme Commander's one-time opponent in Normandy and soon once again to be Hitler's Commander-in-Chief in the West. Here the aged Field Marshal, with the greatly wrinkled face, had indulged himself in fine French wines and good cognac and had, as he was often to remark, 'enjoyed the war because the peace was going to be terrible.'

Now this house, at Germaine en-Laye isolated to a certain extent, had become a security officer's nightmare, especially as Allied security was well aware that the Germans knew every nook and cranny of the place. After all the 'Krauts' had occupied the place for nearly four years and had built certain additions to it, such as its air-raid shelters, an ideal place of refuge for those intent on evil.

The staff officer who was most worried was US Lt. Colonel Gordon Sheen of the US Corps of Counter-Intelligence, who reported directly to 'Ike's' Chief-of-Intelligence, General Strong. This US Corps of Counter-Intelligence of which Sheen was the most senior representative in Europe was virtually unknown in US Army circles. Even at SHAEF HQ, Sheen and his agents were shadowy figures, fighting to survive in a multitude of intelligence outfits, dominated by the OSS, the forerunner of the CIA.

In addition to the fact that CIC was virtually unknown at SHAEF, the organisation had a bad strike against it. The CIC had, in fact, incurred the wrath of a no less a person than President Roosevelt himself. Indeed Sheen himself probably had just escaped being sacked by being posted overseas to England and then North Africa.

It appears that the CIC had bugged a hotel room occupied by S/Sgt, Joseph Lash, an army Air Corps NCO, who was not only a personal friend of the presidential couple, but also allegedly a communist. According to a CIC report, dated December 31, 1943 and later submitted to President Roosevelt, it seemed that a sexual encounter had taken place between Eleanor, the President's wife, and Lash.

As the story goes, once the President learned of this allegation, he flew into a towering rage. He ordered Lash posted overseas within ten hours. Then he ordered CIC operations closed down. So it was that the Counter-Intelligence Corps virtually ceased to exist inside the Continental United States. Sheen, as a senior agent, was then obviously glad that he had managed to escape overseas in time and thus survive.

General Strong, his immediate superior and probably the best Allied Intelligence Officer in Europe, was not particularly interested in counterintelligence operations. He left the petty business of dealing with spies, saboteurs, informers and the like to lesser people. Thus it was that Gordon Sheen , who appears to have been of a highly strung nature-for a policeman, which he was - was left in charge of the whole SHAEF security.

Naturally one of his first priorities was headquarters itself, located in the Trianon Palace. It was the jewel of the French crown, a national treasure, where history was made when the Treaty of Versailles was signed there. Even the Allies had to be careful in such premises. So it was that only a limited number of the highest-ranking officers were accommodated there: the G1,G2, G-3 and G-4, plus a few of Eisenhower's own special staff. Any German agent knocking out the Trianon and those key staff officers who worked in it would naturally deliver a body blow to the Allied war effort.

The CIC chief knew, too, that there were still plenty of German agents and sympathisers at large in France and if they were fanatical enough - or well bribed, they would carry out any plan the Germans devised, however daring. Indeed ever since the D-Day landings there had been examples of French agents in German employ attacking US troops. Even as the GIs had left the beaches and encountered the first French built-up areas, they had been fired on by French snipers *8, had trucks of the vital Red Ball express supply route attacked by bush-whackers and the like. By early September, the CIC was already picking up German born 'sleeper agents' left behind in Paris.

Now as the campaign had commenced bogging down at the German frontier the Germans and their French renegade supporters had become even bolder. More than once Sheen had received reports from both Bradley's 12th Army Group and Devers' Sixth that there had been sightings of 'German commandos in US uniform' At first Sheen probably took these sightings calmly. It was known that the Germans tended to pick up bits and pieces of US uniform and equipment, especially boots, from dead GIs. In this way they could replace their own worn and usually shoddier clothing and footwear.

But as the winter approached Sheen was informed by his subordinate at Sixth Army Group HQ in France that a half-company of the US 15th Engineers had been engaged in front-line road repairs when they had been attacked. This time it wasn't the lone sniper or ambusher, but 'seventy Germans yelling 'GI'. All of them had been dressed in full American uniform. That worried Sheen. It was the first large scale attack of its kind. What did it signify?

The mystery was added to later in that same week. POW Interrogation now began reporting that there had been a small trickle of German POWs who had admitted under interrogation that they had been a secret German order, requesting that all captured '*Ami*' equipment and uniforms should be sent to the garrison town of Osnabruck in Northern Germany. Why Osnabruck? Sheen was unable to find out.

However, these German prisoners did state that at the North German garrison town there was a special unit stationed in the 'Adolf Hitler Kaserne' which trained soldiers in long-range reconnaissance and sabotage. More importantly, the POWs maintained, these men under training were supposed all to speak fluent English.

That certainly must have puzzled Colonel Sheen. It was only later in mid-November that he would receive some enlightenment. Then SHAEF's head of Counter-Intelligence learned of an order signed by no less a person than Field Marshal Keitel.

In it, Germany's senior soldier requested all unit commanders to forward the names of men in their outfits who spoke English, in particular, what the Germans called 'the North American dialect of English'. These speakers of 'American dialect' should, in due course, report to a 'Hunting Commando' (*Jagdkommando*), located at the isolated base at Friedenthal; and Sheen already knew who commanded that particular *Jagdkommando*. It was Obersturmbannfuhrer Otto Skorzeny, the scar faced daredevil who had rescued Mussolini from his Italian captors the year before.

But for what reason were these American-speaking Germans to report to Friedenthal? Sheen didn't need a crystal ball to guess they were going to be used in some sort of long-range mission. That mission would be directed against the US Army. That was obvious, too. Why else should these men be required to speak 'American'? But the US Army in the ETO was huge. What part of it was to be attacked? In essence Skorzeny had a four hundred mile Allied, mainly American, front to choose from?

He reasoned, however, that with Skorzeny in charge, whatever operation was planned would not be low-level. Skorzeny's past record showed that. All the same, Sheen knew that his first priority was, as always, to protect Shaef and, in particular, the Supreme Commander. He'd wait until he had more concrete information before he would start to undertake more intensive measures.

So life at the great headquarters at Versailles proceeded in its customary manner. There were the conferences and the parties. Lovers quarrels and petty rivalries between competing staff officers. Talk was of the rising prices in the capital's black market restaurants and how the troops on their forty-eight hours passes from the line were blackening the image of the US Army with their drunken antics on 'Pig Alley' (Place Pigalle). The 'white Mice', i.e. US military police, the staff officers opinion, were far too lenient with these drunken louts from the front.

Thus Supreme Headquarters spent its time. As Captain Noel Annan, one of Strong's Intelligence staff, recalled, 'it was not as if the vast staff helped Eisenhower to make strategic decisions; they had already been taken by meetings between Eisenhower, his army group commanders and General Patton....The plans SHAEF produced were rarely clear or convincing, since they were a series of compromises; and the staff spent more of their time producing papers to justify these decisions...'As Noel Annan summed it all up,' (it was) all balls and rackets'. And he wasn't referring to a game of tennis...

Thus as 'Ike' tried to keep the allied team together and his staff officers played their games in splendid isolation of Versailles, Eddie Slovik approached the back door of the military government office in a remote village on the German border. Here he found a friendly GI from the 28th Division's 112th Infantry Regiment who was doing KP there as a cook. Tamely Slovik, who was worn and unshaven and looked as if he could do with a good feed, handed the KP a green slip of paper. Later the KP would note the time and date. It was eight o'clock on the morning of October 9.

It was a flower-order form of the kind supplied by the US Army PX for troops wishing to send flowers back home to their loved ones. But this was no request. For Eddie Slovik had written in his poorly punctuated, misspelled fashion on both side of the form the following: 'I told my commanding officer my story (the one he had related to Captain Grotte). I said if I had to go out their again, I'd run away. He said their was nothing he could do for me so I ran away and I'll run away again if I have to go out their'.

Moving into the *Death Factory*.

Now Slovik asked the cook to give the message to an officer. This the cook duly did. The officer, Lt. Wayne Hurd, an officer in the military police, knew his duty. He handed the green paper scribble to Lt. Colonel Ross Henbest.

The latter, a former instructor at Gulf Coast Military Academy, was not a hard case. He called Eddie into his makeshift office and gave him a second chance. He warned Eddie that a written confession and statement of intent might well be damaging if he were placed in front of a court martial. He suggested, looking at the pale-faced, agitated soldier, who wasn't going to fight, that Eddie should take the green paper back. Outside he should destroy it. Then no one of importance would be the wiser.

Eddie refused.

God knows what his motives were. Did he think the US Army was like a state rehabilitation unit? Didn't he comprehend that he was simply 'a body', one of thousands, hundreds of thousands? All the US Army wanted from him was that he should pick up his Garand rifle and march to the music of war, the cannon. In what was to come, that horrific slaughter of the 28th Division in the 'Death Factory' there was no time for the personal problems of Eddie Slovik - or anyone else for that matter.

Reluctantly, Colonel Henbest did what he was supposed to do. He entered on the reverse side of the green scrap of paper, this record-endorsement: 'This statement is made in the presence of Lt. Col. Ross C Henbest, 0237158 and 1st Lt. Wayne Hurd 0463853'.

> I have been told that his statement can be held against me and that I made it of my own free will and that I do not have to make it.
>
> Signed: Eddie D Slovik

> The above statement was signed in the presence of the undersigned.
>
> Signed: Ross C Henbest Lt. Col. Infantry
> Signed: Wayne L Hurd 1st Lt. Infantry

Shortly thereafter Eddie Slovik was taken and imprisoned in the 28th Division stockade. Now there seemed no way to go back. It was true. That October day with the guns rumbling up at the front over the nearby German side if the border, Eddie Slovik had signed his death warrant.

Why - has remained a mystery to this very day ....

III

THE DEATH FACTORY

'This day I felt like a 'little Napoleon.'

Gen. Cota. November 1944

Ten days after Private Slovik made his monumental decision and was consigned to the 28th Division's stockade, General Cota, the divisional commander, was summoned to HQ of the US 1st Army at the Belgian town of Spa. Here General Hodges the dull, plodding 1st Army commander told Cota that he was going into the Hurtgen. A little later General Gerow of Vth Corps filled in more details for Cota.

Another of the 5000 casualties the 28th Division suffered in the Huttgen Forest. November 1944.

The Corps Commander explained that the US VII Corps was about to make the main drive for the River Rhine. To protect the right flank of Collins'VIII Corps, Cota's 28th would capture the Hurtgen township of Schmidt, which controlled the local road network. This network would provide 'additional lateral supply routes for VII Corps'. This mission, the capture of Schmidt, would have to be accomplished by 5 November 1944.

Basically Cota had been given an impossibly short period of time to take over from the withdrawing US 9th Infantry Division, organise his attack and achieve his objective. After all he knew that the 9th had taken horrendous casualties in the Hurtgen for an advance of a mere one and a half miles. One of its regiments had suffered sixty percent casualties to capture a few square miles.

Cota didn't protest. Afterwards he stated he had had 'grave misgivings'. He admitted that he had been worried about the rugged terrain. In the case of Schmidt, he said, he knew that the Germans dominated the high ground on the series of hilltops leading to the township. Yet at the time he didn't state these doubts to Gerow. All he said was that the whole 1st Army was in danger of attacking where the Germans 'looked right down the throat' of the assault force. When Gerow and later Hodges didn't react to his warning, Cota didn't say anything more. He started to prepare his attack.

Although he knew the difficulties, Cota, it seems, thought he had a gambler's chance

Slaughter in the *Death Factory*.

of success. At one point he boasted that his 28th would take Schmidt, even if he 'had to use every medic in the division' (presumably as infantry). In the event those medics would have so much to do tending the dead and wounded; they would never find time to handle a rifle, even if they had wanted to.

Cota's officers were not so sanguine as their divisional commander. Some observers from Gerow's Corps HQ who talked to them before the attack found they had little hope of success. 'None of the officers was in the least bit optimistic. Many were almost certain that if the operation succeeded, it would be a miracle'.

General Cota did not seem to see the problem. As the Division readied to cross the border from the great Belgian training ground at Elsenborn, he heard one staff officer liken the situation to ' a bloody finger pointing into Germany surrounded on three sides by the enemy.' He didn't appear to notice. Orders were orders. They were there to be carried out. Soon hundreds and then thousands of his young men would die and be wounded in those dark fir forests. They would die suddenly and violently-perhaps because 'Dutch' Cota had not questioned those orders from above. As for the General, he would die long afterwards -peacefully -in bed.

October gave way to November. The start of the 28th's attack was only a matter of hours away. Then the rain came. Those who have lived in the Eifel area know it well. It is cold, persistent, exhausting. More often or not, north of Prum, the little cross roads township where the 'Snow Eifel' begins, it turns into snow. The roads become slush. The forest tracks turn to mud. And all the while the snow-rain comes down in relentless, never-ending, soul destroying persistency.

Now as then, the Hurtgen is invariably swathed in fog and a chilling wet mist. Visibility sinks to the limit of the next firebreak or clump of dripping firs. Transport gets bogged down and planes are useless; they simply cannot penetrate the thick ground mist.

Now in 1944, faced with such intemperate weather, Cota made his only attempt to gain some respite. Perhaps for once he perceived the difficulties ahead in those fogbound, soaked forests of tightly packed conifers. Here, under such weather conditions, his armour and air would be of no use. He asked First Army Commander, General Hodges, for postponement. Hodges in his nice comfortable hotel HQ of Belgian Spa turned him down. The 28th Division would attack on November 2, 1944 as ordered. Bradley and, in his turn, Eisenhower wanted it that way. There would be no further discussion....

Dawn, November 2.

Light came slowly. It was as if God on high was reluctant to throw light on the man-made lunar landscape below. The tress dripped mournfully. Frozen snow lay here. The humps beneath were made by the dead of the 9th Division, still unburied. Pfc Bob Graff of the 28th recalled long afterwards, as they moved up, 'another guy took me back in the woods to a blanket, pulled it back and showed me a man laying there with a hole in his back, already mouldering. I though of this guy's family with him layin' there. That was my first contact with what combat was all about'. He'd learn much more about combat before he would leave those woods.

At eight o'clock precisely, 14,000 young soldiers of the 28th, many of whom were green replacements, were shocked breathless by that awesome ear splitting thun-der as it shattered the brooding morning silence, the whole of the divisional artil-lery, plus batteries from other adjacent outfits, flung 12,000 shells at known Ger-man positions. The earth shook like a live thing. Trees snapped like match wood. Bunkers collapsed. Then the whistles were shrilling. Officers were waving their carbines and crying 'follow me'. NCO's, red-faced, as if with rage, were kicking men onto their feet and they were moving into the attack.

But not for long. The attackers stopped on order. They had to wait for promised air support. That puzzled the Germans waiting in their well prepared positions. Why hadn't the *Amis* attacked under the cover of their barrage? That was standard operating procedure.

Naturally the planes didn't appear; the fog was too thick (when they did in late after-noon, they killed 24 US artillery men by mistake. They called it rather quaintly 'friendly fire'). Two regiments, Colonel Petersen's 112th Infantry and the 110th, made fair progress when they finally moved off. The 110th Infantry, always unlucky, advanced straight into well-directed machine gun and mortar fire. Great gaps ap-peared in their ranks. A young Earl Fuller, for one, saw his first sergeant die within second of rising from a foxhole. He'd been an officer in World War One, but he had accepted the loss in rank to fight again in the new war. As Fuller remembers, 'All summer he had said the war would end in November. It did for him'.

It did for a lot of other young men that grey, wet November day. The 110th's regi-ment aid station, code-named 'Honeymoon', was flooded with terrible casualties. And there was nothing sweet and loving about what happened to the injured there.

Desperately officers and noncoms tried to rally their men. To little avail. The intensity of the German fire was too much. The heart started to go out of the young soldiers. Communication began to break down and with it discipline as well. Men left the line at first in ones and twos, then by the dozen. Soon it would be whole companies drifting back and in the end running to the rear.

One survivor recalled a sobbing artillery man trying foolishly, hopelessly, to dig a foxhole in the frozen earth with his bare hands. 'He was the first 'CF' I ever saw. I was going to see a lot more'. The ex-28th soldier was right. 'Combat Fatigue' (CF) would be endemic in the end.

As darkness fell early that terrible first day, the 110th Regiment was fighting desperately to maintain its original start position. Several companies had retreated to the rear area and were being remorselessly shelled by German artillery. Losses were mounting rapidly. In some companies they had already lost two thirds of their strength, without achieving a single objective. A four hour truce was called with the enemy to collect casualties. And there were those drifting back through the grey evening mist who had been neither wounded nor forced to retreat. *They* had already made their separate peace with the enemy. They were going 'over the hill'.

Then the 28th's luck changed for once. A day later they actually captured their prime objective, the village of Schmidt. Cota was overjoyed. Signals came pouring in from fellow general officers congratulating him on his success. The 28th had succeeded where the 9th had failed so lamentably. For his one and only time, General Cota went up to the front, well as far as Vossenach some miles behind Schmidt, to visit his troops. In his diary that day he wrote that he was beginning to feel like 'a little Napoleon'.

The feeling was not to last long. The Germans counterattacked. On the night of 3/4 November they assaulted the 3rd Battalion of the 28th's 112th Infantry. They came with both infantry and tanks and what 57mm cannon the American Infantry possessed were not much use against the German Mark IVs. Here and there the anti-tank solid shot shells bounced off the German armour like glowing ping pong balls.

The soldiers of the 3rd Battalion's K Company started to break. One whole platoon withdrew in panic and without orders. A Colonel Lockett of the 112th was rushed forward on Cota's orders to investigate. He never made it. Colonel Peterson, the C.O., a veteran who had served with the 28th since 1916, seemed to lose control. His 3rd Battalion drifted back through his 1st Battalion. They were infected by the growing panic. They began to break. Officers and noncoms tried to hold them with drawn pistols. In vain. As S/Sgt Frank Ripperdam reported later: 'There was no holding them. They were pretty frantic and panicky'. In the end only 200 stayed in the line. Nearly six hundred fled.

Meanwhile Peterson's third outfit, the 2nd Battalion, was in trouble, too. Even before the Germans appeared some of the men were shaky and nervous. Some were crying as if brokenhearted. Others were slumped apathetically in their foxholes, staring into nothing. They had even to be ordered to eat their C-rations. The battalion commander, Colonel Hatzfeld sat on a box in his cellar command post, face buried in his hands. He was a broken man, who no longer seemed to care what happened.

What happened when the Germans came was predictable. A Company broke and ran. Another company commander seeing this ordered his men to withdraw. Panic started. The Battalion's flank was exposed. Nothing could stop the retreating soldiers now. All of them headed for the rear -and safety.

'It was the saddest sight I have ever seen', remembered Lt. Condon of Company 'E'. 'Down the road from the east came men from F,G and E Companies: pushing, shoving, throwing away equipment, trying to out race the artillery and each other, all in a frantic effort to escape. They were all scared and excited. Some were terror-stricken. Some were helping the slightly wounded to run and many of the badly wounded, probably hit by artillery, were lying in the road where they fell, screaming for help. It was a heartbreaking, demoralising scene'.

As yet not a single German had made his appearance at Vossenach. The regimental staff officers, who had been rushed up to stop the panic, pointed this out to the men. But they wouldn't stop to listen. As Captain James Nesbit, the battalion personnel officer, explained later; 'Yet it was no use pointing this out to the panic-stricken fugitives. They were completely shattered. There was no use fooling ourselves about it. It was a disorderly retreat. The men were going back pell-mell'.

After that German counter-attack, Cota never again visited the front line. But in that one visit to Vossenach he must have seen the state of his men, so many of them reinforcements fated to die before they had begun to live. Still he did nothing about it. He continued to issue orders, as if everything was going to plan. Three hundred man strong battalions, whose battalion 'effectiveness' might mount to a mere hundred soldiers, were commanded to attack again and again. On paper and in reports to his superiors, Gerow and Hodges, it looked good. But more often or not, the battalion commanders and at a lower level, company commanders, simply did not carry out those orders, wherever they could. In effect General Cota had lost control of his 'Keystone Division'. In what was to transpire in the case of the 'US Army v. Private Eddie Slovik' that bitter self knowledge was going to play a role, it had to.

But before the slaughter was over, General 'Dutch' Cota was to suffer yet another bitter blow to his pride in himself as a commander and in the division which he had commanded ever since the summer.

Colonel Peterson, who as we have seen, had served twenty-eight years in peace and war in the 'Keystone Divisions' 112th Regiment', had had enough. He had seen his regiment shattered. Not only that, parts of it had actually run away. Now, for some reason that was never explained afterwards (in fact, the matter was hushed up), he took it into his head to have it out with Cota personally. Perhaps the rumour running through what was left of the 112th that there was a colonel waiting at Divisional HQ to take over the regiment from him might have played a role. At all events, after a great deal of brooding, he handed over temporary control to a Colonel Ripple. Then with one lone companion, he set off down the heights to give 'Dutch' Cota a piece of his mind.

Where Eddie Slovik was sentenced to death.

He descended the so-called 'Kall Trail', but he was out of luck. Just as he and his companion, plus the driver of their jeep, turned a bend, the ditches on both sided littered with American dead, sprawled out like bundles of abandoned soaked rags, it happened. They were hit by a burst of enemy sub-machine gun fire at close range. They dropped from the jeep and fled into the trees.

For a while they were in luck. They dealt with two Germans who tried to stop them. But as they moved forward again, there as an obscene belch. Mortar fire started to descend upon the fugitives. Peterson yelped with pain. He had been hit in the leg. But the Colonel didn't know it at the time. He thought it was his WWI wound acting up under strain.

Somehow the middle-aged Colonel kept going. Once more they ran into an ambush, the Colonel's companion was hit. He took a burst of machine gunfire in his chest. But he saved his superior.

Now Peterson was alone and on his knees. He crawled stubbornly forward. Abruptly he felt a burning pain like that of a red hot poker being pushed into the flesh of his right leg. This time he knew he had been wounded. Now confused and at times almost lapsing into unconsciousness, he continued to crawl through the German positions, which seemed to be everywhere in the dank dripping forest.

He bumped into three Germans. The first two passed. They hadn't spotted him. The third one had. Peterson pulled the trigger of his burp gun. The German he saw through a wavering mist. Whether he hit him or not, he never knew. But when he could see properly again, the third German had vanished.

In the end, he heard German voices, mixing up with those of Americans, But he could go on no longer. He just lay there, bleeding and exhausted. Periodically, or so Colonel Peterson was told later, he called weakly 'General Cota...General Cota...'

Finally the Colonel was picked up and taken to the divisional aid station. Here he recovered sufficiently to ask for the C.O. In due course Cota arrived. Later the General stated he knew of no message recalling Peterson. Thus looking down at his senior regimental commander, ragged, unshaven, bloody and exhausted, Cota thought the worse. He assumed that Peterson had abandoned his shattered 112th Regiment to its fate.

It was too much for the Divisional Commander. Big, tough 'Dutch' Cota, the hero of 'Bloody Omaha' fainted clean away.

Six days before Cota fainted at the sight of Colonel Peterson on his stretcher in the divisional aid post, Private Slovik was given his last chance. At the end of that October he and several other deserters from the 28th were confined in the divisional stockade. The stockade, really a barn and farmhouse, was located in the little German border village of Rott. Discipline wasn't particularly strict as it would have been stateside and the prisoners were expected to work-in relative freedom while they waited for their court-martial. This was held almost daily in nearby Roetgen, where, in what seemed another age, the 'Big Red One' had fired the first shell of WWII into Germany.

But there was no need for the shotguns and manacles that were used in other stockades. Here the men wanted to be sentenced and taken away to the rear as soon as possible. For the fighting front was only a few miles away and at night when the wind was in the right direction, the prisoners in their barn could hear the hollow boom of the guns in Hurtgen. There, they knew from the stockade scuttle-butt, their erstwhile comrades were being slaughtered by the hundred -in the end the 28th Division would suffer nearly five and a half thousand casualties in the Hurtgen -and the deserters wanted to be back in the safety of COMZ before some-one decided to send them into line, deserters or no.

As one of the guards remembered after the war, 'Slovik was a good-hearted kid - never complained. Nice-looking kid too...'But, as the guard recalled ten years after the war, he was like the rest - 'bucking for a court-martial so he could stay out of the line'.

Indeed the same guard remembers two of 'the kids' came back from sentencing to be asked by Slovik, swinging his legs in the hay of the barn, 'How much didya get?' 'Twenty years,' they hollered back ... and they seemed happy.

Slovik's comment was 'I'll settle for twenty years right now. How long do you think you'll have to stay in after the war is over?'

'Maybe six months', was the two prisoner's reply.

As the guard summed it up a decade afterwards, 'That's how it was. They all thought it was the way out... After the war, the business would be forgotten soon and they would be sent home after a couple of months. 'But in the case of Slovik, that guard of so many years ago, was wrong, badly wrong. Eddie Slovik would never see Detroit and 'Mommy' again.

Still he was given a last chance, two to be exact, to get himself out of the mess he had talked himself into. On 27th October he was brought into the presence of the senior legal officer of 'Keystone Division', Colonel Henry Sommer. He was the Divisional Judge Advocate and a trained lawyer, one of the original National Guards-men from Hollidaysburg, Pennsylvania.

Although it was his duty to be hard and punish anyone who committed a military offence which impaired the efficiency of the 28th Division, he wasn't a particularly hard man himself. Still he liked soldiering and indeed he stayed on in the regular US Army after the war. He felt, in essence, that Slovik had 'Assumed a position of defence for which military law said that he should shot'.

In the interview with Slovik at Divisional HQ, a Gasthaus on the road that led from Belgium to newly conquered Aachen, Germany, he felt that the young soldier was 'a nice looking fellow….*not innocent, but calculating*'. (author's italics.) Probably Sommer was the first officer of some authority to have a serious look at the prisoner and decided that, as we would say today, he was 'street-wise'. He was going to play 'I've never had a chance' card. Indeed that would be the impression he gave to most of the lower-ranking people who would have dealings with him over the next three months until he met his fate in that snowbound French village in the Vosges.

But Sommer kept his initial impression to himself. He said, 'Slovik, you're in trouble and I'd like to help you get out of it. We don't like to court-martial anybody. 'Sommer then added that if Slovik would go back to his outfit and 'soldier' he'd ask the general if he will suspend action on your court-martial'. Sommer even offered Slovik a chance to escape the stigma of having deserted by transferring him to another of the Division's three regiments, 'where nobody will know what you have done and you can make a clean start'.

Slovik refused categorically. Although he had never even been in the firing line, he said, 'I'm not going back up there in the line. I can't serve in a rifle company'.

Sommer made one last attempt to make the stubborn young soldier change his mind. He told Slovik that he couldn't have him transferred from the Infantry, as the latter wished, to a safe job in a supply company. He then warned Slovik that if he were found guilty on going to trial, he risked a heavy prison sentence. He said sombrely: 'You're making a big mistake if you don't go back up there and try it'.

Slovik wouldn't hear of the alternative. 'No', he replied, 'I'll take my court-martial'.

Wearily Sommer gave up. He ordered that Slovik should be taken to the makeshift stockade at Rott. Later he said, 'I wasn't particularly surprised at his attitude. I had heard too many like him say, 'I want my court martial…'

Still the US Army didn't give up on Slovik altogether, despite his attitude. He was seen by the Divisional Neuro-psychiatrist, Captain (Dr) Arthur L. Burks. Although Dr. Burks was unlike the usual 'trick cyclist' of the time, disliked by the orthodox regular soldiers, who felt 'trick cyclists' leaned over backwards to explain any sort of antisocial, undisciplined action, he liked Slovik. Or, at least, he said he did later. But as a protégée of the strictly authoritarian General Cota, his report on Slovik gave the latter no means of escape on medical grounds from what was to come.

It read: 'I have this day interviewed Pvt. Eddie D. Slovik, Company G, 109th Infantry and find him to show no evidence of mental disease at this time and I consider him sane and responsible for his actions at this time.

There is no evidence that he was other than sane and responsible at the time of his alleged offences. He has never sought medical attention re garding any physical of nervous complaints by his own admission.'

Signed: Arthur L. Burks
Neuro-psychiatrist

It is clear that the *'trick cyclist'* offered Eddie no way out....

Now it was to be left to Eddie's defending officer. The court, including the Judge Advocate's representative, Colonel Sommer backed up by the several junior officers who had had the first dealings with the reluctant hero, would clearly be prejudiced against Slovik. This prejudice would undoubtedly be reinforced by the psychiatrist's assessment of Slovik. But more importantly, the deck would be stacked against the accused by the gory statistic that the 28th would have suffered nearly six thousand casualties, just over a third of its strength, by the time that Eddie Slovik would face his accusers.

Forget the regular army officer's attitude to 'shirkers', 'gold-brickers' or downright cowards, as they probably perceived Eddie Slovik to be. Their reaction was predictable. As Colonel Rudder , a future commanding officer of Eddies' Regiment would put it, 'an able-bodied man who won't fight for his country, doesn't deserve to live.'

Think instead of average American riflemen of the 'Bloody Bucket' division, as it was now being called in the Hurtgen. They had gone up into the line and done their duty to the best of their ability. Several hundred had admittedly run away, but *they had tried*! They had seen their buddies wounded, maimed, killed What would these ordinary 'dough's' think, say, do, if they saw people like Eddie Slovik getting away with it/

But although he knew he was taking on a probably hopeless case in view of the circumstances and what was happening in the Hurtgen, Slovik's court-appointed defending officer prepared to do battle on behalf of his client. He was Captain (later Major) Woods.

Edward Woods was not a trained lawyer (trained lawyers were not very common in wartime court martials). But he was 'permanently appointed defence counsel' for the 28th's General Court, for all cases brought before it. In this capacity, he had already defended some twenty 'clients' on serious charges. To an certain extent he had been quite successful, having three previous clients to Slovik acquitted, including one charged with 'buggery'. Much later he would take up the 'Slovik Case' once more in the hope of obtaining a service pension for Eddie's widow, who had changed her name and found refuge in an old folks' home. We can assume, therefore, that although Woods was on a first name basis with most of the court and friends with some of those who wished to see Slovik receive the maximum sentence, he was going to do his best to ensure Slovik received a fair trial and, if possible, an acquittal.

But the young ex-businessman, another of the Division's original National Guardsmen, was faced with an almost insurmountable problem when preparing the defence's case. It was Eddie himself. We have seen that Slovik, had been given several chances to withdraw both his written admission and his oral one that he would never go up into the line. By now he had surely been long enough in the US military to have realised that an ordinary soldier does not challenge authority so blatantly. In essence he was saying to the President of the United States, who after all was the Commander-in-Chief of the US Armed Forces, 'you can't make me do anything that I don't want to do'.

Why hadn't he just simply deserted again without making any fuss he did - the confession on the green order slip; the bold declaration that he wouldn't 'soldier' to several officers of the 28th, including its Judge Advocate? What could Slovik possibly hope to gain by cocking a snoot at these men, engaged in trying to maintain morale in an outfit where it was already shaky.

After the trial, the US Army's legal reviewers took the point of view that Eddie Slovik had purposefully set out to challenge the Army. As their report states: 'This evidence leads inevitably to the conclusion that the accused deliberately absented himself on October 8 with the intent of deserting the military service so that he would be tried by court-martial and incarcerated and thus avoid hazardous duty'.

According to William Bradford Huie, the journalist, who first brought Eddie Slovik's case to the attention of the American public half a century ago now: 'Jail, to Eddie Slovik , was a place of refuge - the womb to which he thought he could always return if life became too tough, too demanding on the outside...Returning to jail, as a protective tactic, had been in Eddie's mind since the night he received the draft notice...Perhaps Eddie finally made up his mind there in the hole at Elbeuf: whenever the possibility of his going under fire approached again, he'd make certain his return to his haven; he'd do what, to him, he should have done when he got the draft notice.'

The amateur psychology really doesn't wash. Eddie knew prisons; he'd been in three of them after all. He knew the routine. He could live with being behind bars for a while. That was a risk he could take without being unduly worried. But what about the ultimate penalty that a court martial could impose on an American soldier who deserted in wartime and 'in the face of the enemy?' For a deserter, as Eddie Slovik had already been warned by Colonel Sommer, chanced the possibility of being shot by a firing squad for the ultimate military crime.

It was a piece of information that does not seem to have worried Eddie Slovik unduly as Veterans Day 1944 approached and his court martial would commence. For he knew he wasn't risking much more than a jail sentence if he were found guilty and his own statements pretty well ensured he would be. Then since 1864 when President Lincoln had signed the death warrant personally, no single US soldier had been shot to death for deserting during wartime. Why should he Eddie Slovik, an obscure, harmless ex-petty con, be treated any differently than all the rest who had been sentenced to death for the same crime before him? No, it would perhaps be jail for Eddie Slovik until the war ended and then sooner or later, it'd be home to 'Mommy'.

IV

UNDER SENTENCE OF DEATH.

'The function of a court martial is to preserve security by preserving the armed forces in a state of discipline. Just that, if it can be done with justice, so much the better, but it must be done.

John Terraine.

On November 7th, 1944 while the 28th Division still bled in the Hurtgen Forest, Adolf Hitler personally ordered that there would be no patrolling in the 'Ghost Front area' of the Eifel-Ardennes. The Fuhrer feared that German prisoners taken by the *Amis* on such patrols might inform the latter about the great secret offensive soon to come. For now the most stringent measures had been enforced in the deep forests of the Eifel to ensure nothing leaked. Even the families of deserters would be punished by *Sippenhaft* (arrest of next of kin) by being sent to concentration camps. And when the highest ranking German officers, such as Model and von Manteuffel, commander of the 5th Panzer Army, went to inspect the German front and observe the *Amis* opposite, they did so disguised as lowly colonels of obscure infantry regiments.

The only exception to the Fuhrer's November 7 ruling were members of a varied group of special forces, which came under the nominal command of Obersturmbannfuhrer Otto Skorzeny. They were newly recruited officers and enlisted men of his 'jeep teams' attached to the top-secret 150 Panzer Brigade, all of them fluent English speakers. But there were others, too, who, up to now, have not been mentioned in the vast literature of the Battle of the Bulge. For in 1945 their activities were 'classified' by the US CIC who interrogated the survivors at Colonel Sheen's request. Thereafter these interrogations and what they revealed of a cast no-German network of agents in Allied West Europe were deliberately, or so it seems, allowed to moulder in the CIC files; and when the CIC were disbanded forgotten altogether.

In the main, French renegades and fascists made up the largest group of these undercover Skorzeny's agents. As we have seen some had remained behind as 'sleepers' when the Germans had abandoned France. But three groups had been forced to accompany the fleeing Germans. They were the members of the *SS Division Charlemagne*, the German commanded French SS division, which had been recruited to fight in Russia. It was this division which defended Hitler's Bunker to the last in Berlin in spring 1945. Indeed one of its members won the last Knight's Cross of the Iron Cross awarded by the Fuhrer in WWII.

Then there were the formations of the two French renegades and traitors, Darnard and Doriot. Skorzeny was impressed by the former, who told him when they first met that he could offer 4,000 to 6,000 followers. They (according to the CIC report of 23 July 1945) 'were distributed throughout France, four to ten men in each small town and .. it was agreed that an efficient resistance net could only be built out of political organisation'. This would be known as the 'White Maquis'.

In the meantime Darnard and Doriot offered Skorzeny 60 agents from their headquarters in German Sigmaringen. These would be contracted by Skorzeny and be paid four to eight hundred reichmark a month. For each successful mission completed they would also be given an additional bonus of two to four thousand marks.

Skorzeny, according to his interrogators, liked Darnard. But he preferred volunteers from the Charlemagne Division and Doriot's 2,000 strong Milice formation. For both organisation could supply trained soldiers and fanatics to boot who had not hesitated to kill their fellow French men during the months preceding the Wehrmacht's flight from their country.

In addition to the French, the main body of Skorzeny's agents in the West, there were the Belgian van der Wiele's men and those of the Belgian SS under the command of fascist Degrelle, who was admired by Hitler personally on account of his bravery at the front in Russia. These two fascist leaders were supplying agents for training who would be employed in the Belgian Antwerp area (the ultimate objective of Hitler's surprise attack in the 'Bulge' and the Allies' major supply port), plus thirty Flemish women who could be dropped by air as wireless operators.

According to the postwar CIC investigation (ordered by Eisenhower himself for what will appear as obvious reasons), there were some 'ten to twelve French...and 6-8 Belgian group leaders in training each month at Skorzeny's sabotage and spy schools that autumn, with the French alone running twenty to thirty long range operations deep behind the Allied front line in October and November 1944.

But how did these renegade agents manage to penetrate Allied lines and reach even Antwerp and Paris; both key objectives in what was soon to come? The short answer is they didn't attempt to do so. They were not the usual 'front-runners' ('Passeurs' in French; 'Frontlaufer' in German): agents who were so familiar with that rugged, forest frontier of the Ardennes that they could slip by the American outposts and strong points and reach the rear areas which were relatively empty of US troops.

Instead these long-range agents were transported to their destinations by air. They were carried there by the very mysterious German special air squadron, attached to covert operations HQ, known as 'Kampfgeschwader 200'. Although after the war 'KG 200', as it was popularly known, figured quite often in thrillers and adventure novels such as the 'Eagle Has Landed', Allied intelligence did not succeed in obtaining very much information about the elite undercover air squadron, which flew almost exclusively captured Allied planes.

As one of the surviving pilots has written to this author, 'We knew nothing about other pilots' operations. For security reasons, we were not allowed to discuss our own on the pain of death. In general we were very much concerned with our individual assignments and, therefore, learned little of what was going on in other areas'.

It is clear from the CIC report on KG 200 that this was the case. In fact the CIC interrogators after the war couldn't even place the special squadron's home base. According to their agents it was 'located W. of Berlin'. In fact the base was at Finow outside the German capital. In the event, the KG200 flew its covert missions from fields; many of them simply landing strips all over the Reich and German occupied territories in the East.

Skorzeny had first come into contact with this special air force outfit when it was run by Admiral Canaris's *Abwehr* (Secret Service) when it was called *Staffel Gartenfeld zbV*. Gartenfeld, a tall dark-haired, bold pilot, had run covert ops. for the *Abwehr* since 1939, infiltrating some of the first parachute agents into Britain in the first years of the war. In 1943 Skorzeny started using KG 200's services for long-range operations into Soviet Russia and the Middle East, including 'Operation Long Jump' of the November that year, which was designed to assassinate the 'Big Three', Churchill, Stalin and Roosevelt, at the Tehran Conference.

One year later Admiral Canaris was arrested and his *Abwehr* was amalgamated into the SS's own secret service and Skorzeny was allowed to use the KG 200 planes when and if he wished, providing there was enough gas for the proposed op.

By now the special air force outfit had an interesting and deadly mix of places. As the CIC report states: 'These included suicide bombers, remote control ones, gliders for special purposes, piloted V-Is and Mistel Flugzeuge (pick-a-back planes.)' The force also included, according to the author's informant: Douglas DC-3s, B-17 Flying Fortresses and B-24 Liberators'. It was these latter types which were used for agent drops in the west behind Allied Lines.*[9]

It is clear from the detailed and carefully documented CIC report of July 1945 that the American agents were not able to find out very much about KG 200-its pilots, afraid they might be arrested by the Russians on account of their activities there had gone to ground or had actually fled with their planes abroad, mostly to supposedly neutral Spain. But the Americans did establish one thing. For the 'purpose of the Ardennes Operation...KG 200 was attached to Pz. Brigade 150'.

The question rises now is what did Skorzeny's special long-range penetration armoured brigade, equipped with Allied tanks and armoured cars etc., currently being trained in Grafenwohr, Bavaria, want with an elite secret air force unit, flying captured Liberators and Flying Fortresses? Surely there could be no viable connection between the two outfits, save that they were both on the same side?

We know that the CIC had captured a couple of agents already who had been landed behind Allied lines by aircraft. The records indicate that CIC had picked up Frenchmen who had been dropped or been landed by light aircraft in August and again in September. But no further details of who had carried them to those remote DZ's are given in the scattered CIC files. Nor is there any indication of what happened to the captured agents, probably they were handed over to De Gaulle's counter-intelligence service once they had been grilled by the US authorities. It must be remembered that the Great American Public had to believe that the French, as well as the other 'liberated' nations of Western Europe, were overjoyed at being freed from the 'Nazi yoke'. There had to be no indication that all was not sweetness and light between 'our boys over there' and the gallant French. Therefore accounts of French men and -women-sniping US troops or spying on them as German agents had naturally to be kept under the wraps.

But if Colonel Sheen was unable to draw any hard-and -fast conclusions from these occasional airdrops behind US lines, there was still ample evidence coming from that section of the line held by General Middleton's VIII Corps that something strange was going on.

In the main Middleton's VIII Corps was located on the linguistic border between German-and-French-speaking peoples of the area. The line held by Middleton's four infantry divisions (soon to include the battered 28th returned from the Hurtgen) was located in the German-speaking part,   The rear area, mainly supply outfits etc., was in the French-speaking portion.   The German-speakers were the doubt-ful element as far as security went. In 1940, when Belgium had been conquered by Hitler, they had become Germans again, by official decree. Over the next four years, till the Americans had arrived to 'liberate' them, most of their men folk had been recruited in to the German armed forces. Understandably their loyalty was dubious. Francophones of the rear area were regarded by the American Intelli-gence services, on the other hand, as loyal and reliable.

All the same, both sectors, the French *and* German speakers did make numerous reports that November and early December that something strange was happen-ing in the Middleton Corps area. Reports came in periodically from civilians in the villages and small towns of the 'East Cantons', as that part of Belgium is known., of chance meetings with strangers who asked unusual and sometimes leading ques-tions.

The locals at Middleton's own HQ in Bastogne maintained they had seen stran-gers laying out drop-zones in the fields surrounding the future site of the 101st Airborne's great stand. These reports were poo-poohed by Middleton's Intelligence Officers. The Belgians were great scaremongers, always had been, 'Nervous Nellies' to the man.

But it was the German-speakers of the front line area who came up with the strangest sightings, a multitude of them - all of them seemingly ignored. Virtually everywhere there were meetings with American officers, who smoked German cigarettes; farm-ers and peasants with soft white hands who, to judge from their use of the local dialect, weren't from the area; a whole range of supposed locals, who weren't re-ally locals.

In particular, there were at least half a dozen of these sightings at the cross roads outside Poteau on theN-31 highway between Malmedy and Vielsalm, both sites of US barracks and reinforcement holding units. Here one side of the cross roads was -and is -French speaking; the other was inhabited by those who spoke Ger-man.[10]

The strangers who all spoke German would turn away when their questions were met by a reply in French. Even the Americans who turned up there wouldn't speak to the Francophones, but conversed *in German* with those of the locals who an-swered their queries in that language.

In the main they seemed interested in the road system stretching out from the cross roads towards the bridges across the River Meuse some twenty-odd miles away. But they also were interested in the way to the 'French' or 'Napoleon Cross', located in the woods some 250 metres away. This was is a plain weathered stone cross, supposedly erected by 'Napoleon's troops some century and a half before.

Why, the locals couldn't fathom out.

It was only later when a small-time farmer encountered once more the 'American' he had met that November and who had offered him, not a prized 'Ami' cigarette, but a German cigar (not so prized) that he tumbled to the fact that he had been taken in. This time (December) the 'American' was wearing the uniform of an officer in the Armed SS. Now he waved cheerfully to the frightened farmer and called, 'don't you remember me?...I gave you a cigar last time we met.'

Then the slow-witted farmer understood. The strangers had been using the weathered 'Napoleon Cross' as a convenient landmark and rallying point between major road systems leading westwards through the Ardennes and on to the River Meuse. But as the Belgian chronicler of that strange meeting over a half a century now recorded: 'rallying point for what?'

The German commander who had sent those mysterious 'Amis' to that ancient cross in the woods near the Poteau Cross roads was now back again in the Reich. During the preceding months he had travelled a great deal carrying out his manifold and mysterious operations, which included two kidnaps and one attempted assassination. Now Obersturmbannfuhrer Skorzeny was fully engaged in the planning of the forthcoming attack in the Ardennes, flitting from one remote training base to the other, dealing with commandos, soldiers and agents from a dozen European countries.*[11]

In particular, he was concerned with the training of his special Panzer brigade 150, which contained the English-speaking long-range jeep teams. These were being instructed in a sealed-off part of the Bavarian Grafenwoehr tank training grounds, soon to be known to generations of American soldiers, including future generals like 'Stormin Norman' Schwarzkopf, Wesley Clark and the like.

November 9, 1944. Eisenhower with General Cotta. HQ. 28th Devision, Rott.

There under a guard of SS soldiers, who were Ukrainian volunteers and didn't speak German and, treat Skorzeny's men like prisoners, the latter were being put through their paces.

HQ. 28th Devision today (Rott).

As Skorzeny would have his US interrogators believe after the war, there were two groups of Germans being trained in that remote winter camp. There were those who would wear US uniform, man US vehicles, speak some English and would be used to rush the bridges across the River Meuse for the follow-up 6th SS Panzer Army. Hence the general name of the operation 'Operation Trojan Horse'.

The second group was a more select bunch. These were the men who were fluent English-speakers (some were German-Americans, who had served in the US Army and Merchant Marine), dressed in American uniform and in their jeeps make long-range penetrations behind the US front. It was their mission to spy, sabotage and generally disrupt the American lines of communication.

Typical of the training of the 'Jeep teams' was the learning of GI slang and cusswords plus 'the way the American GIs lounged and didn't take life so seriously as did the

HEADQUARTERS
EUROPEAN THEATER OF OPERATIONS
UNITED STATES ARMY

In the foregoing case of:

Private Eddie D. Slovik, 36896415,

Company G, 109th Infantry,

the sentence, as approved, is confirmed. Pursuant to Article of War 50½, the order directing the execution of the sentence is withheld.

DWIGHT D. EISENHOWER
General
United States Army
Commanding.

2 3 December 1944.

Death Sentence - Agreed by Eisenhower.

German landser', as one of the volunteered remembered after the war. Indeed Skorzeny went to great lengths to ensure these special teams were well trained for their unspecified missions yet to come.

As another of the teams ex-Sergeant Heinz Rohde revealed to the German new magazine *Der Spiegel* in 1950: 'At first we were mostly concerned with learning the idiom of the GIs. The showing of American film, including war films, played a great role in our training. 'But apparently the learning of supposed GIs phrases such as 'Go and shit in ya hat' and 'Ya old man cant suck eggs either' didn't suffice. Skorzeny actually sent his men, disguised as POWs into American prisoner-or-war camps to mingle with the others in the compounds. As ex-Sgt Rohde recalled: 'Then came short visits to nearby POW camps where we mixed with GIs and gained the impression that we were developing into perfect Yankees'.

It was a daring ploy. In the great sprawling POW camps, where starving Russian POWs routinely ate the guard dogs, one of the supposed GIs could have easily disappeared into the great 48-seater 'thunderboxes' if he were discovered. Unfortunately for Trojan Horse, the pseudo-GI's would make a basic mistake right from the start. They would place four men into a jeep, whereas US Army policy was three men in a jeep, especially in Patton's 3rd Army. But that was later.

Still the men under training in Graefenwoehr were puzzled. Rumours were circulating all the time, as the volunteers tried to work out what their role was to be and why they should be guarded in this manner, as if they were prisoners themselves. It was obviously their mission, whatever it was, was highly secret. It was whispered that two of the volunteers had already been executed for having revealed details of their training in their letters home which were censored. It was also said that two SS truck-drivers, both Dutch, had been arrested and perhaps executed too on the same score. They had gotten to know too much in an overnight stay in the now snow bound Bavarian camp.

At first, as Skorzeny recorded after the war, he attempted to suppress these 'latrinograms', as they were called. But in the end he realised that wild rumours might well provide an excellent cover for the real mission. Therefore he let his men indulge in an orgy of rumour mongering. For he knew that his own spies among them would report anything which cam close too the truth about the 150 Panzer Brigade's and the 'jeep teams' real missions.

Then it happened. It was the start of a rumour that would plague Skorzeny for many years: one that hasn't rally been scotched to this very day. *'That is if it were really a rumour?'*.

One morning in November, a young SS officer identified by Skorzeny solely as *'Leutnant N'*, who was a member of one of the jeep teams, asked to see the Obersturmbannfuhrer.

Skorzeny granted the surprise request and when they were 'under four eyes', i.e. alone, *'Leutnant N'* burst out excitedly with: *'Obersturm* I think I know what our real objective is'.

The scar faced commando leader must have sat bolt upright at this statement, if it were ever uttered. Officially he and only two officers in Grafenwoehr camp knew of their assignment. Had someone spilled the beans? But before Skorzeny could react, young *'Leutnant N'* allegedly said, 'Sir, the Brigade is to march on Paris and capture Eisenhower's headquarters'.

Death Sentence - Agreed by Eisenhower.

According to his own account, Skorzeny forced himself to be calm. In a non-com-
mittal manner, he remarked, 'so-so'. Then he frowned , as if he were suddenly dis-
pleased.

That frown convinced 'Leutnant B' he had hit the nail on the head. With 'all the
enthusiasm of youth', as Skorzeny described it, he said, 'May I offer you my co-
operation, sir? I was stationed a long time in France and know Paris well. My French
is good, too. You can rely on me, sir. Now this is my plan…'

According to Skorzeny, the young officer went on to explain eagerly how the 150 Panzer Brigade would enter the French capital from various directions, posing as Americans. With them they would take supposedly newly captured German tanks on transports. According to 'N's cover story these tanks were being taken to the rear to be examined by US tank specialists for any new German developments in the armoured field.

Now all the Panzer Brigade would need was a central rallying point for its various columns. There they would concentrate for a daring raid on Eisenhower's headquarters at the Petit Trianon. German Intelligence, according to the excited SS officer, knew all the details of the place on account of Field Marshal von Rundstedt having lived there for so long. It would be not so difficult to penetrate it and - here Skorzeny stopped and didn't give any details of what 'Leutnant N' had suggested they would do with the American Supreme Commander once they had captured him.

Instead he recalled he pretended to go along with the other officer's wild scheme. He said he, too, knew Paris well. He suggested that the Café de la Paix might be a good place for a rendezvous. He had often sat there in better time drinking a *Pernod* or a *Ricard*.

With that he dismissed the excited young 'Leutnant N' (if he had ever existed) and left him to develop his wild scheme *[12]. Thereafter even wilder rumours swept the camp and Skorzeny would confess after he had been captured that he had lived ever since 1944 'regretting that he had ever mentioned that damned Café de la Paix in Paris'.

But had 'Leutnant N' really been the source of that story? It was a story that would have Eisenhower maintaining that Skorzeny was 'the most dangerous man in Europe', virtually demanding the giant's head on a silver platter. Is it conceivable that a young officer such as the mysterious 'Leutnant N' would approach Hitler's favourite soldier, the man who had created headlines all over the world by rescuing Mussolini the year before? Would that obscure young officer, if he ever existed, have possessed such temerity? Hardly likely in this author's opinion.

The events of that 20 November 1944 when, as Skorzeny recalled in his Memoirs, the interview between himself and 'Leutnant N' took place at Grafenwoehr, were later dismissed by the commando leader as 'a little stone which spread large ripples'. For him it became 'evil (enemy) propaganda....to ensure that three years later I faced a US military tribunal'.

Later when Skorzeny and others of the 'Jeep teams' did face a war crimes court at Dachau concentration camp, it was very convenient for him to dismiss the alleged plot to kill or kidnap the Supreme Commander as the figment of that young officer's vivid imagination. Interestingly enough in this context is that while the US prosecution managed to find all the 'Jeep Team' leaders who had survived the war, they never did succeed in apprehending what might have been a key witness in Skorzeny's favour - 'Leutnant N' .

But as was discovered during in his post-war interrogations and those of the participants close to him during the Battle of the Bulge, his attitude to seizing and possibly assassinating senior Allied commanders had been slightly different during the war. On 14/15 December on the eve of the great attack, a young SS man with the 6th SS Panzer Army recalled at his own trial, he and his comrades of the Peiper Column had been briefed by their company commander.*[13]

'He told us that' Force XYZ' (the sixth Panzer's cover name for the Skorzeny 'Jeep Teams') was tasked to capture corps headquarters, corps and divisional commanders' (author's italics) and general sabotage behind enemy lines. 'The young SS soldier was then told how to recognise Skorzeny's 'Americans'. They would raise their helmets in certain ways and both their helmets and vehicles would be marked in a small 'z'. Not that the young soldier had occasion to have dealings with 'Skorzeny's 'Jeep teams' thereafter. For on the late afternoon of the Saturday 16 December 1944 Skorzeny disappeared completely, only to reappear on 22nd December outside a famed country hotel in Ligneuville where he was wounded and quit the lost battle for good, taking the ultimate secret of his mission with him.

There is, too, just one other item that could indicate that Skorzeny was not altogether being quite honest with his US interrogators after the war. It came during a routine inquiry dated 23 July 1945 made by an unknown American officer at the ' US Forces European Theatre Interrogation Centre.'

It was about the 'KTI (*Kriminal Technisches Institut*), Berlin, internationally known before the war on account of its use of technical means in the solution of crimes. After the summer of 1944 and the imprisonment of Admiral Canaris, the *Abwehr* chief, for treachery, it had come under Skorzeny's control. Skorzeny had started using the *Institut's* facilities for developing special weapons, including parts for the British-invented silence Sten machine pistol; the English one-round pistol with silencer; and the Russian Nagau silenced pistols etc. etc.: all weapons used by assassins; it may be noted.

In July the unknown US interrogator wanted to know from Skorzeny details of 'poison bullets (made) under his direction' at the *Institut*. Readily Skorzeny told the American about the use of bullets, fountain pens, lighters and the like for the concealment of poison capsules. But as the interrogation report reads '(he) at first tried to persuade the interrogators that these bullets were manufactured and issued solely for suicide purposes...He finally admitted that they were intended for assassinations.'

Unfortunately Skorzeny (very wisely for him) didn't state for whom these bullets were intended, but just after his capture in the Austrian Alps he had boasted to his CIC interrogators when queried on Colonel Sheen's behalf whether he had really intended to assassinate Eisenhower the year before, "If I had been ordered to assassinate General Eisenhower you can be sure I would have carried out the operation successfully...."

While all this strange activity was going on 20 miles or so to the south, on the morning of Tuesday 9 November 1944, 'the stars', as the saying went, descended upon General Cota's Command post at the *Gasthaus* in Rott. Leading them there was no less a person than the grim, frowning intended victim General Eisenhower himself. With him he brought the commander of his 12th Army Group, General Bradley who had once advocated that the 28th Division should be disbanded; 1st Army Commander, General Hodges and Cota's 5th Corps Commander, General Gerow.

It must have been an alarming sight for Cota, so many stars on the shoulders of this top-ranking brass and they had all come to see him. And he knew why. His 28th Division had been soundly defeated in the Hurtgen Forest. Indeed it was in such a bad state that its battered regiments were being helped out by another regiment from a different division. Now the Brass were there to discuss what to do next. The division had lost a third of its effectiveness and was in no shape for further offensive action for the time being. Already in the early hours of the morning Cota had been telephoned by Hodges and then Gerow that the 'stars' were on their way and that he, Cota would be expected to make suggestions of how to pull his division out without any further loss of prestige. For as 12th Army Group Commander Bradley always maintained: 'The US Army does not give up ground which has been bought with the blood of its soldiers'. The fact that 'Ike' himself would be present was indicative enough of the seriousness of the situation. For, as Supreme Commander, he rarely came this far forward unless it was a grave emergency.

In essence, a worried Cota must have known, a decision would be taken this Tuesday that affected not only the fate of his 'Keystone Division', but also his own. Understandably after a life time of trying to achieve his own stars and the command of the largest actual fighting formation in the Army, Cota would be fighting for his career and future. Then Bradley was renowned for doing a hatchet job on divisional commanders who had appeared not to have lived up to his expectations in combat. Normandy had proved that.

Although nothing is recorded of what either Bradley or Eisenhower said to Cota that morning the little turn-of-the century stone *Gasthaus*, we do know that Supreme Commander was in a bad mood. There is a photo extant, too which in dumb show seems to express Eisenhower's attitude to his fellow West Pointer Cota. 'Dutch' is standing outside the *Gasthaus* explaining something with an uncertain weak smile on his face, probably for the benefit of the divisional photographer, while Eisenhower watches. The look on the supreme Commander's face reveals all. Its says, 'Dutch, you're bullshitting'....'bullshitting me for all you're worth.'

But the 'bullshitting' must have paid off. For Cota was not sacked, as he might well have expected to be after losing control of his division which had been wasted in the Hurtgen. Instead he was to put in another and last attack with his own and new troops, while the bulk of his division was to be withdrawn to the supposed 'Ghost

Front' of the Ardennes to be reinforced and re-supplied.

All the same those of the 28th who would be expected to fight yet another time while their more fortunate comrade withdrew, sloshing through the ankle-deep mud of the forest trails, dragging their wounded with them, didn't complain. Perhaps they were too exhausted and battle-weary to do so. As one of their equally beat company commanders said afterwards, 'Not one of the men offered any bitches...' As for the survivors who finally neared safety and relief from the misery of the forest, where it had begun to snow again and two signallers were found frozen to death at their posts, 'they were so damned tired', as one of the colonels, Lt. Colonel Sibert recalled after the war', they stepped over and <u>on</u> the bodies of their comrades - they were too tired to step over.'

On 11 November, it was recorded that 33 men of the 28th Division's 109th Regiment slipped exhausted into their own lines. They were the last survivors of a company which had been surrounded for five days. There they had held out in snow and mud without food or drink and with only the ammunition they had carried into the forest with them. The 28th Division's battle was over. In two weeks, one 28th Regiment alone, the 112th Infantry had had 232 men captured, 431 reported as missing, 719 wounded, 167 killed and 655 non-battle casualties. This made a total of 2,093 out of the original 3,000 men who had gone into action. For the Division as a whole, the final score was 6,184 casualties, some 45 percent of the Division's original strength. A tremendous blood-letting.'

But 'Dutch' Cota had survived. He would never get a corps command, as did many of the US generals who had gone to Europe with him. His handling of the 28th and its defeat in the Hurtgen mitigated against any promotion. He would stay a divisional commander till the end of his service in Europe. It is not surprising that he was a disgruntled man that mid-November when he was faced with the fact that too many of his men had run away in the forest, refused orders to attack and had placed themselves effectively out of his control. Now, in addition to all this, he was made aware that one of his men had decided he wouldn't even make the attempt to go to the front in the first place. Not only that, he had actually had the audacity to sign a statement to the effect he would desert once more if he were ordered to do so'.

We can imagine Cota's state of mind when he first read the court-martial documents relating to the 'Eddie Slovik case'. By nature he was an old school disciplinarian, whose ideas were already becoming out of fashion even then. He thought a soldier's first loyalty was to the country and the army. Personal considerations came second. Naturally men cracked in combat. But a rest out of the line, clean clothes and a show, and perhaps a few drinks would soon have them on their feet again, ready to return to the firing line. Admittedly there was a lot of talk about 'combat fatigue', the new name the 'trick cyclists' had given to the 'shell shock' of the trenches of the Old War. But naturally General Cota didn't hold much with 'trick cyclists'. They could be taken in too easily by the 'gold brickers' you found in every outfit.

But such men were dangerous. There was a lot of truth in the old saying about 'rotten apples'. Hadn't that sort of thing happened to the 'Keystone' in the Hurtgen? American youth had become soft. They thought more of their rights than their duties and obligations. The rot had to be stopped.

As General Cota told William Huie in his forthright manner in 1953. 'I was never impressed with what they called our 'orientation program' during the war. I think it is more effective to teach men traditions and obligations. Whenever I spoke to men under my command, I put it simply as I could: 'Men for every right that you enjoy there is a duty you must assume. You have heard a lot of talk about 'rights'; now you'll hear a lot about 'duty'.

This was the attitude of the general who was going to be the deciding factor in the trial of Eddie Slovik up in the small town not ten miles from Cota's own HQ. It was not a very promising one. It boded little good for a soldier who had actually put down on paper, an unprecedented, foolish and provocative thing to do, that he couldn't, wouldn't soldier; and that if anyone attempted to make him do so, he would not hesitate to desert. After what General 'Dutch' Cota had just been through, one didn't need a crystal ball to know which way the 28th's Commanding General would vote if it came to his making the final decision about Private Eddie Slovik's fate.

At ten o'clock precisely on the morning of Veterans' Day, Thursday, 11 November 1944, Private Eddie Slovik's court martial was convened. It was held in the upper storey of the local military government in the Belgian-German border township of Roettgen, its only claim to fame as far as the Americans went being that two months before a battery of guns from the 'Big Red One' had fired the first shells into Germany in WWII. As always, America's premier infantry division had to be first.*[14]

But now the old 'Big Red One' had vanished, decimated in the fighting around Aachen and in the Rhineland. Like the recently slaughtered 28th Division it had already been consigned to history. But in the matter of Eddie Slovik v. the US Army there were a few loose ends to be cleared up still.

The court was typical of such courts at that time. Combat officers, especially if they were infantry were urgently needed at the front. So the men who would try Eddie Slovik, all officers naturally, were from the staff, doctors, dentists, glorified clerks and the like, though in a month's time most of them would undergo their first and only taste of combat. This included Eddie's defending officer, Captain Edward P Woods, who would end the year, wounded and prisoner himself of the victorious Germans fighting in the 'Bulge'.

After the court was duly sworn in, the charge was read out: 'The general nature of the charge in this case is a violation of the 58th Article of War. There are two specifications. The first specification alleges that the accused deserted the service of the United States on or about 25 August 1944 at Elbeuf, France with intent to avoid hazardous duty and to shirk important service, to wit action against the enemy and remained absent in desertion until returned to US military authorities on 4 October 1944. The second specification alleges that he deserted the service of the United States on 8 October 1944 with intent to avoid hazardous duty and to shirk important service to wit: action against the enemy...'

Now Slovik was asked to make his first utterance of the trail. Had he any objection to these 'stipulations'?

His answer was limited to five words: 'I consent to the stipulation'. This laconic approach was typical of Eddie's handful of statements throughout the 100 minute trial -and remember Slovik had been warned his life was at stake if he were found guilty. Later, it would appear that Slovik must have been motivated by two things: 1) Get the trial over quickly, without angering any of the officers composing the court: 2) by not angering the authorities, he was making sure that any future plea for clemency (if he were found guilty) would be favourably supported at 28th Division HQ.

For it must be remembered that Slovik had always got on well with those in authority. Even in reform school he had never caused trouble and run foul of the prison authorities. Those whose reactions have been recorded all spoke of him as a handsome willing young man who gave no trouble. It was the same with those of the 28th

Division who interviewed -and often warned him about his own foolishness-prior to his being arraigned for desertion. As we have seen the 28th Division's most senior officer of the Judge Advocate's Branch thought he was a 'clean-cut, handsome young man' and advised him to tear up that incriminating 'green confession slip'; then Colonel Sommer promised him, if he would tear up the slip, he'd ask General Cota to withdraw charges and Slovik could go to a new infantry outfit of his own choice where his 'crime' was unknown.

Now the prosecution started to wheel out its witnesses and the affidavits of those who were detained due to the Hurtgen Battle. First came Private George Thompson who had been a member of that little group of frightened reinforcements at Elbeuf. He stated that Slovik, who he knew from shipboard, had been with them and that he had been handed out live ammunition like the rest. This meant Eddie Slovik knew that they were soon going into combat and that he guessed that all of them 'had a pretty strong suspicion' that they were soon going to see action.

Slovik's defending officer who like his client remained silent a great deal of the time made a minor objection, but Captain Woods was overruled (as he was generally by the court.) Even when Thompson was asked if the reinforcements had seen any action on their way to Elbeuf, Woods didn't challenge this important point. For it should have been his aim to prove that Eddie hadn't realised that he was in an actual combat zone; and that he had not deserted 'in the face of the enemy'.

But the defending officer failed to do so. Hence Thompson's testimony helped to support the prosecution's case that Eddie Slovik had received ammunition, had been shelled and therefore must have realised that he and the rest were in a combat zone and could be expected to engage in battle with the German enemy at any moment. Thus when he didn't accompany the others to Company G he had deserted in a combat zone not in a rear area for which there were lighter sentences. He had therefore infringed Article 58 of the US Army's Code of Military Justice.

Thereafter the various witnesses for the prosecution stood up and made their points: Lt Hurd, the officer of the Military Police to whom the 'green slip' had been handed; Captain Grotte of Company G who had been used by the authorities to bring the desertion charge against Slovik and so on and so on. Throughout however both the defending officer and his client remained strangely silent, save that the former raised two totally unimportant objections.

Finally the cook, Private Schmidt of the 28th's 112th Infantry Regiment appeared for the prosecution. It turned out that he wasn't a cook after all, but just a soldier doing KP. But he did testify to receiving that fateful green slip from Slovik and that the latter 'hung' three hours around headquarters while what was to be done with him was presumably discussed. In that time Slovik helped Schmidt with the dishes and was fed.

In retrospect, this might have been an ideal opportunity for Captain Woods, Slovik's defending officer, to ask the private soldier, (who might well have been more sympathetic than the officers who had testified before him) what he had felt about Slovik's mood and state of mind during those three hours they were together in the kitchen of that German house which functioned as the military government HQ.

Schmidt might have been able to give the details that could have swayed the court in Slovik's favour. After all Schmidt spent the longest time of anyone with Slovik that October day when the latter had made the decision which led to his trial. But Woods failed to ask him a single question.

At 10.50 a.m. the court recessed for ten minutes. Since ten o'clock when the court martial had commenced, no member of the court martial had asked a question of the witnesses, all of them for the prosecution of the accused, Eddie Slovik. Nor had the latter objected to anything stated against him, while his defending officer, Captain Woods had made mere trivial objections.

What happened in the next ten minutes is not clear, but as soon as the court was in session again at eleven o'clock, Captain Woods rose and made his longest statement so far. He said: 'Accused understands his rights as a witness and elects to remain silent, but the Defence requests that the Law Member advise the accused as to his rights as a witness'.

Why did Woods make this request? Had he given up already on Slovik and was attempting to justify his own position, i.e. making it clear that he had tried his best; and that he couldn't get through himself to his client? Or was Woods hoping that the Law Member would startle, even frighten Eddie into understanding the true seriousness of his position? For Eddie Slovik would have to realise that he was not merely attempting to get out of the firing line by being found guilty and sentenced to imprisonment by the court. No, he was fighting for his very life. For if he were found guilty -and he would be on the evidence so far shown by the prosecution -he could be sentenced to death!

Nearly thirty years later when Major Woods examined the testimony again, he gave no explanation for his obvious lapse at that moment. He wrote that he felt he himself was very young and could not challenge the testimony of the witnesses who, in part, were combat veterans. As he stated with some degree of irrelevancy, 'My chance to prove myself had yet to come during the Battle of the Bulge.'

The Law Member, a Lt. Altman, now rose and addressed Slovik directly. He said, 'Private Slovik it is my duty to explain to you that you have the legal right to be sworn in a witness and testify in your own behalf...(and)' make a sworn statement, either written or oral....(or) remain silent in which case no inference of your guilt or innocence will be drawn by the court nor will the trial judge advocate comment upon your silence in the closing argument. Take time to confer with your counsel and decide what you intend to do.'

Altman sat down and Slovik and Woods went through the 'act' of consulting. I say 'act' because if was a mere performance. For Slovik seemingly didn't want the trial to be prolonged any more than necessary. As Woods wrote three decades later, 'There was nothing to summate. I couldn't plead immaturity because Slovik was almost as old as defence counsel.' i.e. Woods himself.

So the inevitable took place. Private Slovik rose and told the court, 'I will remain silent'. He was followed by Woods, who added, 'The defence rests.'

Now it was the turn of the prosecutor. He rose and said, 'The prosecution has nothing further to add. Woods had the last word. He rose now and said simply: 'The defence has nothing further to offer'. It was almost a death sentence in itself.

It didn't take the court long to make their decision. It was done correctly by secret ballot. But Colonel Williams, the presiding officer, was going to make sure that everything was done correctly. After the first ballot which was unanimous and found Slovik guilty, he said 'I then suggest that we smoke a cigarette and take a second ballot.'

The result was the same. Williams, according to his testimony to Huie ten years after the trial, was still leaning over backwards to ensure that Slovik was being given a fair trial, then said; 'Well, gentlemen, this is serious. We've got to live with this for the rest of our lives. Let's take a third ballot.'

The result was the same, for as Colonel Williams recorded: 'I think every member of the court thought that Slovik deserved to be shot; and we were convinced that for the good of the division, he *ought* to be shot....(But) I don't think that Slovik would ever be shot. I know, I didn't believe it...I knew what the practice had been. I thought the sentence would be cut down, not by General Cota, but certainly by Theatre Command.' Williams added, 'I don't say this is what I thought *should* happen; I say it is what I felt sure *would* happen.

After some preliminary details about Slovik's forfeiture of pay etc., the specifics of the court's findings were read out. Eddie was found guilty on all three charges. Woods listened stoically. He had felt right from the start that his client hadn't much of a chance and that he was 'not entirely without blame.' So he was not 'surprised when the charges and sentences were read out.'

They were phrased in the cold unfeeling officialese of the US Army. It stated that Slovik is 'to be dishonourably discharged the service, to forfeit all pay and allowance due or to become due, and to be shot to death with musketry.*15

Woods thought that Slovik took the news well. For his part, although he felt the sentence unjust and was embarrassed by his own failure as a defence counsel, he shared Colonel Williams' belief: the sentence of 'shot to death with musketry' would never be carried out.

Thus as the defence counsel and his client, now under sentence of death, parted for the last time, Captain Woods felt he could reassure 'my client in good faith'. Quietly he whispered to the already pale-faced Slovik, 'Eddie, they will never carry out the sentence....'

V

FALL GUY

'A coward when he is taught to believe that if he ...abandons his colours he will be punished by death will take his chance against the enemy.

George Washington 1776

According to the US code of military discipline, a deserter could be charged with a 'straight' desertion under the 58th Article of War; or with absence without leave with intent at 'avoid hazardous duty or shirk important service.' This came under 'AOW 28'. thus by October 31, 1945 after the end of the war with Japan, a total of 2,024 US military personnel in the European Theater of Operations had been charged under AOW 58 and a further 1,852 under AOW 28. A total of these, 2,804, were found guilty. But in 923 cases the accused absentees were found guilty under the lesser charge of 'absence without leave (AOW 61).

Eddie Slovik himself was found guilty on November 11, 1944 under AOW 58 to become one of the nearly 2,000 men similarly accused and found guilty. The question now arises why Eddie Slovik, the only one of these nearly two thousand airmen, infantry soldiers and tankers charged, on the ETO, was to be executed? Was his case in any way exceptional, so much so that he would become the only US soldier since the Civil War in 1864 to die for desertion?

It must be noted that in the last two years of the war in Europe there were extreme cases of the breaching of Article 58 which far exceeded that of Eddie Slovik. For instance, there was the case of Keeton and Leming (CM ETO 1610). The two soldiers deserted from their unit in Belgium during the Battle of the Bulge. They fled to that haven of deserters, Paris, where with two other AWOL GIs they went to a dubious print shop. Here they had fake orders and travel documents printed with which they proceeded to that other major deserters' hideout in the latter stages of the war, the British capital, London.

Here it didn't take them long to find another crooked backstreet print shop, where they bought orders allowing them to fly to New York. That stage of their journey complete, they headed for 'outlaw country' in the shape of Springfield, Massachusetts, where they telephoned their relatives for money and then disappeared into the hills. Although Keeton and Leming were finally caught and served a jail sentence, they did not suffer that extreme penalty imposed on Eddie Slovik.

Another more blatant case still was CM ETO 15343 Deason. Private Deason went over the hill in France, where he absented himself from his outfit for thirty-seven days.

He had finally apprehended by Sheen's CIC . A violent fight followed and there was some gunfire reportedly. Deason was arrested in the end and on his person was found to have a small fortune, some 52,000 Francs. But that was the only part of the money that he had accrued his five weeks' absence from his outfit. During that time he and some of his fellow deserters had taken part in a large scale heists of the US supplies etc. and his share take had come to just under a quarter of the million francs!

There was even the case of exceedingly cheeky Private Orem (CM ETO 18159). Orem had deserted like the rest, but he knew he would be captured sooner or later if he remained in Europe. By the fall of 1944 security had been tightened up considerably and the MPs were checking passes all time in the major cities behind the lines. These were the only places where a soldier on the run could find a whore to shelter him and a black market to pay him for what he stole from the US Army and, in many cases, from his former comrades.

Orem quickly arranged a flight from Brussels to London. There he bought fake travel documents to take him to New York and from there to Washington, the nation's capital. Unfortunately those orders landed him on a plane filled with US Army V.I.P.'s. Nonplussed Orem took it all in his stride. Taken out of his "short snort", (the dollar bills that all GI's who crossed the Atlantic carried with them and, in the autograph craze of the time, asked anyone of interest or importance, to sign them) he approached the highest-ranking officer, a Brigadier-General. Without batting an eyelid he asked the one-star general to sign the "short snort". The general complied immediately and without a second's hesitation. Private Orem deserve to get away with it. But it didn't. He was court-martialled too.

But he was not executed! * 16

So why Eddie Slovik?

Three factors played a role in the decision to shoot Eddie Slovik. The first was, as we have seen, the horrific slaughter of the 28th Division in the Hurtgen Forest, taking place at the time of Eddie's trial. This occasioned Eisenhower himself to make his appearance at Cota's C P two days before Slovik was arraigned.

At the time Eisenhower was already a worried man. His forces had been battering away at the German frontier since September 11th now and were making virtually no progress. In the meantime discipline was breaking down to some extent and casualties were mounting rapidly. By December the fighting divisions on Germanys frontier were down to 70 percent of their strength in riflemen. We don't know what Eisenhower said to Cota at his C P in Rott. But we can guess he wasn't handing over congratulatory bunches of red roses to this 'Hero of Omagh Beach.'

Although three weeks after that visit, Eisenhower could report to his mentor Marshal back in Washington: "the moral and conditions of our troops is remarkably high. It is noticeable that each division, after it has been out of line three or four days and has absorbed its replacements, is fit and ready to go back into the line", he quietly sent home at the same time three divisional and one corps commander, who had failed to reorganise their battle shaken outfits. As Eisenhower wrote to General Hanley in Washington, they were coming home for 'sixty days' detached service to 'get some rest and recuperation'. 'In certain instances these officers themselves did not realise that they were momentarily exhausted'. Eisenhower added the proviso that he didn't want them back until Handy was sure that they were fit to resume their duties. In other words they had been in all intents and purposes fired. Why?. Because they couldn't make their outfits fights.

That was something that General Cota must have been quite clear about on November 9th, 1944. He was being given another chance. But he had to pull his division is together. The rotten wood had to be gotten rid of, which meant some very senior officers would have to go. At the same time the rank-and-file had to be shown that insubordination would be punished. Riflemen would not decide whether they would fight or not according to their mood at time when ordered into action. They obey the orders of their officers, whether they'd liked it or not. There'd be no more running away, such as at Schmidt , Vossenach and on the Kall Trail. Anyone who did would be punished

Norman Cota was personally brave. He had shown that on Omaha Beach and he had been prepared to shed blood for his country, as he had again shown at St Lo where he had been wounded. Yet he was incompetent. He had displayed his inability to command a division efficiently in the Hurtgen, where for a gain of thousand yards of useless forest, he had lost a third of his 28th Division. Naturally then and in the years after the war, the great American public was not to know this. Then, as now, they laboured under the illusion that their "boys" were always well led by determined, skilled and competent generals. That was not always true. Some of those World War Two generals were slow, plodding, unskilled and inferior: men who should have been relieved as soon as they had shown just how badly they led their soldiers. But they weren't. The Top Brass wouldn't allow it. These generals were old friends, they were members of the same old West Point network, one that was more influential and powerful and those of any other Allied or enemy army, even that of the British; that supposedly class-ridden, caste- dominated society.

Cota, however, knew how to protect himself and from criticism and he knew, too, to a certain extent, he could rely on old West Point friends and associates such as Eisenhower and Bradley to cover him in the future, especially now if (to use the modern parlance) he "cleaned up his act" . This was what he now intended to do. Eddie Slovik was going to pay the full penalty of the law not only for the military crime *[17] he committed, but also as a first step in General Cota's programmed to whip the 28th Division once more into a proud, *reliable* fighting outfit.

At the same time, most of the senior officers concerned with the Eddie Slovik case were left to accept that General Cota and his Division would take a very hard line with the accused. But most of them, as we have seen, did not expect the Eddie would ever pay the penalty imposed by the court on Veterans Day 1944 - "death with musketry." Hadn't the President of the Court-Martial, General Williams himself, stated that although he felt Eddie deserved his sentence, "I didn't think that Slovik would ever be shot."

However now the third factor entered the decision-making process which finally confronted even those who felt that Slovik should be shot for desertion, but never would be. After all it was the eighty years since the last US deserter had been shot. Right throughout World War One not a single doughboy was executed for the offence. And besides any death sentence had to be confirmed by the Commander-in-Chief of the US Armed Forces, who was no less a person than President Roosevelt himself. Would Roosevelt, just elected for another term in the White House, risk a public outcry by sentencing one single GI in some godforsaken place in Europe to death by firing squad? It seems hardly likely, especially with President Roosevelt, married to "bleeding heart" Eleanor.

So what was this third factor, one that made General Cota's mind up for him that Slovik should die and one which would do the same thing for the Supreme Commander General Eisenhower?

Naturally divisional commanders are busy people and in his case, still fighting the tail-end of the Hurtgen Battle, General Cota was especially busy. So Huie guessed, quite rightly, that Cota's mind was probably made up for him by (if it wasn't already) the review *and* recommendations made by the individual judge advocate, Colonel Sommer

Now we know that Colonel Sommer in his preliminary interview before the trial with Eddie Slovik had generously given the latter a chance to get off the hook by suggesting he tore up the green slip confession and then accepted a transfer to another combat regiment of the 28th Division. All the same, although he thought that Eddie was "a nice looking fellow ", Sommer did feel he was "calculating" and that when Slovik turned down the chance he offered him Sommer " wasn't particularly surprised... I had heard too many like him say, "I want my general court-martialled."

So we can assume, as did Mr Huie, the while Colonel Sommer was naturally on the side of law-and-order, he wasn't aggressively prejudiced against this reluctant hero, Eddie Slovik. As Huie quoted Colonel Sommer in 1953, "I never expected Slovik to be shot. Given the common practice up to that time, but there is no reason for any of us to think that the theatre commander would ever executed a deserter. But I thought that if ever they wanted a horrible example, this was the one. From Slovik's record, the world wasn't going to lose much."

So what was this "record?" Certainly not his civilian one. That had not been included in the prosecution's case in the trial and we know that from the President of the court, Colonel Williams, that the only "record" that he and the rest of the court knew about that Thursday when they had sentenced Slovik had been that of his military misdemeanours.

Huie soon learned, however, that someone *had* asked to see Eddie Slovik real criminal record: that list of civilian offences for which he had been sent to jail in the late 1930s and early 1940s. This, he also discovered, had been forwarded to Germany from the FBI in Washington.

But in 1953 , trying to follow this line of inquiry up, he had been informed by the Department of Defence's Office of the Judge Advocate General that the " Judge Advocate General would not inform him whether the FBI criminal record had been included in Colonel Sommer's 1944 review of the Slovik case." It was a privileged communication.. and a copy thereof may not be furnished."

So fifty years ago, Huie had been forced to use conjecture and substitution in his assessment of what the role the FBI records must have played in Cota's final decision. He assumed, however, that it was Somer who had requested the information from the FBI and had used it in that supposedly damning review.

Huie have been right. Sommer had used the FBI records in his review. But just how damning that review and its recommendations were, Huie could only guess.

In mid-November 1944, the Supreme Commander, General Eisenhower was down in the dumps. For he had serious problems, both privately and professionally. On that same Veterans Day that Private Slovik was sentenced to death, his main concern seemed to have been to explain himself to his wife.

Somehow he felt she had got news of his liaison with the green-eyed, Irish-born Kay Summersby, his "chauffeuse". In addition, his wife, Mamie, was seemingly blaming him for the fact that their newly graduated son, John, were soon going to be posted to the infantry outfit in the European combat zone.

He wrote: "You've always put your own interpretation on every act, look or word of mine..... . It's true we have been apart for two-and-half years (and) because you don't have the specific war job that absorbs your time and thoughts, I understand also that this distress is harder for you to bear.... but you must never forget that I do miss you and I do love you and that the load of responsibility I carry would be intolerable unless I could have the belief that there is someone who wants me to come home- for good. Don't forget I take a beating every day."

Naturally Eisenhower didn't want to come home to Mamie (who was twice Kay Summersby's age), carpet slippers and a nice comfortable, pensioned retirement, playing golf. All his life he worked to get where he was. He was not about to relinquish the power and privilege of high office. Indeed he never would. Eisenhower actually enjoyed the perks of his position, isolated in the middle of his little circle of friends, cronies, hangers-on, cut off from the grim realities of the front.

All the same he *was* taking a beating that November. But not just with the Mamie. Since he had taken over as the commander of all allied ground forces on the 1st September, 1944, he had failed on every front. Montgomery's left flank attack on Germany's frontier in the north at Arnhem had been a disaster. Patton's to the south had been the same.

Ever since then his armies had battered themselves to bloody pieces against the concrete fortification of Hitler's *Westwall* (The Siegfried Line) day after day, week after week. Gains had been measured in yards. On November 11th, two month to the day since the first Americans crossed into Germany, his armies had advanced little more than a couple of miles into the Reich.

At first the Top Brass had blame the lack of supplies for the failure to make any appreciable gains. Then it had been the weather which had made it difficult for the Allies to use their a superiority in armour and airpower. But finally it had been the lack of infantry replacements to make-up for the losses of those murderous frontier battles such as that of the Hurtgen. (By now , 2000 battle casualties were being evacuated from the Allied front each day, equivalent of the division a week).

The reality was that the Germans were better soldiers; were usually better led;

were fighting for the future of their country inside their own country; and were defending it from prepared positions. But Eisenhower and the Top Brass would have none of that. As the euphoria of the summer victory in France began to vanish, he started to think that a new reason for their failure to crack the German frontier defences wide-open was that the moral (or lack of it) of the attackers.

In early November Eisenhower had been aghast when he had visited the forward military hospital at Verviers in Belgium. To his horror he had discovered that most of the wounds were self-inflicted. GIs has shot themselves in hands and feet. They had covered the self-mutilation by having a buddy shoot them from a distance to avoid the telltale powder burns of a close-up wound; or they had shot themselves through loaves of bread to achieve the same effect. Others among the hundreds and then later thousands of "trench foot" cases had deliberately expose their feet to the rigours of the winter weather to achieve that wrinkled look that would turn black and gangreous if the feet weren't attended to within three days. Others rubbed diesel oil in their chest to create an incurable (then) eczema. Older men lost their teeth- a man who can't eat, can't fight. And so it went on.

Behind the lines it was little better. Deserters and non-deserters from their COMZ supply service milked the GI's rations. Anything that could be sold on the thriving civilian black-market went missing or was deliberately stolen. Cigarettes and gas were all at a premium. A whole railway company, together with two officers, were arrested for stealing a trainload of cigarettes. It wasn't only those two commodities that went missing. Anything from bullets (for civilian hunting) to blankets (used to make ladies' coats) were stolen from the depots and the supply columns. Soon Eddie Slovik would find in himself in the Paris stockade with 168 other GI's, including officers, accused of black market activities and thefts in the Paris area, alone.

Eisenhower and his army commanders, Simpson, Hodges and particularly Patton naturally thought American youth had gone soft in the interwar years. They lacked stamina, strength and above all the moral fibre of their fathers and great-grandfathers who had fought in World War One and a war between states *18

Naturally the Brass didn't take into consideration the difference between the rifleman of those old wars and those who were sent to Europe in World War Two. In that war, you stood a better chance of being assigned to the infantry if you were an office clerk, piano tuner or grade schoolteacher, the supposed "Caspar Milquetoasts" of the then society, than if you were burly engineer, a vice cop or boilermaker. The latter usually went into their rearline specialities and not into the fighting Infantry, who made up 17 per cent of the army and a suffered 70 per cent of the casualties.

It seems that in 1944 the Brass gave little thought to the fact that, unlike the British and earlier on the German Armies, only men classified as "A-I" ,ie top fit, were eligible for the infantry. Under the US system, there were merely two cat-egories: "Fit for general service" and "Fit for limited service". Anyone belonging to the former group could become a rifleman "SSN 745" - and most of them did.

Therefore little consideration was given to the question whether the men se-lected for a rifle company under this very broad category could actually carry out the average infantryman's heavy and very stressful duties. Could he hike long distances with heavy loads? How could be stand living -and perhaps dying- in a foxhole for hours on end? Enduring cold, unappetising food or perhaps no food at all?. Stressful and very strenuous experiences before he actually began to fight?

Carserne Mortier, the Paris stockade where Slovik was held till his execution

To the West Point-trained in mind, the civilian now transformed into a rifleman, should be able to carry out the functions of that classification. If he failed to do so, there could not be anything wrong with classification and his training. The trouble was the man himself. In essence the riflemen had been trained to fight and, therefore, he should fight. If he didn't, then he was a shirker, a coward, a gold-bricker, trying to escape his responsibilities as an American, a man, and a soldier of the United States. Men like that ought to be punished and although they were not too numerous in November 1944, there were still enough of them, in the opinion of the generals, to infect their fellows with this discontent, disobedience and finally open rebellion in the form of refusal to obey orders and desertion.

Such men were dangerous. An example had been made of them. And by November, Eisenhower who had been concerned with the ill-discipline and failing morale among the troops since the early fall was now prepared to take severe measures to crack these deficiencies. Every day in Versailles, General Betts, theatre judge advocate, laid death sentences, which Eisenhower had to review, on the Supreme Commander's desk. Thus on November 5th, Kay Summersby noted in her personal diary: "General Betts reports that disciplinary conditions in the army are becoming bad. Many cases of rape, murder and pillage are causing complaints by the French, Dutch etc. E (Eisenhower) has assigned several officers to make a complete investigation and report personally to him. "

On the top floor of Paris 'Hotel Majestic' , Major Bertholet wrote his damning 'review' of the Slovik Case for Eisenhower.

She went on to write: "E discussed with Bedell at length this discipline of our troops, and the Chief-of-Staff has had to report which substantiated Betts' report ."

On the following day, according to Kay Summersby, Bedell Smith was called in to Eisenhower's office again. "E discussed with him the discipline of the 101st and 82nd Airborne Division. It is bad, numerous cases of rape, looting. Strong measures will have to be taken . E suggests they should be a public hanging, particular in case of rape."

This is the other face of the supposedly ever-smiling "Ike", whose public image was of a democratic general, who had few airs and graces, and was one of the boys etc. etc. This was the other, darker Eisenhower, who had been educated and trained at West Point, where some of his superiors and training officers had actually hanged   soldiers back in the old days; He like they, believe that some-times you had to be hard, very hard indeed, to maintain discipline in a demo-cratic, independent nation, which had been the first to cast off the shackles of the class-conscious, caste-ridden European colonial master. As the first the trainer of the fighting in New Republican Army of the United States General Steuben had always maintained in his harsh Prussian manner, "*Wer sich nicht fugt, muss spuren*"[*19]

If on November 5th, Eisenhower had been prepared to hang in public, members of his two elite parachute divisions, which had just arrived back in France after 60 days in the line, first Normandy and then Holland, what must have been the Supreme Commander's mood four days later when he heard the disgraceful behaviour of Cota's 28th Division in the Hurtgen Forest:

In theory, Skorzeny's long range jeep teams were to help
Colonel Peiper's (left) 1ˢᵗ SS Panzer group to capture the
bridge at Huy over the River Meuse. But in fact they had
another objective - the murder of General Eisenhower.

124

We can guess. Someone was going to have to be sacrificed as example for the rest. It couldn't be General Cota. He had done yeoman service until the Hurtgen. Besides he belonged to the West Point "old boy network". He'd fire those regimental officers who had fallen down on the job during the murderous battle of the "Death Factory". But what would convince the 28th Division as a whole and the rest of Gerow's V Corps divisions that they had to obey orders and fight until they were either wounded or dead? Someone would have to pay the ultimate and the overwhelming penalty for having failed to do this.

Today it is clear that by November-December 1944, General Eisenhower was on the verge of the nervous breakdown. He was weighed down by almost impossible responsibilities. He was smoking 60 cigarettes a day in an abortive attempt to soothe his ragged nerves. And he was sick. He was almost at the end of his tether. Nothing seemed to be going right for him, especially at the front. And his senior commanders were no help. They were either plodding, lacking in verve and strategic vision; or they were damned prima donnas like Montgomery and Patton. And things are not going to get any better. Indeed in the next two month Eisenhower's personal and professional crisis would come to head.

The objective: the bridge across the Meuse at Huy (Belgium).

Soon his "football knee" would flare up again. He'd grown a painful cyst on his back and as Kay Summersby reported, "Ike complain that there was no one part of his body which did not pain ." As a result, as she also wrote, and" "his temper was truly vile".

Kay was not alone in their assessment of Eisenhower being close to the end of his tether. As she told it, Bedell Smith, his Chief-of-Staff (also living with a painful nervous ulcer too) thought so as well. "Beetle and I were very much worried. The General's physical and emotional condition was worse than we had ever know it. The two of us were forever having talks about Ike's a state of mind and state of health. Beetle was positive that he was on the verge of a nervous breakdown."

It was not surprising therefore that when in the next few weeks both Private Eddie Slovik and his Supreme Commander General Eisenhower were both "confined" and "imprisoned" (I use the term advisedly in the case of Eisenhower) within 10 miles of each other, Eisenhower wouldn't hesitate. He'd sign Slovik's death warrant.

The document which finally turned the scales against Eddie Slovik that winter at divisional and then later it army commander level was dated "November 15th 1944", It was signed by "J E Hoover Director". It was imprinted with the warning 'NOTICE, THIS RECORD IS FURNISHED FOR OFFICIAL USE ONLY.'

It was, of course, the official FBI transcript of "E. Slovik's" criminal record ". It listed his various crimes, which in officialese seemed very serious, though the actual proceeds from these offences amounted to $60 - and that over a period of nearly 10 years.

But as Colonel Sommer phrased them in his review for General Cota they appeared even worse than in the FBI transcript. "The accused's criminal record to the Federal Bureau of Investigation is attached hereto. The analysis of several entries indicate that the accused was put on one year probation in five different occasions.... between 1932 and 1938 for five offences of breaking and entering and one of assault and battery. ... He was arrested by the Detroit police. ... and convicted of embezzlement and sentenced to imprisonment for a term of 6 months to 10 years.... He was transferred to or Iona Reformatory where he was recorded as having a sentence of 2 1/2 to 7 1/2 years, probably the result of additional time charge against the violation of his first parole offence. It was understood from the statement made by the accused to offices of this division but there was "shooting involved in the latter offence."

On the face of it, it was a damning indictment. From 1932 till 1942, 10 long years, Slovik appeared to have been in constant trouble with the law. There was "embezzlement" involved and also a "shooting". No wonder that Colonel Sommer could feel justified in recommending to General Cota that "The death sentence is deemed appropriate in this case. The accused is a habitual criminal. He has never seen combat, has run away twice when he believed himself approaching it and avows his intent to run again if he has to go out there"

We know General Cota's attitude and that, in the aftermath, he seemed the only senior officer concerned with Slovik case who believe that Eddie would really be executed - at least he told Huie that. Sommer's review and recommendation fitted exactly into his own firm attitude that the accused should be punished for his desertion. He could signed Eddie Slovik's death sentence then with a clear conscience, although he knew that he was signing away young man's life. At the same time, however, he knew, too, that Slovik deserved to die. Not only because he had deserted - many others had done that too this winter and escaped that final awesome punishment - but because, too, Slovik was a hardened ex-con. He didn't deserve clemency; his was a worthless life.

Duly General Cota made his final decision. He fiddled about a bit with Slovik's allowance etc., minor matters. But even clad in the officialese of the time, Cota's decision was hard and unyielding, devoid of any pity or even understanding. Dated 27th November 1944, it reads:

"In the foregoing case of Private Eddie D Slovik, 36896415, Company G, 109th Infantry, only in so much as the sentence as provides that the accused be shot to death with musketry is approved and the records of trail forwarded for the action under Article of War 48

Norman D. Cota, Major-General US a Commanding.

Later Cota explained, "Given the situation as I knew it in November 1944, I thought it was my duty to this country to approve that sentence. If I hadn't proved it - if I had let Slovik accomplish his purpose - then I didnt know how I could have gone up to the line and looked a good soldiers in the face."

We know that General Cota had visited The "line" (well, the rear end of the line) only once during the whole course of the bloody battle of the Hurtgen Forest. But no matter. He had carried it his duty as he saw it. The question now remains that would he have sentenced Slovik to death, if he hadn't known about that FBI records, mentioned in Colonel Sommer's review of the case? Here in this content, we must ask further, what had prompted Colonel Sommer (if it were he who had asked for FBI transcript in the first place?), to make the necessary request to Hoover in Washington? How, too, had it reached Sommers so speedily between the end of Slovik's trial on the 11th November and some time before 27th November when Cota had signed Slovik's death sentence?

Remember this was not the age of instant communications and that a war going on. Millions of communications were passing back and forth between the States and the US Army Postal System in Europe, much carried by boat, a little by air and if the communications were important enough by Wireless Telegraph . Even if Colonel Sommer's requests for Slovik's FBI records had had a top signal priority, it had reached the headquarters of the 28th Division, 'A.P.O.28' with remarkable speed. Or had that request been made *before* the Slovik trial and by someone who had carried more clout than did Colonel Sommers, or even General Cota?

If that were the case, then we might assume that Eddie Slovik was some kind of "fall guy": one of the many soldiers who were sentenced to death for desertion at the front, selected because he fitted the official stereotype of a deserter. He was a weakling, who wouldn't fight for his country and for his outfit, which had recently paid such a high butcher's bill in battle. More over this "yellow slacker" had proved he had no value to decent society before the war. He had a criminal record as long as your arms: Ten years behind bars before he had reached the age of 22.'

One last point must be made in this context. It is this. As Mr Huie pointed out in his book, he had interviewed General Cota and discovered somewhat to his astonishment that of all the senior officers he had interviewed Cota was the only one who expected Slovik to be executed. More, Cota was "not surprised when the theatre commander confirmed the sentence as approved and subsequently ordered Eddie Slovik shot."

At the time Huie was doing his research General Eisenhower had become President Eisenhower, a popular figure especially among the wartime generation, who were the main book-buying population of the time. It is perhaps understandable therefore that Huie didn't draw the obvious conclusion, which might have explained the request for the FBI file, the speed at which it reach the low ranking Colonel Sommer and the fact that Cota was not surprised by Eisenhower's decision. Was Cota not surprised because there had been some sort of agreement right from the time of Eisenhowers visit on 9th October to Cota's HQ that Slovik had to die *pour encourager les autres...*

One month exactly after that November visit to Rott and Cota's headquarters, Prisoner Eddie Slovik found himself closer to Eisenhower than when his fate might well have been decided that November day. For by then Slovik was incarcerated in Seine Base Section stockade in Paris. This was located in the Caserne Mortier on the Boulevard Mortier in a redbrick barracks, which up to August had been occupied by the Germans for the last four years. Ironically enough the man who had been sent overseas to fight the Germans would spend his last week in the erstwhile home of those conquerors of Paris, who, in their turn, had been conquered by the very division, which he had deserted that summer.

Here on December 9th, 1944, Eddie Slovik wrote his one and only letter to General Eisenhower, though it is doubtful at Supreme Commander ever read its; Eisenhower had plenty of staff officers to do that job for him. It was Eddie's plea for clemency, written in his own sloping handwriting - and he began it by getting the Supreme Commander's name wrong:

"Dear General Eisenhowser:

I, Private Eddie D Slovik, ASN 36896415 was convicted on the 11th day of November 1944, Armistice Day by General Court Martial to be shot to death for desertion of the United States army.

The time of my conviction or before my conviction I had no intentions of deserting the army whatsoever, for if I intend too, I wouldn't have given up and surrendered myself as did. I did nothing against the United States Army whatsoever, I merely wanted a transfer from the line. I asked my C.O. when I came back whether there was a possible chance of me being transferred cause I feared hazardars duty to myself and because of my nerves, I'll admit. I have some awful bad nerves, which , which no doubt in my mind we all have. I was refused his transfer. "

In its poor phrasing, the spelling mistakes and the occasional pretensions "I'll admit" and "whatsoever", the letter is sad. Yet beneath all that there is still Slovik strange arrogance; his assumption that he has the right to refuse "hazardars duty" by means of a transfer when hundreds and perhaps thousands of his contemporaries were being wounded or killed without claiming any special favours.

Then Slovik went on explain in his "past criminal life in my younger stage of life" and how he had improved himself since he had been released from jail, learned to stay away " from bad company" and marrying "a swell wife." Then out of the blue he had been drafted, not that that worried him. " I didn't have to come to the army and they called me. I could have went back to jail. ... When I went down to the draft board, I was told that the only reason they were taking a chance on me in the Army was cause I got married and had a good record after being out of jail for two years."

Again Slovik showed that he was blind to the reality of total war. In 1944 the army needed "bodies". They were not concerned with Slovik's past record. All they were concerned with was his willingness to hold and fire a rifle at the German enemy in the near future. The US Army was not one bit interested in working out a rehabilitation course for an ex-con, who felt he didn't like what they offered he would take himself off back to prison.

"I don't believe I ran a away in the first time as I stated to my first confession. ... (because) I couldn't move at of my foxhole. I guess I never did give myself the chance to get over my first fear of shelling. " Naturally Eddie would need a special individual period of accustoming himself to enemy shellfire. Perhaps he would have liked to have specified what the German artillery would throw at him - a mild mortar bombardments or perhaps something larger in the form of the medium length shelling by 88 mms? It was all too self-centred and unreal, as if even now when he was under sentence of death, poor, misguided, self-centred Eddie Slovik could not simply realise that he was merely a very small cog in a great big impersonal machine, he was fated to die.

But in the final paragraph of that terrible, yet sad plea for mercy, the condemned man let his heart speak or perhaps it was a matter of simple naked panic as if he suddenly had realised he had started to come to the end of his appeal to the only man who could save him:" "How can I tell you how humbly sorry I am for the sins I've committed. I dindnt realize at a time what I was doing or what the word desertion meant. What is it like to be condemned to death. I beg you deeply and sincerely for the sake of my dear wife and mother back home to have mercy on me. To my knowledge I have a good record since her marriage and as a soldier. I'd like to continue to be a good soldier."

Of course, Eddie being Eddie, couldn't have realised he had spoilt the impact of his initial opening to the paragraph by his last sentence. He *hadn't* been a good soldier. .... and on his own account, he would never been one.

The rest was just wasted words.

"Anxiously waiting your reply, which I earnestly pray is favourable, God bless you and in your work for victory:

I Remain Yours for Victory.

Private Eddie D Slovik. "

Although Eisenhower was only a matter of miles away, Slovik would never hear from the Supreme Commander. For when the plead for clemency reached Eisenhower's office at Versailles on Tuesday 13th December 1944, the great German surprise attack in the West, soon to be known as the Battle of the Bulge, was only days away. By then Eisenhower was on his way to becoming a prisoner himself in the 18th century, luxury stockade outside Paris. Anyway the Supreme Commander, imprisoned by his own people, would have more important things on his mind than the fate of a humble ex- con under sentence for desertion. In essence, not only was the outcome of the great new battle at stake, but also Eisenhower's own career. As William Huie put it 50 years ago now, "As he (Eddie Slovik) and his wife put it, he was the unluckiest kid in the world. .... Even the Germans were among those who balefully affected his destiny....."

On 12th December 1944 the SS officer and their jeep team who were seen to occasion General Eisenhower so much trouble and, in an indirect way it, seal Private Slovik's fate, were steadily advancing westwards. They were confronted by two main problems in their long and complicated journey to where the new battle would soon commence: the state of Germany's bombed railways, and the need to conceal a purpose from not only Allies, but also from their own people. For they were driving enemy vehicles, armed with enemy weapons and underneath the paratrooper coveralls they had been given, they wore US uniforms.

By now, although they had been told they should remove all American clothing if they were in danger of being captured by the enemy- naturally something virtually impossible to do under combat conditions - they knew that they stood a good chance of being shot out of hand, if they were apprehended. After all, even the Geneva Convention, aimed at protecting prisoners' rights, made it clear that they would be regarded as spies - and everyone knew what a spy's fate would be.

The jeep teams' foreboding were reinforced when they finally reached the line of the 6th SS Panzer Army in the Eifel area between 14th and 15th of December and they were given the final additions to their kit. Placed in tents separate from the lines of the "Adolf Hitler Bodyguard", to which they were attached temporarily , the weary jeep members were approached by "several grinning officers. ... and before our tired eyes proceeded to open several cases", as S/Sergeant Heinz Rohde, one of the survivors recalled after the war.

And what cases they were. "First one cheered me no end when its contents were revealed. It was packed to the top with *Amis* cigarettes, coffee, matches and cans of food of all kinds." These "goodies" were subsequently shared out with "Prussian fairness", as Rohde remembered.

They after Rohde was handed a case of his "sole use" as team leader. It, too, contain surprising "goodies" and a form of thousands of US dollars, English pounds, Belgian and French francs. These, they was told, were to be used to bribe people, such a as Belgian, communists who were currently plotting to overthrow the Allied puppet Belgian government and, more importantly, Belgian dockworkers*[20] at the great Allied supply port Antwerp, the German objective in this new battle to come.

But the last case offered them by the SS officers killed Rohde's good mood instantly. When opened, "it offered a view of numerous lighters of the kind *Amis'* called "Zippo" . At first there seemed nothing special about these lighters. They were of cheap metal with no particular exclusive features. That was until the grinning SS Major told us their use."

He pointed out the glass tube. Instead of containing lighter fuel, it was filled with cyanide. ... All we needed to do was to bite into the tube if were trapped and all our problems would be solved. *"Guten Appetit"*.

That information put an end to the team's appetite for the good that evening. Even for "*Ami goodies*". They knew in addition of the foreign currency (incidentally forged) their jeep also contained special weapons, including silenced sten guns, pistol grenades and the like which would not be used by the normal troops. They realised that if they were captured with such items on them, this cyanide was to be used, *not* to protect them from Allied torture, but ensure the secrets they knew would die with them instantly. Skorzeny, their chief, was leaving nothing to a chance.

Rohde remember , " so we trailed backs to our "wigwam" (he meant' tents). For the first time since he had joined Skorzeny "we realised what we had let ourselves in for - and Ascension Day Commando". "In other words a suicide mission, with a one-way ticket to heaven - or hell!.

Now the brass started arriving in the camps in the wooden heights, some one mile or so from the position of the green US 99th Division in the Ardennes beyond. Here they were forbidden to smoke, light stoves (save with smokeless fuel) or make any unnecessary noise. Skorzeny arrived. Later he said that he had nine jeep teams in the forest around, though he didn't mention one graced by the presence of the mysterious "*Leutnant N*". He took up his HQ in a foresters wooden lodge on the outskirts of the Eifel village of Schmidtheim and said later that he had taken part in a last minute a tactical discussion on Tuesday 14th December. But from the German reports of the time, mainly those of the 1st SS, I cant find any reference to his attendance such discussion. Indeed one might ask if Skorzeny, the man who had rescued Mussolini and since then had only dealt with "*big shots*", would be interested in such low-level stuff.

For in his short career as Germany's top commando, Skorzeny had based his mission on the same basic policy. He was not satisfied merely by military operations. He wanted his operation to have long-term *political* results. His rescue of Mussolini had kept Italy, or part of it in the war until 1945. His kidnapping of Horthy's son meant that Hungary, Germany's one-time ally, had not gone over to the Russians as secretly intended, but it stayed in the German camp, again right to the bitter end.

Just like in his student days when he had been a member of Vienna University's numerous student duelling associations, he always gone for the head. For all that was the basic purpose of the mock duel between students: to get a nice big scar across (*der Schmiss*), which would indicate to all and sundry that you had stood your man. Why bother about the scar that no one can see.

Sabotage and general military destruction, Skorzeny believed, was well and good. But they didn't bring about decisive results; they didn't win campaigns, changed political alliances. A blow to the political head of the state did, as he knew well. Those nine jeep teams referred to after the war did a very effective job in confusing the Allies and creating general chaos. But even at their best it didn't change over a course of the Battle of the Bulge. But what if there were similar teams, perhaps even airborne ones, or armoured columns, as "*Leutnant N*" suggested and which Allied intelligence thought right at the beginning existed, which Skorzeny was too scared to acknowledge *after* his capture? Was it now, after searching for Eisenhower's location since late 1943/ early '44 and finding it, that Skorzeny was prepared to strike?

It must have seemed to Hitler as he planed the great offensive that the assassination of Eisenhower would be a major factor in the success of what would become, in reality, a delayed action. But to 1943, as we have seen, Hitler had forbidden any attempt at the assassination of political opponents. By 1944, and especially after the attempted assassination on his life in July of that year, the Fuhrer had no inhibitions about killing foreign enemies. Marshal Tito, the military *and* political head of the Yugoslavia Resistance, was a case in point. And it was surely no coincidence that the officer played a key role in the execution of the attack on Tito's mountain fortress stronghold was Otto Skorzeny.

So was Skorzeny involved in any plan to assassinate Dwight D. Eisenhower in that third week of December 1944? The short answer is that we have his *postwar* declaration that he wasn't. The alleged plan to kill the Supreme Commander came from the "*latrine-o-grams*" (i.e. rumours) which had circulated in the Grafenwehr Training Camp, in particular that proposal put him by the over-enthusiastic and mysterious "*Leutnant N*".

But did "*Leutnant N*" really exist? For was never reported killed in Skorzeny's own accounts of what happened to his nine jeep teams. Nor was he ever found by US Intelligence, as most of the other survivors of those jeep teams were, after the war.

Why then did American Intelligence, in particular the Counter-Intelligence in the form of Lieutenant Colonel Sheen of there CIC, believes so firmly *at the time* that Eisenhower was the target of an assassination plot (and we can guess that other senior Allied generals believe the same)? [*21]

The answer is simple, as we shall see. Captured Skorzeny men who might have escaped the immediate death sentence imposed upon them by their US captors if they confessed everything that the Americans thought they knew, refused to do so. But one thing they did tell that CIC men who grilled them was sufficient to set the alarm bells ringing all the way from the 1st US Army HQ to Eisenhower's in the baroque splendour of Versailles There were those of their comrades who were on their way to Paris to kill Eisenhower.

And Otto Skorzeny, the mastermind behind the plot, if there was one? Where was he that day when it all started? We know that he spoke a little while with the handsome ill-fated arrogant Jochem Peiper of the 1st SS *Battle Group Peiper*. Then, although the Fuhrer himself (according to Skorzeny's later statement) had forbidden him, to cross the front line, he disappeared. There was a "sighting" of the scarfaced giant at Dietrich's headquarters in the forest village of Meyerode, but nobody could — or can confirm it.

The next we hear of Skorzeny is of his being wounded at the Belgian tourist village of Ligneuvelle and his subsequent evacuation from the front. That was on 22nd December 1944, six days after the great counter-offensive had commenced. Where had Skorzeny been in the meantime?

BOOK TWO

ONE: THE BATTLE

"But the past is more readily lamented than corrected. "

Hannibal to Scipio Africaus 202 BC.

1.

About five thirty on the morning of Saturday, 16th December 1944, a lone sentry stood on the parapet of the water tower of the Luxembourg frontier village of Hosingen. He was a young man, one of the 4000 reinforcements absorbed into the 28th Infantry Division after the bloodbath of the Hurtgen. That freezing December dawn, exactly one week before the last Christmas of World War Two in Europe, his outfit the 110th Regiment was holding 15 miles of front overlooking the River Our, the border river, far below. To North there lay the Division's 112th Regiments and to the south, Eddie Slovik's old outfit (well almost) the 109th.

The young men's spell at sentry duty had been long, cold and boring. Nothing had happened, up here ever since he had arrived at the front, nothing ever did. But it was damn cold and he prayed for the next half-hour to pass so that he could report to the guardroom near the village church and a bum cup of scalding hot "Java". Then he'd hit the sack. But that wasn't to be. Soon that unknown sentry would be fighting for his life together with the rest of the 200- odd infantry and engineers who held the hilltop village. Still he attempted to "keep your eyes open," as he had been ordered by his company commander, a Captain Feiker. But there was nothing to be seen save the vaguely glimpsed outline of the other bank of the River Our, which was the German line, but which for all the young men knew, might as well have been the other side of the moon.

Then it happened. As reported to Feiker a few minutes later from the conical top of the tower (it's still there today), he spotted "pinpoints of light" everywhere down below at the river. For a second or so, our sentry must have been at a loss to explain them. After all he'd never been in action. Then suddenly, startlingly his ears were assailed by the hollow boom and thunder of 554 assorted canon, coming from the 29 batteries of artillery of General von Luttwitz's 47 Panzer Corps. In the centre of the US VIII Corps front, the Battle the Bulge had commenced and as before the "Bloody Bucket" or the "Jinxed Division", as the other outfits of the VIII Corps called the 28th, was going to bear the full brunt of the attack.

The rallying point at Poteau for Skorzeny's commados

Just to the rear of the 110th, Colonel Fuller and his second in command, Colonel

139

Strickler, who one day would command the 28th himself, were awakened from their sleep by the thunder of those guns. Hastily they rose from their beds in the hotel HQ, Hotel Claravillis, in the regiment's rest centre at the pretty village of Clervaux. They pelted downstairs to find out what's going on, to find the former hotel lobby packed with scared, frustrated men. They pushed their way through them to find out that all the lines to the frontline villages held by two battalions of Fuller's 110th had been shot away or sabotaged.

"What do you make of it?", Fuller, a crusty WWI veteran, asked.

Strickler, the only senior officer of the 110th to survive the debacle to come, answered, "All that big stuff is a sure sign that we're in for a fight."

They were. Now as the bad news came flooding in, Fuller pleaded all that day with General Cota in his headquarters at the nearby Luxembourg town of Wiltz to let him have the third Battalion back. Cota refused. Since the Hurtgen Forest, he had become very hard nose with his regimental commanders. In the end Fuller sent Strickler to plead personally with Cota for the return of that reserve battalion and the first of those who might have played a role in the final stage of the Eddie Slovik case was swept away into the maelstrom of the new battle. ....

Caught at Aywaille. The execution of
Skorzeny's Jeep team at Henri le Chapelle

Strickler, who would be one of the few senior officers to come out of the imminent debacle with a clean record, had first encountered Slovik when "one day in October, a large group of replacements came up and reported. I immediately gave them the assignment, usually to the front line, for there is when most of the casualties occurred. A GI by the name of Eddie Slovik. .. said to me he did not intend to get mixed up in the front line. I learned that on his way to the front once before he had deserted and went to the rear. I dressed him down and said no matter what he thought, he had to go to the front, for if he didn't someone else would have to do his job." Thereafter Stickler had had Slovik escorted to Company G near Rocherath where "he was placed among the fighting men by the commander at the time when an attack was jumped off."

Colonel Strickler had heard no more of the young deserter until Slovik had been court-martialled for having refused to go into the line and fight yet once again and had subsequently been sentenced to death. One can guess what this long-term soldier and future governor of Pennsylvania's attitude would be towards a shirker and coward like Eddie Slovik.

But in the next few days he would see cowardice and gross dereliction of duty all around him at Cota's Villa headquarters in Wiltz, with not only enlisted men re-fusing to fight and running away, but officers also. Would that change mind and attitude to the prisoner of Paris still awaiting the answer to the Supreme Commander of a week before? *22

However, what happened in Wiltz in the next two days, as that 110th Regiment of the 28th Division vainly attempted to stop the German advance, did change the attitudes of two of those offices closely connected with Eddie Slovik and, in the end, convince them that he had been wrongly sentenced to death.

The first was Slovik defence officer, Captain Woods, of whom one of the court later wrote "was as dumb as his client ." Woods too had fled to Wiltz, where appar-ently no one could find any use for him. So he was ordered (or volunteered, which-ever way you look at it) to lead a column of 50 vehicles from Luxembourg town in the general at direction of Bastogne, VIII Corps' headquarters to the West. With the vehi-cles went "700 officers and soldiers".

The execution of Skorzeny's Jeep team at
Henri le Chapelle

According to his own statement, 30 years later, his jeep was hit by a mine and he was wounded, for which he was awarded the Purple Heart. Wiltz was no more than 20 miles from Bastogne, now been taken over by the US 101st Airborne Division, which would make its celebrated stand there. But Woods and his force apparently was not tempted to stay there -indeed only 500 survivors of the 3000 strong "Keystone Division" 110th did so and took part in the subsequent siege. Instead Woods, wounded or not, led his group even further westwards until on 23rd December, the same day that in Paris Eisenhower made his final decision about Slovik, he and the rest were captured 12 miles north-west of Bastogne at a place called Ortheuville.

Here, taken by what Woods called the *"Afrikakorps"* (which hadn't existed since it surrender in North Africa back in spring of 1943), he was sent to a German POW camps. Here he remained until his captors fled before the advancing Red Army. But even now Woods was not freed. Instead he was apprehended by the Russians and kept under house arrest as a suspected German agent. Naturally he knew nothing of what was transpiring with his one-time client. But in that period and in the subsequent years he came to reflect upon his defence of Slovik and concluded that he could have done better. For now he knew what combat and the fear of combat could do to a man.

His last words to Slovik before they had parted for good had been, "Eddie, I'll say a prayer for you and you say a prayer for me." Now in the winter of 1944/445 Woods would undergo a conversion and in the future would attempt to do more than it merely pray for the dead Eddie Slovik. In due course he would even allow his defence to be held up to ridicule by a real lawyer attempt to get Slovik a posthumous pardon. " Slovik deserved a good lawyer. He didnt get one, as the other council stated" Woods didn't like it. But as a professional lawyer said over half a century after the event, with Woods' approval, "He (Woods) is willing to take it for the team."

But most dramatic conversation caused by the Wiltz debacle at the 28th Division headquarters that bloody December weekend was that of Captain Benedict Kimmelmann, the dentist, who had been drafted on to the board of the court which tried Slovik on November 11th, 1944.

Kimmelmann, who was a staff officer and had never experienced combat, had been a little worried by Woods, his defence and his clients decision to remain mute. All he remembered of the trial that "grey day with its snow flurries", was that there had been some little discussion about the nature of the death penalty. Should Slovik be hanged or shot? A firing squad was decided upon in the end "as a less dishonourable means".

Thereafter "Slovik, still wordless, was escorted out under guard. We members of the court, satisfied with our morning's work, disbanded and went our separate ways.

'For the next several days the case and its no-nonsense deposition and verdict created some little stir in headquarters, but it was an approving stir. If there was a difference reaction among the enlisted men, we knew nothing about it." What happened to Eddie Slovik thereafter, Captain Kimmelmann would not know to the spring of 1945 when, on release from a German POW camp, he was shopping for a wedding anniversary present for his wife in the States when a noncom from the 28th, recognising him in the Paris PX , called "Hey, Captain, you know they shot Slovik."

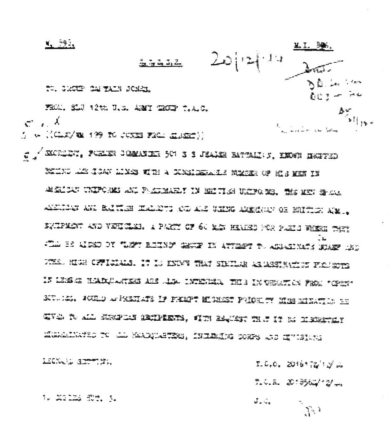

Top Secret signal from the 12th Army HQ. in Luxembourg alerting head of Operation Ultra in Bletchley Park of the Skorzeny threat. Group CaptainJones was the English Officer who incidentally warned Strong, Eisenhower'sChief-of-Intelligence of the coming Ardennes offensive. His warning was ignored.

On the morning of December 18th, however, Kimmelmann had other things on his mind than Slovik's fate. He had volunteered to stay behind as temporary surgeon with the 28th HQ group. But he was in for a surprise when he reported to Cota's HQ, one of the first of many that would change his whole attitude to men in combat. He found men and officers talking off "without orders, empty-handed, running on foot or jumping onto and clinging to every vehicle moving out."

The defenders now consisted of "cooks, clerks, musicians, telephone linesmen," few of them knowing any more how to handle a rifle. Still "scared and furious" as they were, they obeyed orders. "With them were numbers of officers as inexperi- enced in this kind of situation as we all were, but trying to hold things together. Few ever got out."

Kimmelmann now waited for exact orders. As the civilians trooped by outside heading westwards through the snow and in lower part of Wiltz, the German started torching buildings, he observed as the Mayor of Wiltz and a small group of civilians pushed open the doors of Cota's office. "I heard him (the Mayor) say,"what shall our people do? Go and stay in the cellars? If you go, we block your roads."

Cota was on the phone and he hated to be disturbed when he was busy. The night before when Colonel Fuller had pleaded for help from Clervaux, an aide snapped "General Cota can't speak to you. He's at dinner. "Not long afterwards Fuller was fleeing for his life, guiding a blind GI as he did so.
...
Now Cota, still with his back to the frightened civilians, barked, "Tell 'em, I cant do anything for 'em." His Provost Marshal repeated his words to the mayor and "little group walked off slowly and silently."

That night staff departed, even some of the high-ranking medics, leaving the headquarters' wounded in the care of the dentist-cum-acting surgeon Kimmelmann and a brave noncom, Sergeant Mollett.

The two of them did their best. They were determined to get their 41 walking wounded out, though the others with them were simply going to wait for the Ger- mans and surrender . As one of them, a doctor with the rank of major, told Kimmelmann "Don't go. You haven't a Chinaman's chance."

As a German firing slackened off and the German Paras (in name only; none of them had ever jumped) of the 5th Parachute Division, started to loot Wiltz, the two medics and three other brave helpers managed to evacuate the 41 casual- ties up a blazing hillsides and out the main danger. Everywhere in those last hours of the "defence" of Wiltz, culminating around midnight on Monday Decem- ber 18th, officers and men surrendered tamely to any Germans, who had the time or inclination to take them prisoners. American "Camels" and "Hershey" bars were more important for the excited young *Fallschirmjager* than *Ami* prisoners.

At five on the next morning with flames everywhere and dead bodies littering the cobbled streets of the little Luxembourg town, Kimmelmann and his loyal medics were stopped short by a burst of automatic fire close by where they were tending

9-2

HQ NORMANDY BASE SECTION COM Z ETOUSA

INCOMING MESSAGE   TWX

Received - 23 Dec 44

Dispatched - 221917A

NR 180   Prepared by - DC

TO: NORMANDY, BRITTANY, OISE, SEINS, CHANNEL BASE SECTIONS, ADVANCE SECTION AND SOLOH

INFO: THEATER PROVOST MARSHAL; HQ COMZT COM Z; AIR TRANSPORT GROUP

S E C R E T   O P

REF NBR EX-77475

FOLLOWING PARAPHRASE OF MESSAGE FROM 1ST UNITED STATES ARMY AMPLIFIES INFORMATION PREVIOUSLY GIVEN RELATIVE TO SKORZNEY RPT SKORZNEY ACTIVITIES.

INTERROGATION OF PRISONERS OF WAR INDICATES THAT FROM TWO DIFFERENT SS SOURCES HE HAD BEEN INFORMED THAT SKORZNEY LED SMALL GROUP THROUGH LINES WITH 6 VEHICLES PRESUMABLY COMMAND CARS. THEY WERE CARRYING FORGED LETTERS OF RECOMMENDATION AND IDENTIFICATION PAPERS AND WEARING ENGLISH UNIFORMS. INTERVIEW WITH GENERAL EISENHOWER WILL BE ATTEMPTED BY THE PARTY. THAT THEY HAVE RETURNED FROM FRONT WITH VITAL INFORMATION REGARDING OPERATIONS OR AN ATTEMPT ON THE GENERALS LIFE MAY WELL BE THE COVER STORY THEY WILL USE. POSSIBILITY EXISTS THAT A CHANGE OF VEHICLES AND UNIFORMS WILL BE MADE BEFORE REACHING PARIS FOR PURPOSE OF COVERING THEIR TRACKS. POSSIBLE THAT THEY MAY HAVE ONE OFFICER WITH THEM IN GERMAN UNIFORM CLAIMING THAT THEY ARE TAKING HIM TO HIGHER HEADQUARTERS FOR INTERROGATION AS IMPORTANT WITH RANKING PRISONER OF WAR.

Another warning of the Skorzey assassination threat 3 days later.

their wounded. They were exhausted, surrounded and felt they had done the best for their charges. The little group decided that they, too, would surrender. They had no other choice.

Kimmelmann took over. Together with a wounded bandmaster of the 28th, he went forward, "hands on our heads" and gave themselves up to a "brisk German tank corporal posing and strutting as though he had won the war." which in a way he had in his own little battle.

Thereafter Captain Kimmelmann went "into the bag". " In the prison camp, Kimmelmann recalled many years later "there was considerable wild talk about Slovik (among the several hundred prisoners from the 28th). "The harsh sentence had certainly had some impact. .... My fellow prisoners never challenged me to defend my part in the verdict, though I at no time denied that in "throwing the book" and at him we assumed that the death sentence would be carried out. No one then implied that the court had been "ordered" to find him guilty and pass a sentence of death. The consensus was that he had provoked the court martial, gambling on receiving a pardon. .... and there was no doubt the minds of those POWs that he had won the gamble anyway. "

Later when Captain Kimmelmann, released from that POW camps, found out what had really happened to Slovik, he "Railed against the injustice of executing one offender while closing eyes, as a matter of practical or political prudence against injustice of executing one defender to the raft of the new defence's committed in the battle the Bulge of the Bulge." As he summed it up "Assign me to that court now, I maintained, and I would not vote the death penalty knowing that among the thousands of soldiers engage there, there had to be dozens even hundreds who would fail. .. "

And General Cota, had gone with the rest the day before Kimmelmann was captured, transferring his HQ to Sibret some 14 miles to the rear. What of him? Again he had lost his division. His 110th regiment had been destroyed. His 112th and Eddie Slovik's assigned regiment, the 109th, had come under the command of other divisions to the north and south. Thus he was left with his staff and several hundred stragglers. What part would he now take in the further stages of the Battle of the Bulge?

He had an ideal opportunity to do something. Sibret was on the outskirts of Bastogne and in Middleton's VIII Corps which had responsibility for the defence of the town, he was a senior general. He asked McAucliffe, the one-star general, newly arrived to command the 101st Airborne to come and see him. But "Old Crock," as the touchy 45-year old airborne commander called himself, was having none of it. Perhaps he had already seen that Cota's reputation was in tatters. First the Hurtgen and now Wiltz. McAucliffe snapped in his usual grouchy manner, "Tell him (ie Cota) I'am too damned busy!"

Thus Cota would play no further role in the Battle of the Bulge in this year of

1944. Indeed any rational observer might have thought his military career would be over. In this the " rational observer" would have been mistaken.

On the same December Monday when Captain Kimmelmann was transformed from a dentists into some sort of combat soldier at Wiltz, teenage Paul Maquet at the small Belgian town of Aywaille was disturbed by the American MP "Joe", had been adopted by his family. Normally the young MP came to the Maquet household for a cup of hot coffee and a warm-up during his midday spell of duty. His job was to help guard the little bridge over the local river which split the main road to Liege. It was a cold boring task and he was glad to get inside and young Paul, one day to become an internationally known surgeon, was happy, too, to practise his *lycee* English on the American.

But on this Monday the American "white mouse", as MPs were called by the locals, had no time for coffee or English conversation. Today he was flushed, not by the icy cold outside, but by excitement. For he had a sensation of reveal. He and a bunch of black soldiers, now helping to guard the 18th century bridge, had stopped a jeep with three strange 'Yanks' in it

At first the, mixed bunch of MPs and black GI's, who had stopped the jeep at the bridge because the driver didn't seem to know the password, thought the three Americans might well be deserters or runaways, part of the "big bug out", which was taking place at the front. But once they started to examine the jeep's contents, they soon discovered that these were no ordinary GI's. Here hidden in the rear seat, the searchers discovered a huge roll of 100 dollar bills, as fresh as if they had just come off the printing press (which they had; they had been recently forged at Sachsenhausen Concentration camp).

The pass on the River Meuse where British soldiers shot and killed the the last of Skorzeys Jeep team

Engaged and spurred on by this unexpected find, the searchers continued. They dug into the interior of the jeep to discover two British silenced Sten guns, plastic explosives, two Colts, two German Walther pistols six US handgrenades, a radio transmitter, and most incriminating of all, those "Zippo" cigarettes lighters, which S/Sgt Heinz Rodde had also *[23] received. In each the Americans found "L" (for lethal) suicide pills.

Now the smallest of the three suspects started talking. His real name wasn't George Sensenbach as he told his captors at the beginning. It was Wilhelm Schmidt and he was a corporal in the German Army. It was the sensation of that day of battle full of sensations.

He related how he and the rest had set off from the neighbourhood of the US held German township of Monschau on the 12th December. Some days later they had successfully penetrated the lines of the VIII Corps in a jeep captured back in September from the US Fifth Armoured Division when it and the 28th Division had been driven back out of the Siegfried Line positions. Thereafter they had reached the Meuse and had reported the situation there back to Skorzeny's HQ. At the moment no one thought to ask the three Germans what they had done since then. Why had stayed so long in those dangerous rear areas? Had they had another mission?

But now the CIC was on its way from the 1st Army HQ. What methods they used to extract instant information from their prisoners we do not know. We can guess, however. After all "third-degree" methods had been common in certain US police forces before the war and the US police of that time were not inclined to be all sweetness and light when they were in a hurry.

At all events they made the Germans "sing" and what a song it was in the truth. Schmidt told his interrogators that he joined Skorzeny's outfit in November. He had spent three weeks in an American *Stalag* to study GI slang and behaviour. Later Schmidt explained to his CIC interrogators, "I was posted to Grafenwoehr where I was placed in a special unit. ... our training consisted in studying the organisation of American Army, identification of American insignia, American drill and linguistic exercises. "At this juncture, Schmidt really caught the attention of the listening CIC men when he added, that engineers in his group had had the task of "destroying headquarters and headquarters Personnel."

By now the CIC knew that the Skorzeny people had managed to destroy the land link cable which joined Bradley's Army Group HQ with that of Hodges 1st Army so that all telephonic communication between these major army headquarters had ceased at this critical point in the battle. But that admission by Schmidt - "destroying.... headquarters personnel" - really surprise them. "*What headquarters. .. what personnel?* They wanted to know.

The it all came out. Those wild rumours which had circulated throughout Grafenwoehr camp the month before. The dash across France disguised as German POWs to relieve the German garrison at the Breton port of Lorient...the surprise attack on Montgomery's headquarters at the nearby Dutch town of Sonhofen... the column of Tiger tanks being taken for inspection by US engineers which would link up with it assassins assembling at the Cafe de la Paix after they had poisoned the Paris water supplies....

- *"To do what?* Undoubtedly be astonished CIC agents must have queried.

"To kill. ... General Eisenhower."

There was no real record of the interrogation. But one doesn't need a crystal ball to guess the reaction of the US interrogators. Skorzeny .. the kidnapper of Mussolini. .. the man whose subordinates had flooded mines and so-called "battle swimmers" down the Rhine the previous September to attack the "Screaming Eagles" and "All Americans" racing to help the trapped men at Arnhem *24, now his killers were swarming out, disguised as Yanks
to kill the Supreme Commander himself.

Ike had to be warned. ... at once!

3.

That "great flap" commenced almost immediately. As Major Noel Annan, the British Intelligence Officer, working under General Strong ("the Hangman's Dilemma*25), his and Colonel Sheen's boss records: "Gordon Sheen, the officer under Strong responsible for security, burst into a room at SHAEF headquarters in a Hotel Trianon, crying " Skorzeny is driving on Paris".

That did it. Although later, Sheen took the blame for the "great flap" at Eisenhower's HQ, it was, according to Annan, Strong, who "persuaded Eisenhower to incarcerate himself near his headquarters, surrounded by a bodyguards of armoured vehicles."

Now from the 20th to 26th December, while a desperate battle raged at the front, involving 3 million men, friend and foe, Eisenhower was a prisoner at his own headquarters, cut off from the decision-making process. " Yet," as Annan remarked later, "that was the moment when Eisenhower should have been on the move to see Montgomery and Bradley and their army commanders."

Kay Summersby described the situation thus: "Security offices immediately turned headquarters compound into a virtual fortress. Barbed-wire appeared. Several tanks moved in. The normal guard was doubled, trebled, quadrupled. The pass system became a matter of life and death, instead of the old formality. The sound of a car exhausts was enough to halt work in every office, to start a flurry of telephone calls to our office to enquire whether the boss was all right. The atmosphere was worse than that of combat headquarters at the front, where everyone knows how to take such situations in their stride."

Once Eisenhower, according to Kay, grew so angry at the restrictions that he snapped at her, "Hell's fire I'm going for a walk. If anyone wants to shoot me, he can go right ahead. I've got to get out. " And walk he did, followed by the whole company of heavily armed suspicious military policemen. Even when Ike went to eat, he was accommodated in a tank!

Sleep seemed impossible. As Kay Summersby remembered." I lay awake for hours and envisioning death and worse at the hands of SS agents.... with the tramp , tramp, tramp of heavy booted guards patrolling the tin roof."

Captain Butcher, former vice-president of CBS and now a kind of PR man for Eisenhower, was allowed to visit the imprisoned Supreme Commander and told him how he had been stopped by roadblocks all way back from the front. Eisenhower was in a bad mood and Butcher could see why. There were guards everywhere and worried staff officers fussing all the time about his safety. Butcher listened to his boss's complaints, then just before he left, he said, "Now you know how it feels to be a President and always under the watchful eye of the Secret Service." One wonders, if eight years later when he was really President of the United States, Eisenhower remembered that quip

151

It was against this kind of background that Eisenhower, imprisoned in a kind of gilded cage himself, had to make his decision about that other, humbler prisoner at the other side of Paris, Eddie Slovik. With his armies in disarray, the French capital locked in an evening eight o'clock curfew and CIA agents patrolling the streets waiting for Skorzeny and his assassins to appear at any moment, the Supreme Commander now had to make that overwhelming decision: was Slovik going to be executed, the only deserter to suffer that fate since 1864, to serve as example not only to the 28th Division, but also to the rest of his divisions, in which desertion since the commencement of the new battle had become almost endemic?

And in the end, one must ask: did Eisenhower himself make a decision? If he did, did he make it this 4th week of December 1944 to show himself as the strong man, fully in charge of the situation. Why he could even find time to a deal with relatively small problems as that of the ex- con "Pollack" deserter? This at a time when he knew that he was *not* in charge. Instead he was a prisoner of his own officials with three-quarters of the US troops were being commanded by a foreigner (Montgomery); *26 and the Germans were still maintaining the initiative, travelling towards the last natural barrier between them and their objective, the River Meuse.

**The Germans are given ministering by Colonel
P. Schroder, Chaplain to the First Army**

Or had the decision been forced upon him that November day when he had visited Cota's HQ and the Top Brass had realise that *pour encourager les autres*, a soldier must die. Any soldier.

4.

Now Skorzeny's spies, saboteurs and parachute assassins were spotted everywhere in Allied Europe. Eisenhower ordered a 48 hour blackout on what was going to. This was, it was thought, a good measure to stop all alarmist rumours. It had the contrary effect. It only increased the panic, alarmist civilians statements and the rumour mills throughout the Continent and even in that "Island Fortress ", Britain itself, flourished.

A captured Skorzeny team before being executed by firing squad.

Hundreds of Americans and Allied soldiers were arrested and jailed for a while because they could not give the right password or answers to the guards and sentries who were posted everywhere, stopping vehicles. Even generals such Bradley and Montgomery were not immune. It was said that the tyres of Montgomery's ancient Rolls-Royce were shot out by overeager US military policemen and in the end "Monty" had to ask his subordinate US commander, General Simpson, head of the 9th Army, to give him an American ID card.

As Bradley had later to comment, "A-half million GI's played cat-and-mouse with each other each time they met on the road. For neither rank nor credentials spared the traveller an inquisition at each intersection he passed."

153

Skorzeny's spies shot by the British 29th Amour Brigade. December 1944.

And the circle of suspicion spread even wider. The British run " black" Propaganda station, intended for Wehrmacht soldier - listeners , *Soldatensender Calais* reported that more than 250 Skorzeny agents had been captured already. In fact, only three had yet been taken alive, those at Aywaille. We shall never know who the other 247 unfortunates were and what happen to them. *Radio Nice* stated that a local bank had been held up by Skorzeny para-agents, some 400 miles away from the scene of the fighting. The London *Daily Telegraph* informed its conservative readers that specially-trained female agents have been dropped in the general area of Paris at Skorzeny command. It was there task to seduce a unwary GI's. Once the latter had been duly "seduced" and had "revealed all", they were to be killed by their "handy little dagger" that all these German Mata Haris carried it in their purse.

The front was not immune from these rumours and wild tales of Skorzeny's agents and killers, either. The US 2nd Armoured Division "Hell on Wheels" found its point had turned back from setting out to rescue a hard-pressed neighbouring outfit because it had been "ordered to do by" American officer. The "American officer" was never found. The 16th Regiment of the 1st Infantry Division "the Big Red One", was misdirected down a side road by an "American MP". According to an "American NCO", it was no use General Gavin's men of the 82nd "All Americans" Airborne Division attempting to cross a certain bridge on its advance into battle because the bridge had already been blown. It hadn't and the "American NCO" was never located.

As Patton recorded in his diary at the time, "On this day, four Germans in one of our jeeps, dressed in America uniforms, were killed, and another group of 17 also in American uniforms, were reported by the 5th Division as follows: one sentinel, reinforced saw 17 Germans in American uniform. Fifteen were killed - and two died suddenly."

**The bodies are untied and taken to a temporary cemetery.
Later the bodies are exhumed and reburied in the German
cemetery at Lommel.**

It was typical Patton comment - "two died suddenly." But "Ole Blood an' Guts'" attitude changed slightly was some time later a his own plane was buzzed and fired upon by Spitfire bearing Polish Air Force markings. Fortunately for Patton, the pilot was too bold in his attack and fatally crashed his plane in the second attack.

By 22nd December, the US if authorities had begun to take drastic measures to discourage Skorzeny (if he were behind this massive influx of German soldiers in American uniform). Germans dressed in US uniform were being shot out of hand and in his new headquarters (General Hodges had fled yet again, from Chaudfontaine to his new HQ at Tongres on the safe western side of the River Meuse) had to make his decision about Skorzeny men already in captivity.

There were eight of them, who had been apprehended by Hodges 1st Army. But on the 22nd, his main concern was the team under Corporal Schmidt which had been captured at Aywaille. Hodges had already sentenced the three men to death for having worn US uniform. They had appealed, stating that they hadn't wanted to act as spies and potential assassins. Indeed just before they had set off on their own covert mission, one of their comrades had refused to go "on account of the criminal background of the whole enterprise" and had been shot. The three condemned men ended their plea with: "We were sentenced to death and are now dying for some criminal (ie Skorzeny) who have not only us, but also. .. our families on his conscience. Therefore we beg mercy of the Commanding General; we have been unjustly sentenced ; we are *de facto* innocent. "

Their appear had no effect. Bradley had already informed Hodges verbally that he had to pass sentence of death on the three Aywaille captives and carry out the punishment as soon as possible. Hodges understood. He knew the urgent need to reassure the average frontline GI that something drastic was being done about these disguised Germans. All the same, old soldier that he was, he demanded a decision from Bradley in writing; he wasn't going to shoot the Germans off his own bat.

As a kind of ghastly preview up of what was going to happen to private Eddie

Slovik a month later, the execution of the three Germans was going to be stage-managed to achieve the maximum possible effect and impact on the GI's for whom it was intended.

Just as would be the case in a month's time, regulations were consulted. "Preliminary Preparations, SOP No, 54" was pursued on the correct manner for a firing squad and the officers in charge were informed that: "The place of execution will be prepared to provide for a backdrop made absorbent material, before which the prisoners will be placed. An upright post will be placed in front of the backwall and will be used to support the prisoners if necessary."

The wall was soon found. It was at the new US Military Cemetery at Belgium's Henri-Chapelle, near Eupen, packed as it was with fresh American dead from "Bulge" (the Wall is still there, marked with bullets which killed the three Germans and the others who were shot after them).

A firing squad was formed of military policemen. The " SPO" prescribes "In (the) charge of a sergeant, consisting of eight and not more than 12 enlisted men, skilled in the use of regulation rifles." Thereafter came the officials required to be present, as prescribed by regulation: "Three medical offices, a chaplain, a recorder and not fewer than five officially designated military witnesses."

All was finally ready and on the 22nd December, one day before Eddie Slovik fate was also decided, they were told. They took the news that their appeal had been turned down bravely. It was recorded that they were asked if they had one last request. "Yes," they answered. "You have some German women prisoners. We would like to hear German Christmas carols."

Their request was granted.

Thus they went to their death, the echoes of "*Stille Nacht, Heilige Nacht*" still ringing in their ears, bearing what secrets they might still know about that "Eisenhower Murder" with them. * 27

On that same Friday that Hodges confirmed the death sentence of three Germans, in Paris to the south, other American officers were still working on Eddie Slovik's plea for clemency. CIC officers staked out the Cafe de Paix waiting for Skorzeny to make an appearance and every main road leading into the French capital was covered by armed GI's and French security police. (Even the many brothels of the capital were under surveillance, too, including the celebrated "*Sphinx*", reputedly German-owned and during the German occupation Reichsmarshal Georings favourite place to let his hair down. Brothels were ideal places for dubious characters to "take a dive", as the parlance of the time had it). All through this chaos and uncertainty the offices of the Judge Advocate's Branch laboured mightily on Slovik's case.

On 19th December Slovik was informed that his plea for clemency had been received. Then General McWilliams, the Assistant Adjutant-General, wrote him that no "final action had been taken upon your case, but you may be sure that the evidence in the record of the trial and the matters which you have presented in your letter will be carefully examined and that your plea for clemency will be given every possible consideration before the final action is taken."

With that Slovik had to be satisfied. Unknown to him, naturally, working on the top floor of the "Hotel Majestic", the 19th century Parisian hotel which had been taken over by the Americans, one of the team of highly trained US lawyers was reviewing his case. He was Harvard trained Major Bertholet who had volunteered in 1941 for the Army as a private, a very patriotic thing to do. Unfortunate perhaps for Eddie Slovik, he had carried out his patriotic deed from the Department of Justice of the Commonwealth of Pennyslvania".... He was yet another of the Pennsylvanian Establishment who would dominate the "Slovik Case".

We can assume, therefore, that the patriotic Major Bertholet was proud of the state's National Guard " Keystone Division " and that he knew personally some of the more prominent local figures involved in the arraignment and the trial of Eddie Slovik. In peacetime, and in a civil court, Major Bertholet would undoubtedly had been challenged by any halfway astute defence counsel. For any defence lawyer might have concluded he was prejudiced. But this wasnt peacetime and this was the all-powerful US Army. No one challenged the good and patriotic Major.

As Major Bertholet told Huie some nine years after the events "My prime responsibility was for other correctness of the legal findings. My responsibility on the matter of clemency was secondary. .... In the Slovik case no protracted legal discussions were indicated. The record was clean and the facts were clear."

As the legal reviewer saw it, therefore, it was his task primarily to assess the validity of the original court martial and there is an official US document extant in which Bertholet has marked item by item if every step of the trial and relevant discussions and decisions had been carried out correctly. Each entry is marked by a series of ticks and crosses.

However there is one aspect of the review which might well have caused any civilian defence to query its objectivity. It is that final reference to the FBI records. Slovik was being tried on his army record, his desertions and refusal to enter the firing line: as serious military crimes as such. His FBI record surely had no place in an army trial for strictly military offences?

According to ex- Major Bertholet's statement issued to Huie in 1953, "No one attempted to influence my review". In addition, the ex- Major added," I have no way of knowing to what extent General Eisenhower was influenced by my review." All the legal reviewer knew was that "the Slovik case had pained General Eisenhower deeply, as he longed to equal General Pershing's record in World War One (ie.. the fact that the World War One commander had not had one doughboy shot for cowardice). Nor had he, Bertholet, visited Slovik in prison. As Bertholet puts it in 1953, "It was the Officer's duty to confine himself to the records and the accompanying papers."

In brief Major Bertholet felt that he had no influence in any way in his assessment by outside factors or personalities. Yet although in his review Major Bertholet points out under the heading '9 Clemency' " The power to exercise clemency is a trust; it is not to be granted as a matter of course. ... but its exercise should depend upon the facts and considerations of military discipline, "almost immediately he brings in the FBI records.

Audie Murphy.

Bertholet gives the details and then states, at "they (the civilian offences) indicate the persistent refusal to conform to the rules of society in civilian life, an imperviousness to penal correction and a total lack of appreciation of clemency; these qualities the accused brought with him into his military life.

Of course Major Bertholet was correct. Slovik did think that he was doing the US Army a favour when he, the ex-con, attempted to become a soldier, although previously he had been graded "4- F" due to his past criminal record. Slovik also felt that if he didn't want to soldier in the frontline then he could refuse and would accept a prison sentence as result. After all he had done time before; prison life would be nothing new to him.

But under the terms imposed upon Major Bertholet in preparing his review, ie. he was dealing with a military offence and not a civil one, the above considerations should have played no role. But they did. Major Bertholet stated rightly that "confinement (for Slovik) is neither deterrent nor punishment". He concluded " If the death penalty is ever to be imposed for desertion, it should be imposed in this case, not as a punitive measure nor as a retribution, but to maintain that discipline upon which alone an army can succeed against the enemy. There is no recommendation for clemency in this case and none is a here recommended."

III
THE DECISION

"Silent cannon, soon cease your silence.

Soon unlimber'd to begin the real business."

Walt Whitman

Saturday 23rd December 1944.

The Battle of the Bulge had been raging for a week now and the initiative still seem to be in German hands. The point of General von Manteuffel's 5th Panzer Army had almost reached the last natural barrier in their path, the River Meuse, and all the Allies had to hold the length the river in Belgium was one worn-out British armoured brigade.

In fact, the battle would now begin to turn in the Allies' favour. The night before General Bruce Clark, who was defending the Belgian frontier town of St Vith with his combat command of the 7th US Armour, plus a regiment of the now surrendered 106th US Infantry division and Cota's 112th Infantry, had opined that it looked "like Custer's last stand." His remaining tanks were tied down in thick mud and the Germans were in the forest on both sides of him. At 5 o'clock that Saturday morning he awoke to discover a heavy frost and earth solid and hard; his tanks could move again".

In surrounding Bastogne, the old "old Crock," General McAucliffe was still besieged.*28 But Patton had commenced his relief attack from the south, with his ringing orders of the day. "Lets root hog...." If those Krauts sons of bitches want war in the raw, let's give it 'em". It would take Patton three more days to raise the siege, but least he was on his way.

And on the Meuse, an apprehensive British infantry sergeant, who are just set off a mine under a jeep which had refused to stop, approached the wrecked vehicle feeling he had killed its American occupants. A minute later he was immensely relieved to find out the dead men sprawled in the smoking wreckage weren't Yanks, but Germans. It was the last recorded instance of the destruction or capture of one if Skorzeny jeep teams.

The tide had slowly commenced to turn.

General Eisenhower, still a prisoner in his headquarters in Versailles did not know this, of course. In essence, he had been out of touch with what was happening to his troops at the front since Wednesday. In several ways he was unaware of what had transpired since he had last ventured outside his "prison" to Verdun on 19th December. For example, this day he would send a message to General Clarke's boss, General Hasbrouck, congratulating him on the continuing defence of St Vith", not knowing Clarke had abandoned the Belgian town a day before.

All the same, on this Saturday, Eisenhower was preparing to draft a long memorandum on the "Battle of the Bulge", as it was now beginning to be called. It was obviously intended to cover him if there was an inquiry *29. In it he would explain why the Ardennes had been so thinly defended; and why Bradley had allowed Patton to continue his offensive in the Saar to the disadvantage to the rest of his long front, especially in the Ardennes.

He'd turn to the Intelligence fiasco and how and why General Strong's 1000 staff and those of Bradley's and Hodges' armies had failed to notice the German build-up. He'd write: "All intelligence agencies assiduously at tried to find out the locations and intentions of these (German) Panzer formations, but without definite success". He was telling an untruth about the 6th SS Panzer Army, which had originally been lost and then found before the attack. He'd continue with "While it was felt that an attack through the Ardennes was a possibility.... it was not deemed highly probable that the enemy would, in winter, try to use that region in which to stage a major attack."

It is clear that in the light of how Eisenhower was going to spend that Saturday morning and the fact that he was living under armed guard (CIC had set up a trap in the Cafe de la Paix the previous evening, but all they had caught were two US officers breaking the curfew) the Supreme Commander was not going to make Eddie Slovik his major priority of that snowy morning.

Still, as was his custom, before he saw his staff chiefs to discuss the key military matters at the moment, he was "attended" by Brigadier General Ed Betts', his theatre judge advocate. For Betts' duty was to brief Eisenhower personally on

January in Alsace. The Second Battle of the Bulge

important legal and moral business. Today it was a question of whether Eisenhower would extend clemency to one Private Eddie Slovik, who languished a few miles away, imprisoned just like the Supreme Commander, wondering if his appeal of 9th December 1944 would find Eisenhower's favour.

According to Major Bertholet, as we know, Betts' had discuss the Slovik case with Eisenhower and that the Supreme Commander "was pained" by the decision he made. But General Betts' died in Germany almost immediately after the war and we have to take Major Bertholets word for it that there was some time for discussion. Usually Eisenhower could give Betts less than an hour at their daily morning meetings to discuss a whole range of such matters. However what little can be gathered was that Eisenhower relied greatly on Betts' opinion. . For the latter had been with him ever since he had taken over in England after Eisenhower's return from the Middle East. As Betts was fully convinced of Slovik's guilt and didn't believe he should be shown any clemency, we can assume that if Eisenhower was, in any way hesitant, it was Betts who swung him over to his decision that morning. It was that Private Eddie Slovik's sentence should be carried out. Within a month, as military law prescribed, there would be another review and when the time was up, and Slovik still was judged guilty, the sentence of death would be carried out.

But what Eisenhower really thought about sentence he confirmed that December Saturday, with the snowflakes falling outside, is not known. He never made a reference to the matter publicly or privately, as far as it is recorded. Perhaps understandably so. Here was a public hero, a decent man of the people, lauded and admired by millions of ordinary people and soldiers in the Allied camp. Yet at the same time he was a general who was sending - and did send- the only GI to be convicted of desertions since 1864 to his death at the hands of a firing squad. Such an action didnt match up well with that well-known image of a democratic general with his ear-to-ear wide grin.

Naturally his future reputation - and it was clear that by 1944, Eisenhower was toying with the idea of the political career in the post-war world (Patton for instance, had a already made statements on the matter privately to his staff on several occasions remarking scornfully- "Ike's bucking for President") - would not be helped by the death sentence on a reluctant Slovik, especially when Joe Public discovered the circumstances in which it had been made.

For as we know on that Saturday and, indeed for most of the early part of the Battle of the Bulge, Eisenhower had allowed himself to become a prisoner in his own compound, guarded by several hundred soldiers. During the Battle of the Bulge, 80,000 of his soldiers were killed, wounded or captured; and here he was hiding away in the baroque splendour of Versailles," in the French "Sun Kings" Palace. Why? Because there was a vague threat, based on a rumour that's Skorzeny's SS killers were out to get him.

It is not surprising, that when was Skorzeny was finally captured at the end of the war, Sheen made a hurried journey to Bavaria to interrogate the commando leader. He didn't let Skorzeny know who we was, but posed as the local chief of the counter-intelligence. The interview took six hours and later when Skorzeny was sent for trial, the scar faced German who was wanted by the Russians, Polish, Czechoslovak, Danish and Belgian governments as presumably a war criminal was arraigned before a US court on a paltry charge of stealing US Red Cross ration parcels for his jeep teams!

Although Eisenhower had characterised Skorzeny back in the early months of the spring of 1945 as "the most dangerous man in Europe", with wanted posters of Skorzeny plastered throughout Western Europe, he was acquitted of this very minor crime. It was clear that Eisenhower wanted the Skorzeny assassination threat of December 1944 and the impact it had on his life during the key stage of the Battle the Bulge forgotten as soon as possible.

So when Eisenhower signed Betts' paper, reading "The action of the confirmed authority is....approved," he would insist in due course on a codicil which would surprise, even shock General Cota. Private Slovik would not be executed in Paris, where the Press might get wind of the execution and publicise it. Even the soldiers paper "*The Stars and Stripes*" would not, in due course, mention the events in its columns aimed at the average G I. Instead Eisenhower would direct that Slovik would be returned to his unit, the 28th Division, for execution. That division would spend two days looking for suitably remote site in France to carry it out; and all but military personnel connected with the 28th and the corps to which the division belonged would be excluded from the scene.

In retrospect it is clear that Eisenhower wanted to forget that Saturday and the decision he had been forced to make that morning. It was part of his personal war that he would insure was forgotten or swept under the carpet as long as the had the power to control events. Indeed, when Frank Sinatra bought the rights to the Huie book, his studios in Hollywood were told by representatives of the Pentagon that the US Army didn't want a movie made on the Slovik theme. Frank, always insisted that he did it "my way." Nevertheless he dropped the project like a hot potato and it would be another 15 years or so before the Slovik film will be made. We can guess who might well have been behind the Pentagon ban.

The house in Ste Marie-aux-Mines (Alsace) where Eddie was shot

Thus that Saturday which was the turning-point of the Battle the Bulge passed. Eisenhower, however, did not know that. He had demanded that this would be last day of his "imprisonment" by Colonel Sheen. He had intended to go by rail to visit Montgomery, who seemed to be running most of his armies at the moment, whether Bradley or the other US generals liked it or not. But that wasn't to be. It would be another four days before he was "released". The Skorzeny threat seemingly still held sway.

France. Spot where Private Slovik was shot by comrades of 28th Division. January 1945.

So we can assume that the Supreme Commander spent that Saturday evening as he customarily spent his Saturday evenings: perhaps reading one of his cowboy novels, drinking a little and playing poker with his " boys": those hangers-on, visiting firemen and members of the intimate little circle.

And Slovik?

We know little of what happened to the condemned man now.

Although when all the others, the General Betts, Major Bertholet etc etc had disappeared into the dusty footnotes of the history of WWII Slovik was still a known and recognised name. But his last days are much under-recorded. Indeed it was nearly a decade before even his own wife knew exactly what had happened to her husband of two years and that he had been shot for desertion.

From this exit Eddie walked to his death.

We do know, however, that a second review of the Slovik case took place in Paris in the early new year of 1945, just before the Battle of the Bulge was finally declared officially won and the Skorzeny threat had disappeared .*30 This time it was a full board chaired by a
Brigadier-General, B Franklin Riter. Again that FBI evidence played a major part in the board's decision. In his endorsement of the Board of Reviews finding, the case was "found legally sufficient to support this (ie death)", General McNeil, Assistant Judge Advocate General wrote: "The sentence adjudged was more severe than he (Slovik) had anticipated but the imposition of a less severe sentence would only have accomplished the accused purpose of securing his incarceration and consequent freedom from the dangers which so many of our armed forces are required to face daily."

McNeill concluded: "His unfavourable civilian record indicates that he is not a worthy subject of clemency."

Slovik had lost. He had a three more weeks to live. In retrospect it seems as if Eddie Slovik had selected himself as the sacrificial goat which the US Army needed that winter. In the event there were scores, perhaps hundreds of the other deserters in the European stockades who had committed greater military crimes than Slovik. For the most part they had not surrendered voluntarily to the US authorities. They had been caught and arrested. But the one man who had tamely surrendered to the division, from which he had absented himself, had not only signed a statement maintaining he'd deserted again if he were sent up the line, but he had also possessed what had been made out to be a lengthy and serious criminal record in civilian life. Thus he had been portrayed as a hardened ex- con by the courts and the reviewing bodies: a worthless person who would let down both society and the army of his native country. Such a man deserved to die.

If Eddie Slovik had cunningly set out, as some of his officers judging him that December and January thought he had, to be arrested and sent to the safety of jail away from the dangers of the front, he had made a serious miscalculation. If he had been simply a fool, who had acted spontaneously out of the overriding fear of sudden death in the line, then he had played the wrong card. He had gambled and lost. ....

On the 6th January 1945 when the Board of Review forwarded their recommendations to Eisenhower for his approval that the death sentence on Slovik should be carried out, the battered 28th Division was beginning to reorganise itself.

Cota, somehow still in command, began to replace commanders who had failed and again to absorb thousands of replacements to make-up for the nearly 3000 men were being lost in the 110th Regiment alone. The 110th was replaced totally and rejoined by the 112th and 119th regiments which had fought the Battle of the Bulge under the command of other divisions. Cota, for his part, as we know, had filled only a minor function in the defence and relief of Bastogne. Still, it seems, that as a divisional commander without a division, he felt he had carried out his duty. But in reality we know little of General Cota or in this period, for the media were keeping pretty quiet, under orders from Supreme Headquarters about the ill-fated 28th Division and its commander.

On 11th January, however, it started to become clear that, while the battle raged all along Germany's frontier with Belgium, Luxembourg and France, the 28th would be called upon for combat again. On that day Bedell-Smith, Eisenhowers's fiery Chief-of-Staff, conferred in French Alsace with General Devers, the commander of the US 6th Army Group, which consisted of the US 7th Army and the French 1st Army.

Currently Devers was fighting what was known as "The second Battle of the Bulge", the German attack "Operation Northwind" into it Alsace. Forced to retreat under the fury of the German assault, that Army group was now preparing to go over to the attack itself. But just like the combat divisions further north, Devers infantry were running out of riflemen, too.

Bedell Smith suggested that the 28th Division could be sent south from the Bastogne area to help in the coming attack on what was called the "Colmar Pocket", the German foothold on France centred in the area of the Alsatian town of Colmar .The Chief-of-Staff warned, however, that the 28th were still pretty battered from the Ardennes fighting and was capable of limited offensive action only.

Thus the 28th reinforced massively and reformed for the last time in WWII in which it would suffer 30,000 odd casualties, started to move to Alsace in some of the worse January weather experienced in that part of the world since the turn of the century. The Division's task would be primarily to support the elite 3rd US Infantry Division, now part of General Milburn's XXI Corps. In due course, XXI Corps would be placed under the command of the 1st French Army for the attack on the Colmar Pocket, which occasioned protests from every commander within the XXI Corps. But as Bedell Smith had warned Devers, the 28th was really only to be used as fill-in and not as an assault unit. General Cota now felt perhaps he could concentrate on something else than the battle to come.

There was a place where the 28th could shoot its most famous (perhaps Cota would have thought "infamous" was a better word) private soldier, namely Eddie Slovik. Up to now, those American soldiers who had committed crimes against French civilians, rape, murder and the like, had been punished fairly openly so that the French could see that the US Army took care of their interest and did actually punish its criminal elements. This time, however, the punishment of private Slovik was to be hidden from the locals. His execution would be revealed solely to the men of the outfit with which he would have served if he had not been such a coward. Therefore, the site of the execution had to be within the 28th's divisional area, as Eisenhower had ordered. All the same it had to be a remote so that it would attract no outside publicity.

Cota, we know, didn't like that assignment. As he told Huie in the 1950s, " I'll admit it I was surprised - - maybe a little irritated - at first , when I learnt that theatre commander was sending a soldier up for me to shoot. I had thought the execution would be performed back at the Disciplinary Training Centre, were many of the murderers and rapists were executed". However, in the end, "as soon as I thought it over, I conceded the logic in the theatre commander's action: a deserter should be shot by the outfit he deserts."

But was that a latter-day rationalisation on the part of General Cota? Although the information was passed out afterwards that Slovik had been shot, one won- ders how many of the 28th's soldiers going into action that day after the execu- tion knew of it and felt warned to watch their discipline? What effect did the news of the Slovik execution have on the Army as a whole when it was censored and, as we have seen, not publicised in the only newspaper readily available to the troops on a daily basis, *The Stars and Stripes*?

But Cota had survived yet a second debacle in the Ardennes and come out still commanding his division. He wasn't going to rock the boat now when he was being given a third chance, after the Hurtgen and the collapse of his 110th Regi- ment on the "Skyline Drive". He set about the complicated business of shipping his division from Belgium to France and at the same time passed on the order from Paris which had just come through to his Provost Marshal Major Fellman.

Fellman, another old-timer of the National Guard from Philadelphia, was to be in overall charge of the Slovik execution, which meant he'd ensure the site was private and free of civilians. As his assistant he had a Lt. Zygmont Koziak, who would handle the firing squad. These two officers, both known to Cota, would be assisted by two reliable senior sergeants, James Hess and Frank McKendrick, who in due course would guard Slovik when he arrived from Paris and as a final duty bind him to the post at a which the would be shot.

Unfortunately all these four trusted and loyal men had never been engaged in such a dreadful task before - the shooting of a fellow American and a member of their own outfit. How did you go about it?

So while the search for a suitable site in the divisional area in Alsace went on, an urgent appeal was sent to higher headquarters for the "SOP " - the Standard Operational procedure. After all the last time this particular military operation had been carried out and a coward and deserter had been "shot to death with musketry", in the snows of a wintery Virginia, the accused Union soldier had actually been shot by muskets. Thus it was (through Fellman and his team didn't know it) the Provost Marshal received the same instructions which had been used only a month before at Henri Chapelle in the excuse of Skorzeny's alleged assassins. By a strange quirk of fate, the manner of execution of those Germans who had indirectly influenced Eisenhower's decision of 23rd December 1944, one day before they themselves were shot, would now formalise the shooting of Eddie Slovik. Friend and foe united in death. ....

On the same day that the order came from Paris making Cota responsible for the shooting of Eddie Slovik, who complained he was being shot because he had "stolen a loaf of bread when I was 12", another American kid from wrong side of the tracks - Audie Murphy- was earning his country's highest honour for bravery in action, the Congressional Medal of Honor.

Back in 1942 when Eddie Slovik was just finishing his "time", the 18 year old Texan, whose sharecropper father had abandoned his mother and their children when he had been nine, had already been turned down by the Marines, the para-troopers and the Navy. Indeed the only branch of the US service prepared to take the skinny, baby-faced kid, who looked all of 13, was the army. His rejection by the other, more selective marines and paratroopers was understandable. The eager Texan kid was undernourished, barely literate and had a chip on his shoulder which came from being a near-orphan and raised in a state, which according to the "kid", had had nothing to give him but "free advice and malnutrition".

But the youngster made it . More than once kindly superiors suggested he should transfer to the cookhouse or some rearline function; he simply did not have the physique for infantry. He refused. By the time, Eddie Slovik was thinking of marrying his Antoinette, the Texan had been through North Africa and Sicily (where he had collapsed with malaria and exhaustion), and was fighting with the 3rd US Infantry Division in Italy.

By the August when Eddie Slovik had deserted at Elbeuf, the 19 year-old Texan had been wounded, killed a 100 Germans and had about won every medal that the USA had to offer save the most important of them all.

Now baby-faced Eddie Murphy, a 20 year-old company commander of the same company he joined nearly two years before and its only survivor of the original outfit, was about to win that medal, too. On that snowy January afternoon, the only surviving officer of seven with which his company had commenced its action, the survivors were attacked by 125 Germans and tanks. As the attached artillery observer, a Lieutenant Weispfennig recorded afterwards: "Lieutenant Murphy did the bravest thing I've ever seen a man do in combat. With the Germans only a 100 yards away and still moving on him, he climbed on a slow burning tank destroyer (which had been abandoned by its US crew) and began firing the 50 caliber machine-gun at the Krauts'. He was completely exposed and silhouetted against a background of bare trees and snow, with a fire under him that threaten to blow the destroyer to bits if it reached the gasoline and ammunition. 88 mm shells, machine guns, machine pistols and rifle fire crashed all about him."

Murphy didn't run. It wasn't in the baby-faced soldier's nature to do so. As an-other observer, a Sergeant Brawley remembered afterwards: "The German in-fantry men got within 10 yards of the lieutenant, who kill them in the draws, in the meadows, and in the woods - wherever he saw them. Though wounded and covered with soot and dirt which must have obscured his vision at times, he had the enemy at bay, killing and wounding 35 of them during the next hour."

That day Murphy deserved his Medal of Honor. But as he said himself long afterwards, he "felt nothing. No sense of triumph, no exhilaration at being alive. Even the weariness seemed to have passed. Existence had taken on the quality of a dream which I am detached from all that is present. I hear the shells bursting about the trees, see the dead scattered on the ground. But I do not connect them with anything that particularly concerns me."

Indeed that brave man deserved his medal, just as the coward would be thought to have deserved his death which would bring his existence to an end within the next week. Yet the kid who hadn't overvalued his life too much and hadn't run away, would pay the price too. For the remainder of his relatively short life he privately suffered anguish for those months in combat, culminating in gaining his country's highest honour for bravery. In 1971 just before Murphy died, he told his doctor that he had been plagued by nightmares ever since the war. In them he relived his combat experiences. He said, too, that he was unable to seep without a loaded German Walter automatic pistol beneath his pillow. Naturally, by then a Hollywood star, he was on drugs, too.

His waking life was also marked by his preoccupation with his wartime experiences. When an interviewer asked him at the time, how combat soldiers managed to survive war. Murphy's answer was: " I don't think they ever do." He added "a combat soldier always pays the price one way or other, either on the battlefield or later in peacetime."

Audie Murphy might have won his country's highest order for bravery and enjoyed a successful career as a cowboy movie star - "same movie 40 times over," equipped cynically years later, "The only thing they change was the horse". But in the end war caught up with the hero-movie star, too.

Just like Slovik, preparing for his last journey to the spot where the US army would shoot him dead, the state had done nothing for Murphy. But that had not mattered. He had done his duty. Slovik was different. He felt the state owed him something, including the right as an ex-con originally judged to be "4-F" not to risk his life in the line. Slovik had believed he could make his separate peace with the enemy and let other young men such Murphy and all the other nameless thousands to fight and perhaps die in combat that winter of 1944/45.

"I knew they (he meant the state) wouldn't let me be happy," Slovik exclaimed once after being sentenced to death. The outburst has indicated he felt that the state had a duty to let him enjoy happiness. It was a *cri de coeur* that would find resonance in the United States of the 1950s, when William Huie first revealed the details of that hidden execution of the decade before. Undoubtedly it is a heartfelt cry that would elicit approval today. We live in an age when it is generally believed that we have a right to happiness.

But in the last week's January, as the 28th Division prepared to go into action once more to support the badly hurt 3rd Division of Audie Murphy, Eddie Slovik would finally learn that the state owned him nothing, especially not happiness. ...

III

EXECUTION

"Remember me when I am dead and simplify me when I'm dead."

Captain Keith Douglas, Poet. Killed in action, Normandy 1944

On 29th January 1945, the Brass arrived at a Ste. Marie-aux-Mines. Somehow their Packards and command cars had negotiated the deep snow of the steep climb into the mountains and now they were here, ready to warm themselves and have a stiff drink.

They walked into the requisitioned chateau at the edge of the run-down mining town in the Vosges mountains and were immediately ushered into the welcoming warmth of a log fire. If anything else was in short supply up in the mountains on the linguistic border of the German speaking Rhenish plain below where the fighting was and the French-speaking heights, which had once marked the Franco-German border till 1918, there was always plenty of wood. Not that the arriving Brass worried about the natives. Most of them in the immediate vicinity had been forcibly evacuated. For the civilians had been ordered out by Major Fellman and his MPs two days before and what was soon going to happen would take place solely for the benefit of American witnesses. The French were going to have no part in the execution of Private Slovik at Number 86 Rue General Bourgeois.

Two days before Fellman had decided that the 18th century house with its mas-sive walls, patched with damp from thick snow which lay everywhere, would be the right site for their execution. As he recorded after the war: "The location was not adjacent to any town activity. A very important factor was that a stonewall approximately seven and a half feet high surrounded the property. "

Now its occupants had gone, as were those of the nearby houses (not all as we shall see) and, as Felman remembered, "The occupants did not know for what purpose it (Number 86) was to be used. .. A security guard was established 24 hours prior to the execution and all possible points of view were cut off to both civilian and military personnel. But prior to the execution and afterwards the entire matter was kept from the civilian populace". [*31]

With Fellman, feeling that anything was under control, despite the terrible weather and the snowstorms that raged in the High Vosges, a squad of the divi-sional engineers moved in to set up the execution. Paths were cleared. Sites were selected for the brass to observe the execution. The "backwall" was made. Against this Eddie Slovik would be placed, tied to a post in case his knees gave and then crumpled. As for that, it would provide additional protection to the exist-ing masonry wall. For a bullet from that Garand M1 rifle, the infantryman's stand-ard weapon to be used at the execution, was reckoned to kill at a distance of two miles. Fired now at 20 paces, as "Standard Operating Procedure" decreed, any ricochets might well slay a couple or more spectators; and the assistant divi-sional engineer, Captain Humel in charge of preparations, knew it wouldn't be wise to lose any of the Brass in the process of shooting a condemned man.

So that January near its end, the preparations neared their completion, too, down to the black cloth hood which would cover Eddie's head. Unfortunately it was one item which the Division, with all its resources, could not supply. In the end, the Provost was forced to send out into town for a cloth and in a tiny smelly shop in the steep, cobbled main street, a seamstress was engaged to carry out a macabre task of sewing the hood. But as Major Fellman confidently stated after the war: "Neither the person from whom the material was secured nor the seamstress knew for what purpose it was to be used for. "Now, it seems, that after the apparently original intention to publicise what was to happen to Private Slovik as a warning to others, the US Army was doing its damnedest to make sure that only a very select circle knew what was going on.

Today it is not known -at least officially- what prompted the top brass to hold a dinner on the night of January 30th, 1945 at that commandeered chateau at its Ste Marie-Aux-Mines Already on the 25rd, General Devers, the commander the 6th US Army Group had, as we have seen, agreed to place Milburn's XXI Corps under the command of the 1st French Army for the attack on Colmar Pocket. It had been a hard decision for Devers, whose mother was Alsatian, to make. It wasn't liked in Washington. But it had to be done. So there was really no need for him to gather his senior officers together in that snowbound mountain township to discuss the matter again.

Yet here they all were - Devers, Milburn, Cota and three or four lesser generals from XXI Corps and the two infantry divisions involved - the 3rd and the 28th - which were to attack on the morrow. Was it a mini-version of the ball before Waterloo or that of Richmond prior to the outbreak of the civil war?

Hardly likely. As far as we can ascertain, there were no women present. It was an assembly of the Brass, West Point to the man, So why had General Frank "Shrimp" Milburn invited then to dinner on this snowbound evening while 15 miles to the south-east their divisions prepared for the attack on the last German outpost in France? *32

We can only guess.

They had come to view something unique in history of the US Army in the 20th Century - the ceremonial shooting of the only US soldier to be executed by his own comrades for desertion since that snowy January day in Virginia in 1864. Professional soldiers, are acutely aware of the history and traditions of their armies, like to be part of such events. Perhaps it gives them some sense of immortality?

For on that same evening with the wind rattling the blackout shutters outside and the lights wavering in the air that swept through the draughty chateau at periodic intervals, "Shrimp" Milburn, the undersize Corps' commander, took the opportunity of establishing — indirectly- his own part in these historic proceedings.

One of the two lowly colonels who were present, the Corps' Chaplain Colonel Edward Elson, chanced to bump into Milburn. The former knew nothing of what was going to happen at this remote place. Now Milburn enlightened him. Drawing aside the colonel, who had once been forced to decide whether he would go to West Point or into the ministry, he said, "Chaplain, tomorrow morning the 28th Infantry Division is executing a soldier by firing squad for desertion."

Elson, who one day would be US Senate chaplain and preacher before President Eisenhower himself, nodded and wondered what the news had to do with him.

Milburn soon informed him. He continued with, " This is the first firing squad execution since the Civil War. I must give full attention to the battle which begins tomorrow or I would attend. I wish you would attend as my personal representative and give me for a full report when it is over and you can reach the command post. This is VOG. "

For a moment the divisional Chaplin wondered what the initials signified. Then he got it. They meant - Vocal Orders of my Commanding General. "Naturally the Colonel hurried to agree. But neither then nor later when he finally revealed his part in the Slovik Execution, over 40 years after the event and some three in a half decades after Huie's breaking of the Slovik story did Colonel Elson query that his sudden task was placed upon him under some strange circumstances. Why, for instant, a vocal instead of a written order? Why, too, had he been summoned to the dinner without any previous knowledge of what was soon to happen at number 86 Rue de Generale Bourgeoisie.

We could only conclude that the "Shrimp" was taking his orders directly from SHAEF, and perhaps from Eisenhower himself. The emergency had passed in the Bulge. There was no need to make a great public example of Slovik. Hence the remote location of where the execution was being carried out. Still Eisenhower, who probably wanted to disassociate himself from the whole unpleasant affair, knew that there was no going back now; the penalty of death had to be carried out. Hence a private and concealed line to the place of execution so, in an emergency or an inquiry, he, the Supreme Commander, could always maintain he had followed the Slovik case to the end. So, indirectly the lives of " Eddie", a humble private and " Ike", the Supreme Commander, were linked to the very last moment.

Although he hadnt know it in the time, Colonel Elson, the chaplain, who had once toyed with the idea of going to West Point, was now appointed the secret official observer of what would happen on the morrow.

Back in 1953 when Huie interviewed the main surviving participants in the "Slovik Affaire", he knew nothing of Colonel Elson's secret role in the proceedings and especially of his narrative accounts which he penned the very same night of the execution, written "by candlelight and seated at a field desk", with

Colonel (Chaplain) Ralph Smith of the 3rd Division, huddled in his bed wrote in the freezing stone chamber to next him.

For his part, Huie had described the execution through the eyes and the words of those who carried out necessarily "military ceremony" of the execution: those who comforted Slovik professionally; and those who observed. Being the campaigning journalist, anti-establishment and, in particular anti-US Army writer that he seemed to have been, he made most of these people - conformist, typical products of their service and social class. They were most definitely in favour of the execution - at the beginning ".

But as Huie assessed their reaction, feelings and selectively used their subsequent statements when it was all over, it appears in his written account of the dreadful day in Alsace that they had changed their attitude to Slovik and the necessity of his execution. With perhaps the exception of the key member of the firing squad quoted, Private Morrison, they seem to show both sympathy for Slovik and horror at the execution. More importantly they began to think that Eddie Slovik, was being shot for cowardice and refusal to go into combat, was no coward after all. Indeed, Slovik emerges as a brave man. As the tough little Catholic chaplain of the 28th , Father Cummings, who according to Huie had no time for deserters and cowards, the man who gave Slovik his final absolution that day, expressed it to Huie eight years later: "Slovik, was the bravest man in the garden that morning. "

So, for this writer it seems better to set out the details of the execution of Private Slovik as they occurred that January morning, without subsequent comments of the participants which Huie recorded*[33], not always very objectively. Those recollections of Colonel Elson are perhaps the most apt and less subjective.

For as he explained, "I have written my own narrative that evening (the 31st of January 1945) for two reasons. First, acting on a sound psychological principle by writing a description of what I had seen, I would thus exteriorize any inward burden and harassment of memory and secondly; since it was known at the time to be the first execution by firing squad since the war between States, it was certain to have an unusual meaning in history of World War Two. For me it evoked deep reflection."

In the event as Colonel Elson discovered later, "As it turned out the narrative I set forth on this evening of January 31st, 1945 appeared to be the only unofficial account of an on-the-spot eyewitness " For our purposes, therefore, let it be the basis of what happened on that date.

It was the morning of Wednesday January 31st, 1945.

All along the Allied line from Southern Holland to near the Swiss border to the south, the Allied armies -Canadians, Britons, Americans, French, were attacking for the last time. Their aim was to get over the German border and then onto the last natural German barrier in the north, the River Rhine. That morning nearly 2 million Allied fighting men were attacking or about to attack. It was a tremendous number of men and the assault signalled the end of Hitler's vaunted "1000 Year Reich".

The secret burial place

In far off, bombed ruined Berlin, the lair of the Nazi beast, Dr Goebbels informed his listeners and readers: "It is just before the hour of twelve (the German expression for the last minute). The hands of the clock of history are veering, undecided whether to move nearer to the danger point or to move far away from it. .. We are faced with a flood from the east and an onslaught from the west. We must defend ourselves"

This day, too, was the 12th anniversary of Hitler's takeover of power in 1933. From some secret location on the east, the Fuhrer broadcast a few words of encouragement, bidding every German, man, woman and child, to do his duty to the last. Ironically Eddie Slovik had been a 13 year-old "dead-end kid" then and had probably never even heard of Adolf Hitler. Now by some complicated process they had been brought together like this and one of them, who hadn't wanted to come here, would die on account of what happened in Berlin back in 1933.

"At 900 hours," Colonel Elson wrote that night using the military twentyfour hour calendar, "we travelled in a command car about three quarters of hour up to the site of the ceremony at the edge of the town. ".

"The place selected a 86 Rue de General Bourgeoisie, was quite like description in fiction stories and historic accounts I have read (It was) a very large and well-kept three-storey grey house with orange shutters and tiled roof.... (it) rested at the foot of one of the Vosges Mountains. A mountain stream flowed past the walled garden, winding its way through the centre of towns. The approach to the house was accomplished by a bridge about 30ft long. We walked across the span of the high iron gates.... and we were checked by military police, who admitted us, one at a time, carefully checking the name, rank, and serial number and organisation of each officer. We walked up the short distance to the front of the house where another MP admitted us to a large reception room in the centre of the house. Here we awaited until ceremony began."

Oisne-Aisne Cemtery, France, where Slovik was buried in
the secret 'Plot E' for over 40 years (author's photo)

While the Colonel and his fellow officers and spectators waited, General Cota had already visited the firing squad, all first-class marksman, personally selected from all companies of the 109th regiments by its regimental commander on the basis of their shooting record. They were all young working-class men from the same background as their intended victim. But it is clear from the subsequent statements that at first at least they had little sympathy with the condemned man, whom they had yet to see. After all he was one of them, who had let his fellow "working stiffs" down. The day before Cota, on his first visit to the firing squad had assured them they are doing their duty; all he expected of them was to aim at the white paper heart pinned to Slovik at the appropriate spot. He had ended by telling them that they would have nothing to reproach themselves with afterwards.

Now, clad in his smart "A-class" uniform and carrying a cane in the fashion of an upper-class British officer, he repeated the statement, occasionally pointing the brass handle of the cane at the 12 enlisted men for emphasis. Satisfied he had made his point to the somewhat subdued firing squad, which now realised perhaps for the first time what was expected of them, he ordered Lieutenant Koziak, who was in charge, to gather up the squad's rifles. These were carried into another room. Here Koziak and Major Fellman loaded the magazines. One blank round was inserted. Then the rifles shuffled around until as Major Fellman reported later, "Neither Koziak nor I knew were the blank was. We had locked them. Thereupon the squad was called in to pick a rifle."

A firing squad was ready *[34]

Inside the freezing cold "reception room", Chaplain Colonel Elson, who would describe this day with the dry precision of the staff officer, allowed his feelings to wander for a few moments. "Within (the reception room) the waiting atmosphere was grave and realistic in the awareness that, only a few miles beyond us at the front, men were killing and were being killed, that this is war and we are soldiers. " Milburn's private agent noted the officers and MPs coming and going, concentrating on their task with grave set faces. Once he saw the 28th's judge advocate enter. Under his arm he carried "a piece of black cloth and some nylon rope." No one, even the padres, needed to be told what they were intended for.

Presently "Dutch" Cota strode in. Carrying his brass-handled swagger stick, he took his position in the centre of the room. After all, he was in command. He nodded formally to several of the officers. Then he spotted Elson. It called "Good morning Colonel."

"As my collar was buttoned and my helmet was in my hands, he could not see my cross in either place (the chaplain's cross)." So Elson pushed by several other offices and presented himself as the corps' chaplain.

The information didn't disconcert Cota, though he might have wondered what the corps chaplain was doing here in addition to his own catholic divisional padre who was currently confessing the condemned man. Instead "Cota remarked immediately that he needed five chaplain replacements. Four of his chaplains had been wounded or were missing in action in the von Rundstedt breakthrough further

north. .. and another had been hospitalised due to wounds". Cota naturally didn't add, that although the 29th Division had lost so many
" men of God", seemingly so many of his staff, all combat soldiers, had survived the debacle of Wiltz.

Elson assured the Divisional Commander that replacements would soon be on their way and Cota went out to return a few minutes later (perhaps it was now that he spoke to the firing squad) and stand alone in the centre of the big cold 18th century room. Elson did not know it, the but General Cota was waiting to start the execution.

Major Fellman and gone to great lengths to ensure that the execution soon to come would be attended and observed only by those who had right to do so. Colonel Elson had made a surprise appearance, one with which Fellman and his boss, Cota had not reckoned. But at least he was an American. But there was an unknown French witness, too.

She was Madame Steiner who lived on the opposite side of the valley to the place of execution. The farmer's wife had pooh-poohed her husband's fears the previous day when he had maintained apprehensively that they should keep their heads down. If the Americans caught them, they'd be in trouble. Madame Steiner would have none of it. She was curious in her peasant fashion; besides how often did anything happened in that remote valley? The Americans were up to something; she wanted to know what it was.

Now Mademe Steiner and her 10 year-old son positioned themselves well so they could watch and hear what was going on in the place requisitioned by the Americans, who had acted so unnaturally secretively for such an open people. Thus it was that she heard the first command in a language didn't understand around 10 o'clock that morning. The site of the execution was quite a way off, but she heard them well enough in the stillness of that snowbound January morning. What she didn't know that moment was that she was eavesdropping on the commencement of the ceremony, macabre as it was, which would have repercussions across the ocean in far off USA for years to come. It was as if a rock had been thrown into the centre of a still pond, with a ripples expanding ever outwards, as if they would go on forever.

Father Cummings, Catholic divisional chaplain of the 28th was a tough little fellow who chewed tobacco. He might well have stepped out from a hard-nosed serial melodramas from one of those pre-war "Dead End Kids" movies. The no-nonsense, Irish priest, played by say - Pat O'Brien. He hadn't much time for men who didn't do their duty and in the past, he had "dissuaded" men of the "Bloody Buckets'" from running away in the line in his own tough manner. Still it seems he looked after Eddie within those few final hours that he had with the condemned man.

While General Cota waited for "the ceremony" to commence, Father Cummings confessed Eddie, gave him a bundle of letters from his wife to read before he went out to face the firing squad - "I noticed him wipe a tear or two away as he read" - and then he consoled Eddie with: "Son, the decision in your case is not ours to question. This is war. The moral responsibility for your death has been accepted for the people of the United States of America". "Finally he admonished Slovik with the words, "Today I want you to walk out there and die with courage." It was the archetypal death-row scene, vintage James Cagney - Pat O'Brien's stuff.

"Will you be with me, Father," Slovik asked.

"I'll be there."

"Then I'm all right," Slovik's said.

It was now that Slovik made an amazing statement. According Father Cummings as quoted by William Huie, the condemned man said, "And Father I want you to tell the fellows in the regiment that Eddie Slovik wasn't the coward at least not today." It was the kind of statement that characterised the Tinseltown's scriptwriter at his worst. In the late thirties it had been the same kind of final dialogue that had been used in a dozen or so movies. The hoodlum makes a deal with his priest in death-row before he headed for the chair. It was hackneyed, corney, throwaway. But it gave the movie an uplift ending. It showed that even the worst of human beings, the petty hood, the dregs of depressions slum society had a streak of good in them, wanted to be rehabilitated, even through their crimes were so great that there was no hope for them. After all, Tinseltown wanted to give the public best of two worlds - crime and repentance. All the same. The movie had to confirm to the standard "message " insisted on by the Hays Office - crime there does not pay.

But what regiment was Eddie saying goodbye to? Was it the one he *almost* joined when he deserted at Elbeus back in August 1944? But that Regiment no longer existed. "The fellows" in that regiment had been wiped out either in the Siegfried Line, the "Death Factory" or the Battle of the Bulge. They had become ghosts in khaki.

Then, according to Mr Huie, in those final moments before Eddie Slovik walked out that snowy January morning to meet his fate, he told Father Cummings, "Father, I'm getting a break the fellows up on the line don't gets. Here I get to sit here with you and I known I'm going to get it. I know I'm going to die in a few minutes. But it there on the line you never know when it's coming and it's that uncertainty that gets you. I guess that's what I couldn't take - that uncertainty. "

A long speech, full of feeling for a fellow soldiers, from a man who had so little time to live and in the past had shown scant attention to the fates of those soldiers of the 28th Division whom he had a deserted and refuse to support on three occasions. But it was the kind of fake Hollywood *sentimentality and compassion which swung the American* reading public behind Eddie Slovik, behind a lone soldier been sacrificed to the authority, (when his case became known, in the early Fifties).

But there was still more to come. Now, again according to William Huie, Eddie asked Father Cummings about the firing squad waiting for him. Supposedly the Catholic chaplain replied: "I told him the boys didn't like the job... That they were good guys."

"Then before we go out, father," Slovik said, "you be sure to tell them that I didnt hold it against them... and.. please.. shoot straight so that I wont have to suffer." Noble sentiment to the end.

Saying he would tell the firing squad and would inform the 12 GI's assigned to it of Eddie's last wish, Father Cummings, put away his tools of his trade and went out.

It was almost over now...

5.

At a few minutes before 10, Major Fellman directed that the enlisted men inside the building should leave for the execution. As Colonel Elson described the moment, "They' marched off with dispatch' and took up a positions facing the house's door. Then the officers were directed to the assigned places..."

" As senior officer this group, my position was directly of the front file facing the stake, there being two files of officers- almost eight or ten in all." Thus the corps chaplain was in a prime position to observe all that went on that "grey, overcast and slightly warmer" morning. Waiting and watching, he thought how magnificent the scenery was and how beautiful the day".

But the good Colonel didn't have long to survey the scenery. "Soon we heard the command "attention" crisply given by the General who saw that a officiating party just emerging from the doorway. Everyone came to attention and there was an atmosphere of solemn dignity."

The "officiating party" came out like a crocodile of the uniformed children, two by two, all save Slovik who came into the yard alone. He was repeating the Act of Contrition, *"Mother of Mercy, pray for us.... Most sacred Heart of Jesus have mercy upon us."* There was no other sound save the boots on the damp path swept by the divisional engineers. It was not surprising. No one was given to talking, even whispering. The occasion was too solemn. Even if anyone had been tempted to say something, they desisted. Cota's eagle-eye surveyed the scene all the while. On the "officiating party" came, with to the rear, two MPs carry the "collapse board". And the name alone sufficed to explain its purpose.

The fire squad made a right turn. Slovik continued at a "slow but steady pace" mumbling his prayers. A few steps more and "the march" ended. The prisoner was placed in front of the posts facing us. "There was no sound. Slovik heads ceased praying". The time for prayer was obviously over.

Fellman stepped forward. He read out the order of execution and asked, " Do you have a statement to make before the order directing your execution is carried out? "

"No," Slovik replied, looking into the grey sky, as if he half-expected God to send a thunderbolt winging to the ground to relieve him. But this morning, God was obviously looking the other way.

Now it was the Catholic padre's turn. He asked, "Private Slovik, do you have a last statement to make to me as a chaplain before your death? "

Again Slovik answered in the negative, whereupon Major Fellman ordered, "Prepare the condemned for execution. "

Now Fellman's assistants began to truss the prisoner up ready for the execution.

187

As Elson described it that night in the freezing cold of his chamber, with candles flickering in the breeze and casting gigantic, distorted moving shadows on the walls, "The MPs completed the physical preparation. Tapes were drawn across the prisoner shoulders, another about his knees and another across his feet to secure him to the stake." According to Colonel Elson's account, Slovik made no protestations; he let it happen. Instead he continued with his prayers under Father Cummings' guidance.

When the MPs commanded by Fellman were finished Sergeant McKendrick, one of them, produced the black hood.

Just before he placed it over Slovik's pale face, blotting out the world that January morning for ever, Cummings said, " Eddie, when you get up there, say a little prayer for me ."

Slovik answered - and his reply was pure Hollywood, that last happy note Tinseltown's scriptwriters always used to lighten the grimness of the celluloid melodrama. He said, " OK Father, I'll pray the you don't follow me too soon." Those were the last words that Private Eddie Slovik ever uttered.

Now cut off from the world and blinded by the hood, Slovik could not see the squads of riflemen under the leadership of Lieutenant Koziak. The young officer of Polish descent like Eddie brought them up at a quick pace, rifles at the trail, when Father Cummnings stepped back hastily, still reading from his breviary.

A crisp command. The firing squad halted at the path in the snow dug for them. They faced Eddie. Another command. They brought their rifles up to the position of "Port". Yet another order. They unlocked their rifles as one, nobody fumbled their safety catch, although as we will see these expert marksman picked personally by the regimental commander, Colonel James Rudder, were nervous.

A moment's silence. The commands echoed and re-echoed in the hollow circle formed by the mountain backdrop. Clutching her ten-year-old son, Madame Steiner strained her ears in an attempt to hear what was going on. She knew it had to be something important. Why else all the fuss?

In the courtyard, they waited. The wait seemed interminable, though in fact, it was a matter of seconds. Colonel Elson, as tense as the rest of the officer witnesses, felt "I could almost reach out and touch one of the boys (of the firing squad) on the shoulders."

Even the firing squad, all combat infantrymen, were somehow awed by the spectacle: the lone hooded figure tied to the stake waiting for it to happen, that brief electric instant between life and death. One of them Private Morrison's, watched Slovik for any sign of the emotion. There was none. Perhaps they had half-drugged the victim in advance. Then he realised just how cold it was and forgot his nervousness. He stated, " I wanted to get it over with and get out of the weather." He concluded "I didnt imagine that Slovik was enjoying the waiting either. "

Now Major Fellman went into action. Elson started as the MP barked, his breath fogging in the air in grey clouds, "Ready....Aim....FIRE!"

In the skeletal trees around the courtyard, the birds rose cawing in hoarse protests. People jumped. No one noticed. Everyone was concentrating on that lone hooded figure. Elson swallowed, as "The black-hooded head dropped to the chest. The doctors, three of them, went forward and one by one examine the body with stethoscope and fingers." Elson, from his position, felt Slovik was still breathing, but at that range with 12 men firing at the victim surely that couldn't be.

But it was. Slovik was not yet dead. The most senior doctor present, Major Rougelot, thought the "shooting had been very poor. Not one of the bullets has struck the heart....But there had been no intentional misses; all eleven bullets had struck the body." He concluded "Since these riflemen were used to killing human beings, I discounted the emotional effect resulting from the requirements of killing one of their own buddies."

How ironic! Here was Slovik, who had risked all by refusing to go into battle in case he was killed in action. Yet eleven aimed slugs at close range had not finished him off. Now the firing squad was going to have another try doing so. For as Colonel Elson noted in his account: "During the examination, which was the longest part of the ceremony, an MP lieutenant past behind each member of the firing squad taking each rifle and placing another round of ammunition in the rifle so that, if necessary, another volley could be fired. "

Lt. Koziak, the officer in question, was still keeping up the charade that a firing squad shouldn't know who had fired the blank and not the live ammunition, though naturally each man of the squad knew exactly what kind of round he had fired.

Elson, who for a padre seemed to know a lot about firearms, thought the squad had been badly handled - hence the inaccurate shooting - now noticed that Lieutenant Koziak was not observing incorrect fire procedure. In his haste the young MP officer in reloading his men's rifles was "pointing them directly at the enlisted men witnesses. This caused me to speak my only informal words. In a voice that only a few could hear, I said, "Be careful, Lieutenant. Let's not kill one of our own accidentally here this morning."

It seemed that the good Colonel, probably like most of those presence that moment, no longer thought of Eddie Slovik as one of theirs. He was already almost "on the other side. "

As Major Rougelot, the senior doctor, recorded, "I applied the stethoscope to the man's chest. His body was quivering slightly; his breathing was extremely shallow; the heartbeat faint, rapid and irregular." He knew Slovik had only moments to live and as a Koziak reloaded rifles, he pretended to examine Eddie further so that the he would die and that there would be no need for a further volley.

Fellman, it seemed, couldn't wait. He ordered the men to reload and not surprisingly enough (according to a Huie) the tough Catholic padre called, "Give him another volley if you like it so much."

Colonel Elson does not mention this uncharacteristic interchange between the priest who had no time for battlefield shirkers and Major Fellman. Seemingly Rougelot did, however. For he called over to the padre 'something like' "take it easy, padre, none of us are enjoying this. "

Fellman was annoyed. He took the doctor to task. He snapped backs that Rougelot should either the pronounce Slovik dead or stand back so that the men could fire.

Coolly Rougelot replied, "The second volley won't be necessary, Major. Private Slovik is dead."

It was 1008 hours. As Colonel Elson described what happened then, the military 'ceremony' continued, as if it was part of the well-rehearsed drill through which the participants had been before. "The firing squad did a right turn and marched out of the yard behind the house. The Provost Marshal directed the enlisted witnesses to return to their room in the house and then ordered the officers to return. I gave the command, "Right face! Forward march! And we returned to where we disbanded." All very objective, without emotionalism and pathos.

William Huie fills in these final details in a much different manner, calculated to arouse emotion, respect for the dead man, perhaps even anger that it had had all to happen. He quotes one of Major Fellman's helpers Sergeant McKendrick, who cut the body down, while Father Cummnings anointed the bloody corpse with oil. "I pulled off the right shoe and sock so that the chaplain could anoint the feet. Then the grave registration details took over, went through the pockets, pulled off one of his dogtags and slipped him into a mattress cover.

Another of Fellman's assistants, Captain Hummel, came on the scene. He pointed to the 'collapse board' and remarked, "It turned out that we didn't need that bit of apparatus, did we? "

That NCO answered, "No, not Slovik. I came nearer needing it than he did. I cant figure that guy out. If he was a coward, he certainly didn't show it today."

It was the cue for Father Cummings. In the best Hollywood style he pontificated, "Slovik was the bravest man in the garden this morning..." He added, according to the Huie, "If you ask me where Eddie Slovik found his courage, I'll give you the 'commercial'". For 2000 years the Catholic Church had been supplying what Eddie Slovik needs on the day he meets his death. From were else can a little man find strength. .."

On the hillside, the hidden civilian witnesses Madame Steiner and her son watched as the American soldiers started to leave. After an hour she saw soldiers burning something at the house. At first she thought they were igniting the body of the American they had shot. Later she realised they were burning the stop board, firing post to which Slovik had been tied and the celebrated 'collapse board.' The US Army was being careful. There was going to be no trace of Eddie Slovik left at Ste-Marie-aux-Mines. Indeed if Eddie Slovik's execution had been meant as a warning to the troops, precious little publicity was given to the event then or later.

As Brigadier-General S. L. A. Marshall, the doyen of WW II military historians wrote in his 1954 review of the Huie book *The execution of private Slovik* for the *New York Times Book Review* : "Private Eddie D Slovik was the only soldier shot for cowardice on the battlefield since 1864. It happened in the European Theatre in WWII. Until today the incident has remained as deep buried as the corpse. If, as the author implies, Private Slovik was shot for the effects of the example, it should be worth mentioning that though the Chief Historian of the Theatre, I have just heard of Slovik for the first time."

A telling point. But by January 1945 things were a lot different than they had been in November 1944 when Eddie had been sentenced to death and morale in some combat outfits was rock-bottom. Now the Army, in particular at the Top Brass, wanted to forget the whole thing. Soon Eddie Slovik would vanish from the 200 year history of the United States Army as if it had never existed. .....

At zero ten thirty hours , military time, half-an-hour after Eddie Slovik had died so, violently, the a top-secret high priority TWX was flashed from the Ste-Marie-aux-Mines to Eisenhower in Paris.

It read -

TO: COMMANDING GENERAL ETOUSA.

FROM: HQ 28TH INF. DIV

PURSUANT TO GCMON 27 HEADQUARTERS ETOUSE 23 JAN 45, PRIVATE EDDIE D.SLOVIK 36896415, FORMERLY COMPANY G, 109TH INF. WAS SHOT TO DEATH BY FIRING SQUAD AT 1005 HOURS 31 JAN 45 AT ST, MARIE AUX MINES, FRANCE.

COTA

'Ike' and 'Eddie' finally parted ways. St Marie-aux-Mines had completed its role in this strange chain of events which had commenced long before. Now the Americans were departing. One who did so was burly ex- Ranger officer, Lieutenant Colonel James Rudder, who had taken over Eddie's 109th Infantry Regiment after the debacle at Wiltz. He had witness the execution and had experienced no doubts, soul-searching or qualms. Slovik had deserted his regiments and his comrades; he had deserved what he had got.

Now Colonel Rudder issued a message to his regiment, which clearly expressed his own feelings: "Today I had the most regrettable experience I have had since the war began. I saw former soldier of the 109th Infantry, Private Eddie D Slovik shot to death by musketry by soldiers of his regiment. I pray that this man's death will be a lesson to all of us who have any doubts at any time about the price we must pay to win this war. The person that is not willing to fight and die, if need be, for his country has no right to life.... "

Rudder spoke as a soldier and a patriot. There were no half measures with him; no mealy-mouth desire to make concessions to public opinion then or afterwards. He would not tell Huie, as General Cota did afterwards, that the Slovik's execution was "The roughest 15 minutes of my life." He stuck to his principles even in the Fifties, when it was becoming even more difficult to do so in the face of the changing mood of the public opinion. By then even ex-Supreme Commander and now President Eisenhower wavered when faced, for example, with a rabble-rousing Senator McCarthy.

But as the Grave Registration people took away Slovik's body, Colonel Rudder, the only officer to use Slovik's death as a warning, need not have feared. Slovik might have let his 109th down, but now the 109th was not going to let him or the United States down. No sir.

At nine on the morning of February 2nd, 1945, the three battalions of Eddie Slovik's "old outfit ", the 109th Infantry Regiment attacked the major Alsatian town of Colmar. Working south along the West Bank of the River Ill, the men of 'the Bloody Bucket' division met surprising little resistance. Here and there they overcame lone German machine-gunners. Now and then last-ditch defenders held them for a while. But soon they reach their first objective: a line running east to west along the northern outskirts of Colmar, the picturesque prewar tourist town, famous for its heavy cuisine and medieval timber-framed houses.

Now the Infantry started to infiltrate the place. But the speed of their original advance had caught the Germans by surprise. As one eyewitness recorded: "It was Sunday and all the people were dressed in their best clothes walking down Beethovenstrasse going to church. Here in the dirty, misty sky several Messerschmidtts were slipping inside the flak, peeling off, diving to bomb the city's outskirts. Shells were zooming so low over the city that you kept wanting to fall flat on your face. Tanks, trucks and the troops were rushing through the streets of the city in several directions. And on Beethovenstrasse lying in it sticky pool of blood there was a German sniper. But except for a small circle of kids staring at the dead Nazi, the civilians didnt seem to notice him, just as he didn't seem to notice the trucks, nor the tanks, nor the shells nor the planes. It was as if they were trying to separate themselves from the war by ignoring it. Or was it just that they had been seeing and hearing war for weeks now and it had become part of them? Now it was Sunday and Colmar was free and there were going to church."

It was a justified comment. Who cared about the infantry men once he had completed his bloody handiwork? Kipling knew all about them when he wrote of his 'Tommy Atkins'. Perhaps some might have thought that the recently dead Eddie Slovik had been right when he had refused to lay down his head for unfeeling civilians, whatever their nationality. But a great nation cannot tolerate such self-indulgence and independence of thought. Whether the 'poor bloody infantry' wanted to fight or not for meaningless causes as it might turn out, they had to. Their country demanded it and whatever sacrifice that went with it for them.

So Eddie's might-be comrades of the 109th Infantry had their victory after all. They had been defeated in his Siegfried Line, the Hurgen and the Bulge. Now finally they achieved victory at last . ..

AFTERWORD.

"But why was it Slovik? What was there about this dead end kid to win such a role it in a nation's history? Are there giant wheels that start turning somewhere, long before a man is born, which eventually deliver him, alone among millions before a dozen aimed rifles in 15 inches of snow?"

William Bradford Huie: *The Execution of Private Eye Slovik.*

Years after the event, Mr Huie had Private Morrison, who had helped to shoot Slovik to death, proclaim, "I think General Eisenhower's plan worked. It helped to stiffen a few backbones. When the report of the execution was read to my company formation, the effect was good. I'm just sorry that the General didn't follow through and shoot the rest of the deserters instead of turning them loose on their community. I want my children to be raised to believe that this country is worth dying for. .. and that if they did won't fight for it, they don't deserve to live "

It is harsh, still a suitably patriotic sentiment. Yet that winter of 1945, there still seem to be one law for the rich and powerful and one for the poor and powerless. Cota who had had Slovik shot on Eisenhower's orders, committed a most grave misdemeanour exactly five days after they took Eddie away to be buried secretly. On the night of February 5th, 1945 he became responsible for one of the most serious breaches of the secret battle behind the scenes of the whole of the World War Two. That night one of Cota's signal officers left a truck containing secret cryptographic apparatus untended and unguarded. That apparatus was so secret that its existence was not reveal to the general public until Group Captain Fred Winterbotham published his 'Ultra Secret' in 1973. In it, the member of the British Secret Service (M 16), explained for the first time just how the British, and later the Americans and the Western Allies, had been able to read Hitler's top secret orders to his commanders just as quickly as a Nazi generals could. The 'Ultra' was the war- winning secret and one of Cota's officers, for whom the General was ultimately responsible, had lost it.

A truck, complete with all its top-secret equipment, seemed to vanished off the face of the earth. Almost immediately there was tremendous consternation at Supreme Headquarters when the loss was reported. A massive search was launched throughout the European Theatre. Eisenhower was beside itself with rage. For he knew that if it had been the Germans who had stolen the truck, the whole of his intelligence would be compromised. Perhaps he'd have to go personally. The truck was found abandoned weeks later in the depth of a French wood, with two of its safes intact. The third was never discovered, and in fact the search went on till the end of the war. But in the meantime, both London and Washington bayed for blood.

A top-level investigation team was sent to France to look into the matter. Their findings were disastrous. The senior investigator recommended that Cota, his Chief-of-Staff, and his four senior signals officer should be relieved of their commands. In addition the four signal officers should be court-martialled.

But that wasn't to be. Eisenhower intervened. He called Devers, commanded the 6th Army Group to which the 28th Division now belonged. Although there was no love lost between Eisenhower and Devers - 'Ike' and 'Jake' strictly for the press - the latter obliged. Perhaps he needed a favour, for now those generals who wish to command in the Pacific had to have Eisenhower's recommendation. Thus it was that the senior investigator's recommendations were quashed. Cota's 'punishment' was reduced to an official reprimand -something that the general public never was aware of.

Still despite the fact that there was no court martial, Cota's career was virtually ruined. He continued to command the 28th Division for the last few weeks of the war until the 'Keystone Division' was 'nipped out *35 of the fighting.

He had commanded the 28th during what General Gavin, "Gentleman Jim" of the 82nd Airborne Division called ` our Passchendaele" and what British war historian R.W. Thompson felt was the worst disaster on a divisional level to befall the US troops in the campaign in North Western Europe.

Now in August 1945 he would return to the States to prepare to go to the Pacific for the invasion of Japan. He did not make it. The bomb saw to that. The 28th Division was deactivated at Camp Shelby, Mississippi and Cota was left without a job. But Cota was kept on limited duty attached to the War Assets Administration for a year. Retiring in 1946, he took a civilian job but soon graduated to federal employment in various civil defence jobs until he retired in 1962, moving to Wichtita, Kansas. There he died in October 1971, aged 78 years, blessed with a daughter, five grandchildren and two great-grandchildren. Naturally he died peacefully - in bed.

Cota's *crime*, if we can characterise it as that, was dereliction of duty and supervision which, could have caused the death of hundreds perhaps thousands of Allied soldiers, if the Germans had been able to lay hands on that truck. Although Kay Summersby and General Bradley told the story of the massive search in their memoirs, they did not give a reason for it. It remained a secret, just as now the reason for Eddie Slovik's execution started to be hidden from public and non-military scrutiny. ..

Immediately after the execution, Eddie Slovik's body was borne away by members of the US Grave Registration people, mostly black, on January 31, 1945 to the pleasant French spa town of Epinal, some 30 miles away on the West Bank of the River Moselle. Here there were buried nearly 6000 of America's youth, most of who gave their lives in the campaign in North Eastern France and on the Rhine.

But Eddie was not feted naturally to join the honoured dead who had died for their country in battle - or at least he wasn't for long. Already there were voices raised against the executed rapists, murderers etc who were scattered all over Europe in US cemeteries be allowed to remain among those who died in battle. Soon as matters settled down (and it is to be remembered that dead US soldiers were being found everywhere for years to come, even to this day, who when found would be interned in official army cemeteries) the US quartermaster General asked the Battle Monuments Commission if it had space to intern all those outcasts in one segregated location.

General Marshall, Eisenhowers's wartime boss, supported the measure. Together with the Battle Monument Commissions, he chose a plot just outside the First World War cemetery at Oise-Aisne in France. Here ironically enough the World War One 28th Division had fought one of the last battles of the Great War and in the main part of that beautiful cemetery, which had been respected by the German occupiers through their occupation of France, there lay bodies of men of Slovik's World War One company G, who had died honourably in combat only 400 yards from where they now rested.

But Eddie Slovik and his fellow at 92 outcasts were not destined to 'rest for eternity' with the 'honoured dead'. They were destined for a special plot 'the dishonoured plot', as it was called later. This was "Plot E".

This 'Plot E'; surrounded by a high stone wall, was (and is) located beside the Superintendent's house of the Cemeteries quarters at the other side of the road (see plan). Here in 1949 when it was completed, there were laid down strict instructions for entry and publicity connected with the criminals' burial area. Public entry is forbidden and all enquiries with reference to 'Plot E' have to be directed to Arlington, Virginia. *36

It was here that the body of ex-Private Eddie D. Slovik was, to be interred under Headstone 65 in Row Three - and presumably forgotten. Naturally the US military authorities weren't too keen to have him and what happened to Slovik remembered.

Thus as 1945 gave way to 1945, more bodies were brought from hidden graves in military cemeteries throughout Western Europe to be re-buried in 'Plot E'. They even included the notorious 'Cleft-Chin Murderer', Karl Hulten, a deserter from the 101st Airborne in Britain, who involved a 18 year old British stripper in his crime and who was one of the only ten women to be hanged in the UK in the 20th Century. The US army, the victorious army of the world's new superpower was to clean up its mess before it set off on new adventures in a world that had now become its oyster.

It was during this period that the man who had indirectly contributed to the reason for Eddie Slovik been in 'Plot E' came down from his mountain fortress in the Bavarian Austrian Alps to "place myself at his disposal of the US authorities", as he phrased it himself. Cocky and swaggering, with the Knights Cross of the Iron Cross dangling at his throat, a pistol holster at his waist, the only sign that he had come in peace, a white armband around his upper arm, the scarfaced giant Otto Skorzeny now thought it better to surrender to the *Amis* before the feared Russians in Austria got their paws on him.

But although still angry Eisenhower had had ordered notices posted in all army installations in that area, stating that "the spy, saboteur, assassin, Public enemy" should be placed under immediate arrest if spotted, no one seemed to want to detain the frustrated giant. Finally Skorzeny turned himself in to a US sergeant, a Texan in a jeep, who had never heard of him. Thereupon Skorzeny explained in his broken English that he had rescued Mussolini in 1943 - and the penny dropped.

The Noncom explained, "Then you must be the guy that led those Germans wearing our uniforms behind our lines during the Battle of the Bulge."

Skorzeny admitted he was, whereupon the Texan cried, "Well, I'll be damned!" he added, "Buddy I'm going to get a bottle of wine so that you enjoy the rest of the trip to Salzburg. When they get their hands on you at divisional headquarters, they're gonna string you up real fast."

But Skorzeny was saved that fate. At Werfen, the village to which he was taken, it was suddenly realised that they had landed a big fish. Here the situation changed dramatically. He was seized, his pistol removed, given a strip search for 'L pills' and placed under armed guard. From the village he was taken to Salzburg to the office of Sheen's 307th Counter-Intelligence Corps (CIC) and interrogated for six hours by a man, whom Skorzeny characterised as "A pleasant gentleman who understand my position well".

The 'pleasant gentleman' should have, for he was no less a person than Sheen himself, using the cover as head of Counter-Intelligence for the US 7th Army. In his report (or the one published for Sheen), he stated, "Despite the short time allocated for the interrogation of Skorzeny, it is believed he is sincere in his desire to give all possible information. ..." Due to his Austrian ancestry he is clear minded and pliable but politically short-sighted to the point of naivete ."

And this is an amazing statement in view of the fact that Hitler, Eichmann and Katlenbrunner (the last head of the SS police *apparat*, including the Gestapo) were all fellow Austrians and Skorzeny was already wanted as a war criminal by

Russia, Czechoslovakia, Yugoslavia, Belgium, Holland, Denmark, France etc etc. But it is a clear indication that after Sheen's interrogation -we don't know what kind of deal was struck up during it - there was going to be a cover-up. A further indication of what was taking place is the fact that almost immediately the world's press was allowed to descend upon the place to interview their 'Captured Lieutenant Colonel Otto Skorzeny, head of HSHA, AMT VI Sabotage".

Naturally the US press knew from their wartime correspondents attached to SHAEF that Skorzeny had been accused of attempting to assassinate "Ike" the previous December. Now representatives of *The New York Times*, *The Washington Post, The Christian Science Monitor*, etc etc flocked to Salzburg to ask about the incident. Skorzeny refused to answer their questions as long as he was handcuffed. Colonel Gordon Sheen, who was deliberately stage-managing the whole business ordered the manacles removed and while a US Signal Corps crew made a movie of the interview at Eisenhower's express order, the correspondents started to ask questions.

A well-briefed and warned Skorzeny fielded the newsmen's questions easily, especially the ones about the alleged attempt to kill the Supreme Commander. As *the New York Times* reported the next day, "Handsome, despite the scar that stretches from the ear to chin, Skorzeny smilingly declaimed credit for leading a mission to murder members of the Supreme Command". The *Christine Science Monitor*, however, was not so convinced as the *Times*. Its correspondent wrote that Skorzeny had "an aggressive personality to go with his physical equipment and a mind adapted to subversive activity." But two things emerged from the various correspondents' reported. Skorzeny had convinced them that he had not intended to murder Eisenhower in 1944, though the *Times'* statement seems to hint that such a mission had taken place. Skorzeny had also played ball with Sheen. He personally had made no reference to Eisenhower, which it is clear the Supreme Commander wanted, and he had purposefully steered the correspondence on to other topics, such as the fate of Hitler, when they kept harping on about the Trojan Horse operation. Soon Skorzeny would be suitably rewarded by Sheen for his co-operation.

In September 1945, Skorzeny was transferred to Nuremberg where the trials of the major German war criminals was about to begin. His exact role there is unclear. He wasn't charged himself but he did seem to enjoy special privileges while he was there. Perhaps, this author suspects, he provided the prosecution with inside information about the defendants.

Seven months later he was again transferred, this time to the old concentration camp at Dachau, where another series of war crimes commenced, this time against the military leaders of the Waffen SS, such as Dietrich, commander of the 6th SS Panzer Army in the Ardennes and Obersturmbahnfuhrer Peiper charged with the Malmedy Massacre. Again Skorzeny was kept in the wings, although his 150 Special Panzer Brigade had been attached to Peiper's Battle Group. He was busy, so it was reported by the US authorities, in writing up his special operations during the war for presumably the US Army Historical Division.

It was 27 months after the end of World War Two that Skorzeny himself was charged. While his old comrades of the SS were been handed out sentences of death and life imprisonment (even former 16 year-old members of Peiper's Battle Group were given such sentences), Skorzeny was accused of having used US uniforms in the Battle of the Bulge and stealing Red Cross parcels intended for US PoWs - truly heinous crimes. Defended by an American military lawyer and cleared by the evidence of a British undercover operative Yeo Thomas, the celebrated 'White Rabbit' who told the court he, too, had used German uniforms during action and would have killed in them if necessary, it was inevitable that Skorzeny would escape serious punishment.

He did. He was acquitted and placed in an interment camp run by the West Germans in Darmstadt in the US Zone of Occupation (it was clear right from the start that the American authorities were going to keep a tight control on the scarface giant right to the end). There on July 27th, 1948, he was rescued by 'three former SS officers', or so the US military alleged.

On that day a car carrying the three 'former SS officers' left Hanover for Darmstadt. At Wurzburg, again in the US zone, the three put American military licence plates on their car and changed into khaki uniforms and white helmets of the US Constabulary. Where did they get their gear? Was it stolen? Years later Skorzeny maintained it had been provided by the *Amis*. And for once, he was probably telling the truth.

Late that day, the three convinced the German guards that there were Americans. With their forged documents they got Skorzeny out and he disappeared for good to start his career as anti-Israeli saboteur, lover of Eva Peron, an arms dealer, CIA agent etc etc. ..... taking the secret of the deal he had made with the Americans with him...

In December 1945, Eisenhower, now the new Chief of Staff of the US Army in Washington, was informed by the Secretary of War, Robert Porter Patterson that there was a demand in the Senate for an account of the Battle of the Bulge the previous December. On the day after Eisenhower received Patterson's requests, he wrote the latter a confidential letter.

In it he stated that "I am unalterably opposed to making any effort to publicise at this time any story concerning the Ardennes Battle or even allowing any written explanation to go outside the War Department. To do so would inevitably create the impression that there is some reason for seizing upon a flimsy excuse, such as the anniversary of the outbreak of the Battle, to defend something where no defences are necessary."

Patterson thanked Eisenhower for the letter and a confidential memo from the Chief-of-Staff which followed the same day stated he felt that " the whole performance in the Bulge was highly creditable to the Army and you." All same he still thought that the main feature of the Battle should be made known to the public, "Otherwise they will hear nothing but fault finding and many of them would think that the Army is covering up."
In the end the two of them compromised. There would be no press release on the Battle of the Bulge that Christmas. Instead Patterson thought that there should be series "of short narratives on the European campaign, with one of them being devoted to the Ardennes ." *37

In a way Eisenhower had won the encounter and his own personal battle with the events of that December of 1944. As Eisenhower insisted in a memo to Patterson on December 18th, a year to the day before he had gone into hiding in his own and luxury bolt hole in Versailles: "(The Battle of the Bulge) was a mere incident in a large campaign. It was one about which one should say nothing whatever except in response to casual enquiry from one's friend."

Since that time there have been indeed more than enough inquiries into Eisenhowers's role in the Battle of the Bulge. They haven't always been casual; and they haven't always been from friends. All the same 'Ike's' luck seem to have held. Nearly sixties years have passed since those dramatic events took place. Yet Dwight D. Eisenhower, Ex Supreme Commander and one-time President of the United States, has emerged from those decades of examination, re-examination and revisionist history with his reputation intact. Yet there was a time, just one year after he had taken over the nation's Supreme Office in the White House, that a somewhat cranky and inconoclast writer seemed about to shake that intact reputation mightily. ....

"On a red and gold afternoon in 1954, I drove northeast from Paris through the 'Marne Country', towards those two little river alleys, the Oise and the Aisne, where already in this war tortured, half spent century, two waves of Americans, a generation apart, have done battle for the cause of freedom. For those of us who value the Western heritage, this is hallowed ground. Here in 1944, youths riding with Patton rumbled over the selfsame hillocks into which their fathers had burrowed; and more one dumbstruck son, spelling out the name of the village, suddenly recognised it as a bright page in his father's memories."

Thus in a rather overblown prose, fashionable in the southern states at the time, William Bradford Huie, a native of Scottsboro, Alabama, began his account of his search for Eddie Slovik and what had happened to him. He had commenced it, according to his own account, seven years beforehand when he had been preoccupied still with the "struggle between a nation which seemed unsure of itself and its reluctant soldiery." He had felt then that the "war was particularly cruel to the individual; it was never presented as a crusade - no music, no poems, no flags - and it's cruel to ask a man to risk his life in any war which isn't fought for the highest purpose." Any observer of America's most popular form of wartime art, Hollywood movies, would have opined to the contrary. Like no other country, foe or friend, the average American had popular patriotism rammed down his throat to an excess by the celluloid merchants of Tinseltown.

Be that as it may, the 36 year-old writer, had noted in 1946, what he entered into his notebook as the "Fascinating Statistic": one single American soldier had been shot for cowardice in the World War Two. In all of the 10 million or more US servicemen, serving on three continents and a dozen different fronts, one humble private shot for a crime of which there had been thousands of offenders, according to the Pentagon. Huie didn't know the man's name. All the same he was intrigued enough by the statistic to type a note and enter it in his files. It read: " The one man in such a situation always deserves to be known. Some day I must dig him up. I must also examine the significance of the fact that in its struggle to inspire its youth, to discipline them, to make them stand and fight, the United States, as late as 1945 had recourse to one full dress execution."

It was clear that although he didn't know the executed man's name and the real reason for his execution, William Huie, already known as an anti-establishment, crusading journalist/writer, had spotted a *cause celebre*; perhaps even American Dreyfus case.

For the writer, proud of being an eight generation southerner had fought bigotry ever since he had left the University of Alabama in 1930. Beginning on the *Birmingham Post,* founding the political journal *Alabama Magazine* in 1936, he would be proud at the end of his life that "I wrote and I upset them and proud of it because they need it." Naturally there 'they' was the establishment.

Throughout his career he would campaign against prejudice in whatever form it came, writing such works as "*The Klansman*", the "*Revolt of Mamie Stover*" and "*The Three Lives Of Mississippi*" (all later made into movies). He would call Alabama Governor George Wallace, "the biggest S.O.B. I've ever seen ." He would be jailed for contempt of court for his involvement with James Earl Ray, who pleaded guilty to killing civil rights leader Martin Luther King in 1968. Huie had paid Ray about $35,000 for information on the assassination because as he told the court, he wanted "to get to the truth." He added, "I paid Ray because I knew no lawyer in the world would call him to testify and no one would ever know the truth." Indeed one year exactly after a set out on that 'pilgrimage' to find Eddie Slovik's grave in France, he was again accused of illegal activity. Investigating the case of 'Ruby McCollum', a black woman accused of killing a white doctor in Florida, Huie was convicted of contempt of court for trying to influence a psychiatrist who had been a witness in the case.

Now this collector of lost causes had reached the end of his seven years to find Eddie Slovik, both figuratively and literally. As he wrote at the time, standing in front of Eddie's grave in 'Plot E' that autumn afternoon in North Eastern France, "I had ended a long journey. I have never met Private Slovik while he was alive, but I have travelled over a continent talking with people who had known him. ... Now there at his grave, I felt that I knew Eddie Slovik better than any of the others could have known him. ...... better than his mother or his wife."

"But why had I worked to know Eddie Slovik?" Huie reflected that day. "Why had I bothered to travel so far, to ask so many questions, all just to get to know one dishonoured Polack private from Detroit? He had been dead nearly nine years and I was the only human being on earth who had ever inquired as to the location of his grave, much less visited. .. Why had I bothered?"

Huie then and later gave three basic reasons for having done so. Private Slovik had been "Killed by the United States for the crime of refusing to serve the United States with a rifle and bayonet"; he had been put to death for "crime of omission"; and because he felt "the United States had wronged him".

Slovik was, in essence, as far as Huie was concerned, the epitome of the little man fighting the giant state. He was a type of individual Huie would seek to epitomize and glorify to the end of his working and writing life.*[38] For as Huie concluded on that day so long ago in that silent French graveyard, surrounded by those dead tributes to America's glory - and shame -" Slovik assumed a singular position in the annals of freedom; he's the only authentic, adjudged, actually executed American coward in the age of Freud." ..
But that autumn when his '*Execution of Private Slovik*' was already with his publishers in New York, Huie knew that he was on to a winner. Not only had he uncovered a sensational story, which the Pentagon seemingly had tried to cover up for nearly a decade, he was publishing it at a point, when the times in the States were changing. The old GI generation of World War Two might well, he knew, have turned against Slovik, the deserter and coward. After all they had been in combat; they knew, sometimes to their cost, how lives had been endangered at the front by those who had deserted and left the firing line dangerously thinned

out. The most recent generation of young readers, however, would, Huie felt, be more receptive to the struggle between "little guy from the wrong side of the tracks" fighting the West Point military establishment.

But that particular thesis, which was Huie's main concern in the book, was vastly overshadowed by the relationship of Eddie and his crippled, sick wife, Antoinette. Antoinette, the wife of a mere two years, had not really known exactly how Eddie had died overseas; the military authorities have been very cagey with her. During Eddie's imprisonment, it seemed that her mail to him, had been held up. In consequence Eddie had not been in a position to reply to non-existent letters. In addition whatever he had written had been censored by the authorities, something that Antoinette had come to expect. After all a husband, as she thought, was on active service overseas and military secrets had to be protected, even if they were mentioned in all innocence in a family correspondence.

One thing that had puzzled her, however, in 1945 when she learned of her husbands death 'on active service' was that she did not receive the customary $10,000 ' GI insurance', into which Eddie had paid right to the end. No one was able to explain why. And in those days when information was not ready accessible as it in our times with its 'Freedom of Information Act', she was prepared to accept the mystery although she was badly in need of the money.

It was here that Huie stepped in after he had contacted her from Garden City, Alabama, where he wrote his book. First he told Antoinette what had really happened to Eddie. Then he offered her money for the use of her and Eddie's wartime letters. It was a brilliant move. It turned the account of Eddie Slovik's military service and execution from what might have been a pamphlet-sized polemic into full-sized book, which was emotional, moving to an extreme, and made Eddie a recognisable human type instead of the khaki-clad figure onto which one simply hung an argument.

In the framework of what Huie visualised as a confrontational affair, he build in the details of the humble everyday worries of the typical wartime romance. The fact that Eddie's allotted pay to Antoinette was $70 dollars a month. Yet the payments of the furniture of which they were so proud was $70 a month. It "Then there was the rent, the car, everything else. And Antonette was pregnant." It was the kind of detail every average American could recognise and empathise with. After all, so many of them had been through the same thing and perhaps were still doing so.

When a March 1st, 1944 Eddie wrote from Ford Sheridan that he might not pass out of the rifle range and that "I don't care. I'm not trying to be a good soldier. I want a discharge and if I don't get home soon, I'll go crazy," many of Huie's readers would feel for the homesick, love-sick soldier, worried out of his mind about his crippled wife trying to manage back home.

As Antoinette told Huie in the early 1950s, "I wrote not only letters; it was more like a story. He lived from one mail call to another; and if the mail was delayed he worried. He lived only for me, and I lived only for him."

A professional writer of the romances popular at the time couldn't have produced a better line, the "*He lived only for me, and I lived only for him.*" It was a line meant strictly for Tinseltown.

Or what about this, dated July 24th, 1944 when the Penn Furniture Store was beginning to worry Antoinette about her delinquent payments on that prized furniture that they had bought together the year before. The landlord was threatening eviction if they didn't pay up back rent and for the first time Eddie Slovik learned that his wife was not only crippled but also epileptic. Not only that, it was becoming ever increasingly clear that Eddie was not going to get that discharge. "It seems, mommy, that ever since I was born I've had bad luck. I spent five years in jail, got out when I was 22, got married when I has 22, lived 15 month with my darling wife and was so happy with her and now they break up my happiness, put me in the Army and try to kill us both and take everything we've got. Oh mommy dear, why don't they leave us alone. We didnt do anything to anyone, did we?"

Hand me the Kleenex....

It's no wonder that in that year of publication that Huie's publishers announced "This book is considered so important that both hardcover and paperback editions are been published simultaneously to reach the widest possible audience." Naturally the film rights to this 'tragic story' of the humble star-crossed lovers has already been sold. How could it be otherwise?

But what did Huie's *"The Execution of Private Slovik"* really tell us of Eddie Slovik? Forget Huie's thesis of the David versus Goliath. Forget the sentimental star-crossed love affair. Let us even forget the sick, penniless post war widow Antoinette Slovik, whose husband had been take from her so mysteriously and allegedly, so cruelly. What do we learn of Eddie from Huie's 50,000 odd word account of his life?

I think it would be fair to say that we can forgive Eddie for his petty crimes at the height of the Depression. His mother was a drunk; his father shiftless and often out of work; and he already had had one brother behind bars when he commenced his own sentence. With that kind of background at that time, Eddie could have been forgiven for resorting to crime to alleviate this sordid misery of his teenage years.

But what about in 1942 when he had been released from jail and been given a new chance in a wartime America that was beginning to boom? Why they were even employing blacks from the south in the plants in Chicago and Detroit. Any-one was welcomed who had a pair of hands and was prepared to work - even if he were an ex-con with a five-year long criminal record. This should have been the 22 year-olds opportunity to make a fresh start, the past forgotten.

But what did Eddie Slovik make of that second chance when he was a man with responsibilities and not a teenage 'dead-end' kid? The short answer is not much. Married in haste at a ceremony, which according to some accounts, lasted for three days, celebrated by over hundred guests, drinking and dancing - ('*The beer barrel polka*' seemed to have been the party's favourite tune) - Eddie started to run up debts swiftly. Apartment, new furniture, carpets, weekends out at movies and beer joints.

Clearly up to then, Eddie, the jailbird since his early teens, had not been used to handling money. But his new wife was a book-keeper by training, a profession notoriously careful with money. Who convinced her to get so deeply into debt (for their circumstances) so quickly? We don't need a crystal ball to guess. It had to be Eddie. For it is clear that Eddie wanted to make up for the years he had lost behind bars. In short Eddie Slovik wanted a good time without worrying about the responsibilities of paying for that good time.

Such an attitude is understandable. It is common among young people, then and now. Eddie was one of thousands, perhaps hundreds of thousands. There was only one difference about the time when Eddie Slovik started to run up his debt. There was a war raging in Europe and the Pacific and it was obvious that a fit young man, even if he was 4-F as an ex- con, would sooner or later be reclassi-fied and drafted. That would be the end of his little dream, the protective home womb of family life in which he could hide away from the harsh realities of the real world outside.

Yet again Eddie Slovik was no different from many other young men of his kind. Why not live for today? Forget about tomorrow. Worry about it and its problems when they arrived. That was -and has always been the motto of careless youth. Unfortunately in wartime that rule no longer applies. The interest of the state overrides those of giddy young men. In times of conflict there is little opportunity for living as if there is 'no tomorrow'. There *is* a tomorrow. Unfortunately the armed service is often grey, hard, brutal and ends in sudden violence. In wartime the youth is perforce to become a cog in a great unfeeling machine.

Huie's book was a success. It was well received virtually everywhere. Briga-dier-General S.L.A. Marshall, the revisionist US military historian who had some strong things to say about American soldiers engaged in World War Two and Korea, gave 'The Execution of Private Slovik' a positive four-page review in the Sunday supplement issue of The New York Times. The Saturday Review did the same with a four-page account. Even Look a more popular magazine, gave it a long summary.

Most reviewers made it clear that Huie had succeeded in his overall intention. He had written a dramatic, thought-provoking book. His theme was justice. The form was drama, tinged now and again with sentimentality, but then US audience had always liked their dramas clothed with occasional sentimentality. And it centred on this unremarkable Polack ex-con as a victim of history.

It was not surprising that Frank Sinatra bought the film rights straight off. One year before he had made his own comeback in "From Here to Eternity" for which he had won an Academy Award as the best supporting actor in the role of the ballsy little buddy of the anti-establishment Montgomery Cliff, beaten to death by a sadistic sergeant. In contrast two years before that, real hero and winner of the Congressional Medal of Honor, Audie Murphy played the role of a coward in John Huston's 'Red badge of Courage' based on Stephen Crane's celebrated Civil War novel. It with a brave thing for Murphy to do -play a coward. As one critic noted, however, it was really a 'study of fear of fear '. Houston elicited an uncom-monly sensitive performance from Murphy, the cowboy star, and the soldier who had won his medal for bravery only a few miles away from where Eddie was shot for cowardice. But the Murphy movie didn't win any awards.

But then days of the traditional heroes like Murphy were over.*[39] Murphy's own story, filmed as 'To hell and Back', one year after Huie's book appeared, might have been a box-office success. But he was an artistic flop. It was all too obvi-ously a gung-ho semi-fictional account of Murphy's combat experience with the willing support of a post-Korea Pentagon (they even lent the producer Murphy's old division, the 3rd Infantry, as extras!)
But the 'Slovik property', as it was called in Hollywood, wasn't going to be easy to make as Sinatra had thought. Sinatra was informed, that if there was any attempt to dramatise the story by using Slovik as the hero, which might make Eisenhower a the villain - "remember Eisenhower is the "heavy" - Pentagon's assist-ance was out. Finally at the singer movie star was informed that the "White House doesn't want it (the movie of Slovik) done."

Sinatra share didn't let himself be intimidated by the Republican president, how-ever. After all he was close to the Kennedy's as a democrat. He prepared to meet his challenge. On July 20th, 1960, the New York Times carried a front-page story about the "first open defiance by it producer-director of Hollywood's blacklist." Otto Preminger had hired a "blacked" screenwriter Dalton Trumbo for his movie "Exodus". Almost immediately Sinatra announced that he had hired Albert Maltz for the " Slovik property".

Maltz, too , was a member of the "Hollywood Ten" who had been cited for contempt of Congress in November 1947 and like Trumbo had also served one year
in jail for his offence. But almost immediately the new script writer was in trouble
with Sinatra.

For now, not only Eisenhower, but the new presidential hopeful, John Kennedy
and his powerful family were putting on the pressure. In mid-March when the
announcement off the Maltz appointment was made, political hell broke loose
from the Kennedys. Their handsome young presidential hopeful was denounced
by Republican governor of New Hampshire, as being "soft" on communism.
Other joined in the attack. The Hearst press naturally attacked that Maltz appointment, as did Hedda Hopper, the gossip columnist, John Wayne — naturally
followed by an American Legion too, with *the Los Angeles Examiner* advising
Sinatra to '' dump Maltz and get yourself a true American writer".

Sinatra at first appeared to make a stand. But he knew the writing was on the
wall. He stated that "I do not ask the advice of Senator Kennedy on whom I should
hire . Senator Kennedy does not ask me a how he should vote in the Senate". ..
I'm prepared, to stand all my principles and await the verdict at the American
people when they see "*The Execution of Private Slovik*". His stand was however
of short duration.

Ten days later he fired Maltz....

Maltz wasn't particularly hurt. He could understand the pressure Frank was
under - the American Legion had threatened to boycott the movie theatres as
soon as the " *Execution of Private Slovik*" was screened. He concluded that the
future President's father Joseph Kennedy was behind the dismissal. After all the
Kennedy family head had known to be interested only in money and power for the
Kennedy's.

It was a view with which Huie concurred. He had thought that " Maltz was a fine
choice" to direct the Slovik movie. He had written him and Sinatra congratulating
them on taking up the Slovik project. He felt, too, that although Slovik was the
"most, interesting off -beat story of World War Two, it wasn't the kind of film that
makes much money"

So the project lay fallow, until the rights to the movie were sold to Richard
Dubelman, a television producer. In his turn he sold them to two TV specialists,
William Link and Richard Levinson. For the memory of Slovik, that sale to the two
TV veterans, plus director Lamont Johnson was a breakthrough.

Then between the three of them, they must have had over 100 films and TV
credits to their name. With such men at the helm and eventually backed by major
TV network, they could give a new dimension to the Slovik story. With people no
longer going to the movie theatres so much, preferring to stay at home or watch

TV, this seemingly catered for more mature people than the kids who went the movies for their weekly dose of dumbing down pap. Eddie could be brought into millions upon millions of Americans sitting rooms. They'd make it a TV film.

By the early 1970s the three had their project under way. It was an ideal time for such a theme as that of Eddie Slovik's trial and execution. At that time TV networks in States were discovering 'made for TV' features. They were shot on healthy budgets about serious issues and they use top-quality actors, some of them older Hollywood stars who no longer could find employment in Tinseltown where youth was at a premium.

In a case of the Eddie Slovik movie, the producer picked Martin Sheen not a major star, but one seems to epitomise the Slovik's attitude and confused soul-searching. Even if the average viewer was not moved by Slovik -Sheen's refusal to fight, he could not help but would be by Sheen's interpretation of Slovik's last moments in Ste-Marie-aux-Mines.

The two and half hour *'The Execution of Private Slovik',* meticulously related, well-documented and equally well-acted, could not help be a success when it appeared in 1974. Besides, Link, Levinson and Johnson must have known they were onto a winner right from the start. The country was sick of Vietnam and what most people thought were the lies of the military and officialdom. After all, even the troops were calling their commander in Vietnam, General Westmoreland - "Waste More Men". In the wake of the post-Vietnam disillusionment the film-makers could be sure that the viewers, even the older ones would

sympathise with Slovik and that sympathy would carry the movie, whatever defects it might have otherwise.

They were right. It was a success. Even when the directors never showed the audience the kind of combat that Slovik was attempting to avoid and what happened to other young Americans, who gritted their teeth and did their duty just as Uncle Sam expected them to do, the movie was accepted without any noticeable criticism. Indeed, although it concerned itself with strictly American themes, the movie was a success, too, outside the USA.

It was shown in dozens of other countries, such as Britain, France, even Germany, though not, be it noted, in Soviet Russia. Even two decades later when the author visited the Ste Marie-Aux-Mines, the locals still remembered Slovik thanks to the movie which had been shown on French TV. In contrast no one there had ever heard of the hero, who had fought to free their Alsace, Audie Murphy. ..."Murp-hee,non M "'sieu...ne le connais pas'."

But apart from being a commercial success and achieving good reviews, due to its solid structure and good acting, *'The Execution of Private Slovik '* made the Slovik case an issue once more. People started talking about the case. Some even went further in that age of issues. They decided that something should be done about Slovik and his memory. Abruptly Slovik's execution had become an historic injustice. ....

But had it been? As we have seen Slovik himself had gone out of his way to get himself convicted. But had those who might well have been forced to try him done so fairly as they should have done? Had military justice that Veterans Day of 1944 been blind in one eye?.

One of the few survivors of that court martial, Captain Benedict B Kimmelman, the dentist
turned doctor at Wiltz, thought not. Originally at the time of the trial, he had believed that Slovik deserved to be sentenced to death. But after his experiences at Cota's HQ in Wiltz and the mass bugout of staff officers, leaving the rank and file and the wounded at the mercy of the enemy, his attitude had changed. As he wrote in 1987, just after Eddie Slovik's remains had been returned from France to the country of his birth, "The executions stands ....as an exercise in injustice". "That Slovik contributed to it by his transparent quasi cunning does not adore exonerate the authorities. Justice is the responsibility of the legal system."

That is plain-speaking enough for one court member. But on what did Kimmelmann and those others who have examine the trial and found it lacking in justice base their statements?

Firstly, all agree on the total incompetence of Eddie's defending officer, 24 year-old Captain Woods. According to his own admission, he felt awed by the court and the combat experienced witnesses from the infantry. At the same he was probably inhibited by the fact that he was on buddy-buddy terms with several of the court and attendant officers, in particular Major Fellman, the provost marshal who was later in charge of the actual execution. Why should he rock the boat on account of a soldier, who wanted to be sentenced and who, no one in the court thought, would be subjected to the ultimate penalty - death?

Time and time again, he fumbled the case. Why, for instance, did he not question the legality of the affidavit signed by people such as S/Sgt Ellis, Captain Grotte and Lieutenant Hillingsworth and demand that they be present in court (which they weren't) to answer questions? It was the same with the evidence presented by the divisional 'trick cyclist', who was clearly a doctor who worked according to General Cota's dictates. Could he, Woods, not to have suggested that there had to be something wrong mentally with Slovik due to his insistence that he wanted to be tried and risked a sentence of death? What normal man would take that attitude?

Later when Slovik had been sentenced and Woods had promised his client that the sentence of death would never be carried out, Woods simply let things go their fatal prescribed way. As he wrote himself, "In the military courts as constituted, I had no right of appeal. It was, however, within my premise to recommend clemency." But as the amateur attorney admitted, " I failed to do so."

An ex-army man and trained lawyer, who took up the Slovik case for free (with Wood's help) half-a-century later, said of his new friend, who was soon to die: "Slovik deserved a lawyer. He didn't get one." Ex- Army Captain Wilkow, an expert on court marshals, said he had listed Woods' failings as a defending attorney, "Woods didn't like it, but he went along. .. He's willing to take it for the sake of the team"*40

But if Woods' failure as a defending officer was the most obvious defect of that court martial, there were others. As a Kimmelman wrote "Nothing said at the trial altered for me the picture of nonentity openly defiant of the rules that we believed bound us all.. . .." Kimmelmann, however, believed that " The reviewing authorities, having the benefit of a little distance, might have shown less prejudice, but did not. " Kimmelmann pointed squarely to the Divisional Judge Advocate of the 28th, Colonel Henry Somer, as one who set the tone. (He), 'wrote the dentist-doctor', "exhibited his personal distaste for Slovik ". Kimmelmann maintains that it was Somer, who seemingly was the first to bring up that damning piece of information about Slovik's pre-service criminal record: one that we have noted should not have been used in a strictly military trial. He quotes Sommer's own review of the trial two weeks later in which the Judge Advocate wrote: "The accused is a habitual criminal. He has never seen combat, but has run away twice when he believed himself approaching it and avows his intent to run again."

It was the line followed by other reviewers, in particular Paris-based Major Fredrick Bertholets. In his own review he stated "If the death penalty is ever to be imposed in this case, (it, is) not as a punitive measure nor as retribution, but to maintain discipline upon
which alone an army can succeed against the enemy." It was, as we have seen that, on the basis of these reviews that Slovik was apparently picked out from all the other deserters sentenced to death to be executed. As Kimmelmann, probably rightly, pointed out, "Those endorsements were beyond the knowledge and competence of the reviewers and did not address Slovik's culpability and the appropriateness of the sentence."

Kimmelmann has a strong case here for maintaining then that Slovik's execution was 'a historic injustice'. Of the 49 American deserters who were tried between the 1st January 1942 and 30th June 1948 and sentenced to death, only one was executed, Eddie Slovik. That execution, the only one in six and a half years was undoubtedly due to the fact that Slovik was the sole single deserter who possessed a criminal record before he joined the service.

But who supplied those reviewers, in particular Somer, the first, with Eddie's civilian criminal record? How did that record arrive so quickly at the front from the FBI in Washington? Why had it been thought necessary for court martial proceedings, i e army business, in the first place?

The date on the FBI transcripts sent from Washington is November 15th, 1944 and it is signed 'J. E. Hoover'. Who at a lowly divisional headquarters located in the Siegfried Line, some 3000 miles away from Washington, could have had the clout to obtain that transcript exactly *six days* after Slovik had been sentenced to death at Roetgen on Veterans Day? Or had the transcripts been requested beforehand? And again, had the person who at requested it been much more important?

All present at Cota's HQ that day came into the frame. They all had problems. Eisenhower was concerned and angry about this second failure of Gerow's V Corps to breach the Siegfried Line. Bradley was dissatisfied with the slow, plodding progress of Hodges 1st Army. General Kean, Hodges' Chief-of-Staff, of whom many said actually ran Hodges's 1st Army, was concerned about his boss and his own future; and Corps Commander Gerow, was not only worried about Cota's performance, but also about his personal problems. His wife of French origin was from a family that was being currently accused of collaborating with the *boche* while they had occupied France.

But although we know virtually nothing about what took place that grey, rainy day when the Brass met at Cota's HQ, we can guess, apart from the tactical problems in the Hurtgen Forest, the Brass were very perturbed about the 28th Division's morale. By now the Division had to be regarded as a veteran fighting force. After all it had been in combat since July 1944. Yet here was an experienced fighting division, still led by offices and senior NCO from its old National Guard days, which had apparently fallen apart in a matter of days in a third major engagement of the campaign. What was to be done with their 'Keystone Division'?

We can only surmise on what was suggested. When back in Normandy, the 28th's leaders had fallen down on the job, even the divisional commander had been sacked. This time Cota obviously intended that he was not going to be fired. People like Colonel Peterson might have to go. But not 'Dutch' Cota.

Already he had made provisions to protect himself. Cota's 'periodic reports', intended for higher headquarters, had turned his reverses in the Hurtgen into a kind of victories. Panic-stricken routs by companies for instance had become 'withdrawals' for the purpose or of 'regrouping and 'reorganisation. False entries had maintained that 'original positions' had been regained after they had been lost to the enemy. They hadn't. And naturally 'combat efficiency' has always been described as 'excellent'.

But even 'battlefield tourists', as Eisenhower and Bradley really were, were not altogether taken in by Cota that day. Unlike his current opposite number, Field Marshal Model , German commander of Army Group B, 12th Army Group Commander Bradley, had never rallied his shaken companies on the battlefield or led them into the attack in a crisis -a field-marshal commanding a 100 men! It was not surprising that Model had been wounded in battle four times in the course of the war. Bradley for his part got piles. All the same, the 'battlefield virgins' could not have but seen that something was wrong with the 28th. that November day at Cota's HQ.

The actual battlefield casualties were bad enough. But they at least were indication of the men's determination to fight. But how did you explain the large number of prisoners of war and combat fatigue casualties? They were numbers that Cota could not hide in his daily reports, which in this instance, went rights up to SHAEF. Didnt these figures, higher than normal, even in the conditions pertaining in the Hurtgen, indicate to Eisenhower and Bradley that there was something wrong with the moral of the 28th?

On the day before, Hodges, it 1st Army Commander, had first become aware that something was wrong when he was suddenly confronted by a request from Cota to withdraw his men from one section of the Hurtgen. The 1st Army leader gave his permission, but he didn't like it. Thus it was that when he met Cota at the top brass conference that November Wednesday, Hodges gave Cota a piece of his mind. In a sharp exchange he told Cota that he was "extremely disappointed" is in his performance. He was also angry because Cota's "divisional headquarters appear to have no precise knowledge of the location of its units and was doing nothing to obtain the information." Later an incensed Hodges spoke to Cota's corps commander, Gerow, and told him he should "examine the possibility of command changes within the division."

In the light of Hodges' attitude and the facts, as the comment and assessment of the US Army 2nd Information and Historical Service (which had assess the 28th throughout the Hurtgen Battle), expressed it: "The division was destroyed as an effective fighting machine", it was clear that something had to be done. But who should do it and what should be done?

On that Wednesday when I think the decision was taken which would determined Slovik's fate in seven days' time, four men at the top had the power to make that decision. They were Eisenhower, Bradley, Hodges and naturally Cota. We can discount Gerow, who would be soon going home to Washington and who had professional and personal problems enough as it was. If Slovik were to be picked as a kind of scapegoat and a warning to the rest of the demoralised 28th Division - and he was the most likely candidate and currently under arrest awaiting trial - it had to be one of the really Top Brass, who had to make that fatal decision. For it was only men with clout who could get away with a death sentence without reference to the Commander-in-Chief of the US Armed Forces, ie the President's, for approval*41. Moreover it could only be such powerful men who could obtain this speedy response from Hoover of the FBI, that actually took place.

We know that it was Cota who signed Slovik sentence of death and we know, too, from William Huie that the former was the only officer he questioned who not surprised that Slovik was actually executed. But would Cota have signed Slovik's death warrant, if he had not had the backing from higher up? After all, here he was, a lowly divisional commander, whose position was very shaky after the Hurtgen fiasco, recommending a cause of action - *and believing that course of action would be carried out its* - that had not being proposed in the US Army since 1864.

But who of his three superiors - Hodges, Bradley and Eisenhower, in ascending order - might be the one who would have encouraged him to take this unprecedented step? In theory it could have been any one of them. Each of them knew that Cota was prepared to go to virtually any length to avoid being sacked. They knew, too, that he was an old style disciplinarian who would not hesitate to carry out an order which would mean the death of one of his own soldiers at the hands of his comrades. And they knew, too, that Cota felt he had been let down by the men of Slovik's type who would refuse to fight and had run away from battle. From Cota they would get no quibbles.

Could it have been Hodges? He was the only one of the three who was a combat veteran: one of those who had been through the hard bloody school of the trenches in the Great War, where human life had counted for virtually nothing. But Hodges was dull, slow-moving and not given to make quick clear-cut decisions. He had twice refused to shoot the captured Skorzeny's men at Henri Chappelle, although he had Eisenhower's and Bradley's oral permission to do so? He had scruples, he wanted written approvals.

Or perhaps Bradley? But the 12th Army Group Commander was really not much more than a schoolteacher in uniform. He had started his combat career, short as it was, at the elevated position of corps commander. He was outraged when Patton, then his boss and future subordinate (after Patton's disgrace) slapped a soldier. Could a man of his type, whom Patton scored as ineffectual, be the man who would ordered the death of one of his own soldiers as an example to the other shrinking violets of the 28th Division?

Finally there is the unthinkable. Eisenhower himself. 'Ike', of that ear to ear grin, the seemingly most democratic and widely loved of all the Allied generals. Wasn't he a man of the people himself? He relaxed by reading cheap cowboy paperbacks, said he liked "GI chow", loved - at a distance - is homely wife. Surely he was the typical example of the downhome middle-class American just as Slovik was of the working-class American ethnic melting pot. Could 'Ike', as he was universally known among his admiring troops, have colluded in the death of Eddie Slovik?

Surely not Ike!

Yet he was the same 'Ike', as the Supreme Commander, the leader of some 5 million soldiers in Europe, who had received Eddie's final explanatory-apologetic letter of 9th December 1944. It had ended with a "To my knowledge I have a good record since my marriage and as a soldier ... I'd like to continue to be a good soldier. " Finally Slovik had realised that the jig was up. The military were going to shoot him, it he did not make his plea. It was Eddie's last and only chance of escaping death. He had come to the final authority. Now only General Eisenhower could save him.

What did Eisenhower do? Nothing. He didnt even read the letter. Perhaps now we know why. ...

ENVOI

"A pardon is not really a problem of innocence or guilt. It's forgiveness. "

Matthew Wilkow, lawyer of the Eddie Slovik pardon appeal, 2000.

They're are all dead now, of course - the Top Brass. Eisenhower, Hodges, Bradley. With them they have taken their secrets to the grave. The members of the Court Martial Assembly, too - Sommer's; the brave dentist turned surgeon; even Woods, one of the youngest, who in 1974 first set out to get a pardon for Eddie Slovik. For nearly quarter of a century Woods and his associates " Rocky" DeFinis tried to get a pardon from a succession of presidents as far back as President Carter. Without success. In 1998 Eddie's old buddy, in ex- private Tandy succumbed to the 'Grim Reaper' too. Now there is no one left, who knew Eddie back in those wartime days when his fate was decided and he became -unwittingly America's most famous (infamous - to some still) private soldier of World War Two.

But still there are good selfless people in America (and outside of the States, too), who had only known of Eddie Slovik and his dreadful fate since the Martin Sheen movie of 1974 , again battling to restore his name and obtain some sort of rehabilitation for a man who died well over half a century ago now.

Even as I write this, 15 years after the death of William Huie who first brought the case of Eddie Slovik to the attention of the American public, new supporters under the leadership of Polish-American lawyer Steve Osinki, aided by Bernard Calka, are presenting a "Pardon Petition" to the US Army. If the 'St Clair Shores' team[*42] are successful, they hope the case will be forwarded to the President of the United States himself. After all, President Clinton, just before he left office, gave pardons to a whole host of soldiers who were offended one way or another back in World War Two, including Freddie Meeks, a still living US Navy veteran, convicted of the mutiny in 1944, the same year which Eddie was sentenced to death. [*43]

The army and the President's option in the 21st century is clear: a free or conditional pardon can be given using the prerogative of mercy. A full pardon can be given only when there is clear evidence that the finding of the court and the sentence were illegal. But naturally it would be genuinely impractical and impossible to re-judge Eddie Slovik today after all these years.

So where does that leave Eddie Slovik - and the United States? Most of those American soldiers who were tried on charges similar to Eddie in World War Two were rogues. Some of them had never even seen action - and all of them were looking for a soft option. Just like Eddie they were prepared to break military law to save their skins. They might well have been 'victims' of the war as Huie felt Eddie was. (All combat soldiers were in a way). But at the same time these 'victims' of Eddie's type *did* know the military law was the foundation of discipline; and that discipline was essential for a combat unit to survive in the line. After all military law is only of use when something goes wrong in a combat unit. It is the threat that forces - in most cases - the individual to conquer his own fear or else!

So what is the alternative?

In reality there wasn't one - and there still isn't. But Huie misguidedly must have thought there was one when he took up Eddie's case and first brought it to the na-

tion's attention. He thought that Eddie and his like, those poor unreliable replacements, basically cannon-fodder, were sent to the firing line, because the top brass
had got their strategy and tactics wrong. For "despite all our sea, air and possibly
atomic power .... it was decided to stage mass infantry assaults, not only on Fortress
Europe, but also on the main islands of Japan".

According to Huie, " The decision to assault both Germany and Japan was challenged by able Americans". Their argument was that Japan could be forced to
surrender by air, sea and atomic power; that the power of Germany could be
broken in this manner, too. "

Huie concluded that, "For the United States to try to match its enemies man for
man with bayonets was an indefensible waste. " This grand strategy, according
to Huie, resulted in the drafting of poor quality men such as Eddie. Naturally this
was 'a total loss' and not 'fair' to that doomed young man. As if war was ever
"fair".*44

In the end, however, it seems from his 'The Execution of Private Slovik' that
Huie could not support his thesis that the execution was unjust. After all the
atom bomb could not have entered the calculations of even General Eisenhower
back on 23rd December 1944 when he approved the execution. So at the end of
his account, Huie switched from the past to the present. He posed what he
called "The final inescapable question". It warned: "WHAT OF DUTY IN 1954? ...
WHAT OF THE AVOIDANCE OF DUTY?" he added to these rhetorical questions the point t hat "If the Slovik case can contribute to understanding and reso-
lution on this point (Eddie) will, in death, have served the same cause of
America".

They were questions that many young Americans must have asked themselves
a dozen years later when the Vietnam war started to make an impact on national
thinking. Could one leave war to machines? Air power, even the unthinkable:
nuclear power? Did one really need to become a 'grunt' and sacrifice one's life
in a war that most people didn't want and didn't understand? Did the fact that one
was an American, and that alone, require one to drop one's inhibitions, preju-
dices, personal considerations, fear of death, and rally to the flag? America right
or wrong?.....

Today, 30 years after Vietnam, America is the world's sole superpower. For
better or worse, the USA's is involved in military and political intervention in the
four quarters of the world. Can a country of such might and importance allow its
young men in times of crisis to decide whether they will or will not fight for it?
After all the nation's policy makers, both military and political, represent the will
of the people. They are the servants of those who elect them - the nation. How
can any nation, superpower or not, survived if its youth is allowed to make its
individual decisions on every crisis issue?

It goes without saying, I think, that an army made up of Eddie Sloviks, would be
fatal for that country. Thus if the Eddie Slovik of the 21st century wont serve willingly,

222

some means must be found to make them. If they don't, what of those who *do* serve their country? How do they stand? Are they just stupid, blinkered, gung-ho patriots? Or merely bovine like cannon fodder?

General 'Dutch' Cota, who has not come out of this book very well, once said to Huie that he couldn't reduce Eddie's sentence. His reason was simple. If he did, he told author Huie, *"How could I have gone up the line and looked a good soldier in the face?"* And for once perhaps General Cota was right.

But now let us forget the cowardice - and the courage - of battle so long ago. Lets leave the bloody, bitter world of our grandparents where it belongs. It wasn't a 'nice' story but then in those days there weren't many a 'nice' stories, were there?....

C.Whiting. 2005, York/England/Roetgen - Germany/Ste Marie-aux-Mines - France

FOOTNOTES

1   See *'Massacre at Malmedy'* (Charles Whiting), for further details.

2   See *'The Ghost Front'* (C.Whiting - De Capo Press 2002) for further details

3   The bold commando raid captured some two score American prisoners and an old freighter. Huffmeier rewarded his 'commandos' with iron crosses and more importantly, for the starving soldiers, a spoonful of looted jam each!

4   Gen. Gerow, commander of the V Corps, to which, as we have seen the 28th belonged, had arranged the parade and the subsequent US move into Paris. His action had incurred de Gaulles's wrath.

5   Hitler's two senior military advisers.

6   For example, all the city of Philadelphias's 21,000 employees at that time were expected to vote the way the party bosses wanted them to. Moreover they were to convince those they had business with to also vote the party ticket. If they didn't, a person could expect the Sanitation dept. to turn up, declare his bathroom a health hazard and tear it out there and then before his very eyes.

7   A play on the popular British song of the time.

8   Several had been reported to have been women.

9   For an account of one such operation, read the author's 'Werewolf', in which a captured US Flying Fortress was used to drop the agents who murdered the senior Burgomaster of Aachen, Openhoff, in March 1945.

10   This was the old border between what the Belgians call 'Old Belgium' and the new one, given to Belgium after WWI. Here the 'East Cantons were St Vith, Eupen and Malmedy.

11   When the author met him after the war on one of his illegal visits to Western Germany, he was surrounded by a bodyguard of heavy built foreigners who had once served under him. Seemingly, Skorzeny trusted the foreign renegades more than he did his fellow Germans and Austrians.

12   After the war what would have been a key figure in the 1947 Skorzeny Trial was never produced by either Skorzeny or his accusers, the Americans.

13   Obersturmbannfuhrer Jochen Peiper led the 6th SS's attack, aiming to capture the bridge over the R.Meuse at Huy.

14   It had seen the first action against German troops in WWI and also against Germans in N.Africa in WWII.

15   In view of what was to come later in the various official reviews of the sentence of death it is important to bear in mind that the Court knew of only Slovik's military crimes, i.e. desertion and refusal to obey an order. It knew nothing of his 'civilian criminal record', which would play an important role in subsequent events, as we shall see.

16   This summary of typical cases does not take into account the probability that hundreds of air crew who deliberately aborted their bombing missions over Germany and landed their planes in neutral countries such as Sweden and Switzerland. The latter country ended the war with a mini-air force of US bombers belonging to those who opted to save their skins.

17 Back 1953 William Huie, who first revealed the details of the Eddie Slovik case, thought that third factor might have been the post-trial case review required by the military code of justice. According to military law, only a divisional commander can convene a court empowered to pass the death sentence on one of the soldiers. After this has been passed that same divisional commander has to review the proceedings. He can't decline to intervene as can a civilian authority in the USA. In other words, a divisional commander *must* act and no sentence can be carried out until he, personally, signs and seals the sentence documents.

18 Stock according to the official US historian of Patton's campaign in Lorraine and in the Ardennes this: (Panton) head troops home (sic) fall rate but just as he had Troop shot for cowardice in the front of the enemy, this despite all the latter business about one man been executed in World War Two.

19 Roughly "he doesn't obey, must feel", i.e. with the drill masters cane across his shoulders.

20 They were to go on strike as soon as the German offensive commenced and thus hinder supplies and reinforcements getting to the front.

21 The author's own inquiries at the Luxembourg City "Hotel Alpha", which was Bradley's HQ at this period, confirm that Bradley felt he was a target, too. The then hotel staff told me Bradley blanked out the stars on his helmet, slept in different bedrooms every night and always left by the back entrance. Once when told by the then manager not to stand close to the window because he made a good target for a sniper in the railway station opposite, Bradley started back and "refused to go into that particular room any more".

22 It didn't. It was something that was to be expected from General Stickler, who would be commanding the 28th Division himself in 1950.

23 Rohde's jeep team successfully got as far as the River Meuse and managed to return to report without discovery.

24 The 101st and 82nd US Airborne divisions.

25 Due to the fact that General Strong virtually lacked a chin, his malicious staff thought it would be difficult for any hangman to fix a noose around his neck and secure it.

26 It is without Ike's permission and have his own volition, on the night at the 18th and 19th December .

27 Unlike the grave of Eddie Slovik, which for four decades was located in place of dishonour, the very spot where he was buried unmarked, save for a number, the three Skorzeny men are still buried among their comrades at Lommel Cemetery near where they were shot to death.

28 McAucliffe always maintained he wasnt surrounded and he had never been relieved. But that never got into the history books; it would have detracted from the Patton legend

29 There was a secret inquiry into the intelligence conducted by General Bedell Smith, which Strong told the author even he did know about a quarter of the century later.

30 After been wounded in the face at Ligneuville on December 23rd, 1944 Skorzeny returned to the Reich where he was treated by the Fuhrer's own personal surgeon.   Thereafter he returned to the Eastern Front for a while (perhaps he thought he was safer there after the great Eisenhower scare), where he commanded a division defending a section of the River Oder against attacking Red Army.

31 Even today five decades after the event, the third generation of Ste Marie-aux-Mine citizens know a lot about the execution of Private Slovik as the author found out when he went there and started asking questions. Security hadn't been that tight as the strict Major Fellman than thought.

32 There were still German outpost holding out in such ports as a Dunkirk and Lorient, but they were in reality POWs camps with the imprisoned Germans guarding themselves.

33 As we will see, William Huie, unknown to many sympathetic readers of his book in 1954, which sold a tremendous 5 million copies, did tend to distort facts and buy his information with generous amounts of money. It was for this reason that he received two court sentences for what we better call undue influence of witnesses".

34 The idea of the blind round dated back a century. It was to leave doubts in the minds of the firing squad who might have fired the killing shot. In fact, there was virtually no recoil from the M-1 Garland when a blank was fired. So the squad would soon know who had fired live round.

35 I.e. squeezed out of the combat formations, due to the large number of these involved on an ever decreasing German front.

36 When the author requested information from the current superintendent of the Oise-Aisne Cemetery in 2001, he was politely referred to the US Battle Monuments Commission in Arlington, although the remains of Eddie Slovik - as we have seen - had been removed from 'Plot E' for over 14 years.

37 These must have been the start of the US Department of Defense' huge tomes of military history , which purported to be very objective, but which have been found to be pretty one-sided, though it must be said very through, almost pedantic in the German academic manner. Not surprisingly really when one thinks that most of the German side of the battles were written by the tame captive Germans, who were relying upon US handouts and food in Germany's immediate post-war hunger years.

38 At his death at the age of 76 in 1986, Huie was engaged still in his usual theme. He was writing a novel, based in part on a role of the Alabama National Guard in Kennedy's Cuban fiasco, the 'Bay of Pigs' invasion. Significantly enough, the novel was going to be called *Deep Dixie '*.

39 See C Whiting: *Audie Murphy: the last American Hero* for further details

40 The team trying to clear Slovik's name.

41   Contrary to what those who had concern themselves with the Slovik case believed, the President, ie Roosevelt, was not the final authority. When Lincoln approved the last execution for desertion, the desertion had taken place in the Continental United   States. In cases that take place overseas, the President's approval of the death sentence was not needed; that was the right of the Supreme Theatre Commander, ie Eisenhower.

42   Their stateside location.

43   They based their case for appeal on violations of the 5th and 6th Amendments - Slovik's right to due process of law and to counsel; and the 8th Amendment, which offers protection from cruel and unusual punishment.

44   This argument was spurious then and is now. It has resulted in the attitude off , let's bomb them back to the stone-age" and we must avoid casualties and the bringing home of body bags to the States. Bad publicity for the government, you know.

BIBLIOGRAPHY

BOOKS.

AMBROSE, Stephen E,. Eisenhower: Volume 1: Soldier, General of the Army, President Elect, 1890-1952. Simon and Schuster, 1983.

AMBROSE, Stephen E,. Eisenhower. Simon and Schuster, 1983.

AMBROSE, Stephen E, The Supreme Commander: The War Years of General Dwight D. Eisenhower Cassell, 1968.

BLUMENSON, Martin, Mark Clark: The Last of the Great World War II Commanders. Congdon & Weed, 1984.

BRADLEY, Omar, and Clay BLAIR. A General's Life: An Autobiography. Simon and Schuster, 1983.

CHALFONT, Alun, Montgomery of Alamein. Weidenfeld & Nicolson: 1976.

THOMPSON, R.W Montgomery, the Field Marshal: The Campaigns in Northwest Europe, 1944-45 Scribner, 1970.

CORNS & HUGHES· Blindfold and Alone. Weidenfeld & Nicolson. 2002.

HUIE W B: EXECTION OF PRIVATE SLOVIK. SIGNET. 1954

IRWING D: The War between the Generals. A. Lane 1981.

KESSLER, L: SS Pieper. Pen and Sword 1992

TREES & HOCHENSTEIN: Holle im Hurtgenwald. Triangel Verlag 1975

WHITING, Charles, 44: In Combat on the Western Front from Normandy to the Ardennes Century 1984

WHITING, Charles, America's Forgotten Army: The Story of the US Seventh Spellmount2001

WHITING, Charles. American Hero. Life and Death of Audie Murply. Eskdale Publishing 2001

WHITING, Charles. The Battle of the Bulge: Britain's Untold Story. Sutton 2003

WHITING, Charles.The Battle of Hurtgen Forest Spellmount 2000

WHITING, Charles. Bounce the Rhine. New York· Stein and Day, 1985

WHITING, Charles. Bradley. Ballantine, 1971

WHITING, Charles.Decision at St Vith. Spellmount 2002

WHITING, Charles. Field Marshal's Revenge, The: The Breakdown of a Special Relationship Spellmount 2003

WHITING, Charles.The Ghost Front: The Ardennes Before the Battle of the Bulge Da Capo 2002

WHITING, Charles.Jochen Peiper· Battle Commander. Pen and Sword1999

WHITING, Charles. The Last Assault: the Battle of the Bulge Reassessed. London: Leo Cooper, 1994.

WHITING, Charles. The Last Battle: Montgomery's Campaign April-May 1945. Crowood, 1989.

WHITING, Charles.Massacre at Malmedy Corgi 1972

WHITING, Charles. Operation Kill Ike. Sphere 1975Whiting, Charles Patton. Ballatine, 1970.

WHITING, Charles.Patton's Last Battle Spellmount 2002

WHITING, Charles Skorzeny: The Most Dangerous Man in Europe Pen and Sword1978

WHITING, Charles West Wall: The Battle for Hitler's Siegfried Line Spellmount 2001

PERIODICALS.

Aachaner Volkszeitung
Grenzechohuie
New York Time
Der Spiegel
Washington Post

Index

Symbols

101st Airborne 123, 141, 146, 199
110th 79, 140, 142
112th 33, 81, 82, 146, 169
1s 51
28th Division 15, 34, 36, 37, 63, 66, 39, 42,
    44, 46, 51, 61, 72, 73, 77, 79, 84, 85,
    87, 88, 93, 97, 105, 106, 108, 109,
    116, 117, 118, 124, 125, 128, 141,
    142, 149, 152, 166, 167, 169, 170,
    174, 185, 186, 197, 198, 199, 218
29th Division 64, 184
29th Amour Brigade 154
4th 32, 34
5th 33
82nd Airborne Division 123, 154, 198
82nd

A

Aachen 36, 51, 52, 53, 55, 85, 108
Abraham, President Lincoln 16
Abwehr 26, 38
Alabama Magazine, 204
Altman, Lt. 110
Annan, Captain Noel 71, 151
Armoured, 2nd Division 154
Armoured, 3rd 51
Armoured, 5th 32, 33
Army, 12th Group 70, 105, 216
Army, 1st 46, 61, 77, 105, 149,
    155, 216, 217
Army, 3rd 101
Army, 6th Group 169, 197
Army, 7th 169, 200
Army, 9th 153
Army, Seventh 42
Army, st 217
Army., 1st 169
Aywaille 148, 154, 155

B

B, Leutnant 102
Bastogne 97, 141, 142, 146, 163, 169
Battalion, 1st 81
Battalion, 2nd 81
Battalion, 3rd 81
Bedell-Smith General 'Red, 68, 169
Bernhard, Prince of the Netherlands 40
Bertholet , Major Fredrick 123, 157, 158,
    159, 165, 167, 215
Betts General 123, 165, 166, 167
Birmingham Post, 204

Bollendorf-Pont 33
Boston Globe., 11

Bradley, General Omar 40, 57, 63, 64, 70,
    79, 105, 117, 149, 151, 153, 155,
    163, 164, 167, 198 216, 217, 218
Brawley, Sergeant 172
Brown, Major-General Lloyd 63, 64
Bruce, General Clark 163
Burks, (Dr), Captain Arthur L. 85, 86
Butcher , Commander, Lt. 40, 68, 151

C

Cagney, James 185
Calais, Soldatensender 154
Calka, Bernard 11, 12
Canaris, Admiral 95, 104
Cemtery, Oisne-Aisne 182
Champs Elysses 38
Chaudfontaine 155
Christian, Science Monitor 201
Churchill, Winston 25, 27, 52, 95
CIC 69, 70, 93, 94, 95, 104, 115, 135,
    149, 150, 156, 164, 200
Claravillis, Hotel 140
Clark, General Wesley 99, 163
COMZ 84, 121
Condon, Lt. 81
Corps, 5th 105
Corps, LXXX 33
Corps, V 33, 34, 36, 125, 216
Corps, VII 77
Corps, VIII 77, 96, 97, 139, 141, 146, 149
Corps, Vth 77
Corps, XXI 169, 178
Cota, General 15, 16, 18, 51, 64, 65, 77,
    78, 79, 80, 81, 82, 83, 84, 85, 105,
    106, 107, 108, 109, 111, 116, 117,
    118, 119, 124, 125, 127, 128, 129,
    130, 140, 141, 144, 146, 152, 163,
    166, 169, 170, 172, 178, 183, 184,
    185, 187, 192, 197, 198, 214, 216,
    217, 218
Coutanche, Alexander 25
Cummings, Father 180, 185, 186, 188, 190

D

Daily Express, 44
Daily Telegraph, 154
Darnard 93
De, Cafe Paix 150, 156, 164
Deason, Private 115
Definis, Robert 'Rocky' 13
Devers, General Jacob, 35, 169, 178, 197
Dietrich 135, 201
Division, 3rd 174, 180

Division, 5th 154
Division, 8th 105
Division, 99th 134
Division, 9th 79
Division Kanada', 24
Division, Charlemagne 93, 94
Division, Keystone 42, 44, 46, 62, 63,
    65, 82, 84, 105, 107, 142, 157,
    198, 216
Doriot 93, 94

E

E.T.O. 34
Earl, ames Ray 205
Ed, General Betts 164
Edward, Captain P Woods 108
Eifel 30, 32, 78, 93, 133, 134
Eisenhower, Commander, Supreme Dwight
    18, 27, 28, 29, 31, 38, 39, 40, 56, 57,
    64, 68, 71, 79, 94, 104, 105, 116,
    117, 118, 120, 121, 122, 123, 124,
    125, 126, 129, 130, 131, 132, 133,
    135, 150, 151, 152, 153, 157, 163,
    164, 165, 166, 169, 170, 171, 179,
    192, 197, 200, 201, 203, 216, 217,
    218
Elbeuf 16, 42, 44, 46, 61, 88, 108, 109, 172
Ellis, S/Sgt 214
Elson, Chaplain, Corps' Colonel Edward
    179, 180, 182, 183, 184, 187, 188,
    189, 190

F

FBI 118, 119, 127, 128, 129, 157, 158,
    168, 215, 217
Fellman, Major 177, 178, 183, 184, 188, 189,
    190, 214
Fifth, US Armoured Division 149
Frank, S/Sgt Ripperdam 81
French Vosges, 16
Fuller, Colonel Earl 79, 139, 140, 144

G

Gaulle, De 37, 39, 40, 95
Gavin, General 154, 198
George, Governor Wallace 205
Georings, Reichsmarshal 156
Gerow, General 32, 33, 39, 77, 78,
    82, 105, 125, 216, 217
Goebbels, Dr 25, 181
Grotte, Commander, Company Ralph
    66, 67, 72, 109, 214

H

Hanley, General 116
Hasbrouck, General 163
Hatzfeld, Colonel 81
Henbest, Col., Lt. Ross C 73
Henri-Chapelle 156
Hillingsworth, Lieutenant 214
Himmler 53
Hodges General 51, 77, 79, 82, 105, 122,
    149, 155, 156, 164, 216, 217
Horthy 52, 55, 134
Hosingen 139
Hoover, E J 127
Huffmeier, Admiral 25, 27, 29, 30, 31, 32, 39
Hughes, General Everett 68
Huie, Bradford William 14, 15, 18, 59, 88,
    107, 111, 118, 119, 127, 128, 129,
    132, 157, 166, 170, 173, 179, 180,
    185, 186, 190, 191, 192, 195, 197,
    204, 205, 206, 207, 208, 217
Hulten, Karl, 199
Humel, Captain 177
Hurd, Lt Wayne 73, 76, 109
Hurtgen, Forest 16, 51, 61, 65,, 77, 78,
    84, 87, 93, 97, 105, 106, 107, 109,
    116, 117, 118, 120, 124, 125, 128,
    139, 140, 146, 170, 216, 217

I

Infantry, 109th 44, 61, 85, 128, 192, 193
Infantry, 109th Regiment 193
Infantry, 109th Regiment. 16
Infantry, 112th 79, 81, 106, 163
Infantry, 112th Regiment 72, 109
Infantry, 112th regiment 33
Infantry, 1st Division 154
Infantry, 28th 32, 34
Infantry, 28th Division 16, 33, 37, 68, 179
Infantry, 28th Divisions 34
Infantry, 30th 51
Infantry, 9th Division 77
Ionia 58

J

K

Kean, General 216
Keitel, Field Marshall 56
Kimmelmann, Captain Benedict,
    42, 143, 144, 146, 148, 214, 215
King, Martin Luther 205
Kliemann, Emile 27
Koziak, Lieutenant, 183, 188, 189

L

Lincoln, Abraham 18
Lockett, Colonel 81
Luttwitz, General von, 139

M

Manteuffel, General von 93, 163
Maquet 148
Maquet, Paul 148
Marshall, Brigadier-General 18, 57, 191, 199
McAuliffe, General 146, 163
McCarthy., Senator 192
McCollum, Ruby 205
McKendrick, Sergeant Frank 170, 188
McNair, Gen. 35
McNeil, General 168
McWilliams, General 156
Meade, Fort 44
Meuse, River 55, 56, 97, 98, 100, 124,
       148, 149, 152, 155, 163
Meyer, Ist Lt. 29
Middleton, General 96, 97, 146
Milburn 169, 178, 179, 183
Milice 38, 94
Model, Field Marshall 42, 93, 216
Mollett, Sergeant 144
Monschau 36, 51, 149
Montgomery, Field Marshall 27, 28, 64,
       120, 125, 149, 151, 152, 153, 167
Morehead, Alan 43
Morrison, Private 180, 188, 197
Mortier, Caserne 122, 130
Moselle, River 199
Murphy, Audie 172, 173, 174
Mussolini 52, 55, 70, 103, 134, 150, 200

N

N, Leutnant 101, 103, 134, 135
Nesbit, Captain James 81
New, York Times 201
Nice, Radio 154

O

O'Brien., Pat 185
Odegard, First, Private Class Verner 37
Oise-Aisne 199
Orem, Private 115
Ortheuville 142
Our, River 139

P

Panzer, 150 Brigade 93, 99, 101, 103
Panzer, 150th Brigade 55
Panzer, 47 Corps 139

Panzer, 5th Army 93, 163
Parachute, 5th Division 144
Patterson 203
Patton 40, 63, 64, 71, 101, 120, 122, 125,
       154, 155, 163, 165, 204, 218
Peiper, Colonel 104, 124, 135, 201, 202
Pennsylvanian, 28th National Guard 44
Peron, Eva 202
Pershing, General 157
Petain, Marshal 38
Petersen, Colonel 79, 81, 82, 83, 84
Pruetzmann, General 52,53
Prum 78
Putz, Hermann 32

R

Regan, President 12
Regiment, 109th 106
Regiment, 10th 169, 170
Regiment, 110th 44, 80, 139, 141
regiment, 110th 146
Regiment, 112th 33, 82, 83
Regiment, 16th 154
Regimenta, 109th 66
Regiments, 112th 139
regiments, 119th 169
Rhine, River 77
Ripple, Colonel 82
Riter, Brigadier-General, B Franklin 168
Rohde, S/Sgt Heinz 10, 101, 133, 134, 149
Roosevelt, President 18, 27, 39, 52, 54,
       57, 63, 69, 95, 118
Rott 84, 85, 105, 116, 130
Rougelot 190
Rougelot, Major 189
Rudder 192
Rudder, Colonel James 87, 188, 192
Runstedt, Field Marshall von 33, 42, 184

S

St. Lo, 117
St Marie-aux-Mines, St 177, 178, 192
St Vith, 163
S/Sgt, Joseph Lash 69
Sauer, River 33
Scharnhorst, Battleship, 25
Schellenberg, General SS Walter 31
Schmettow, Count Von 25, 29, 30
Schmidtheim 134
Schoenberg 32
Schroder, Colonel P. 152
Schwarzkopf, Norman', Stormin 99
Seine, River 15
SHAEF 28, 69, 70, 71, 151, 179, 201, 217

Sheen, Colonel, Lt. Gordon 69, 70, 71, 93, 95, 104, 115, 135, 151, 165, 167, 200, 201
Sherer, Mary 28, 29
Shrimp, General Frank 178, 179
Sibret , Colonel, Lt. 106, 146
Siegfried Line 33, 36, 38, 51, 61, 65, 120, 149, 185, 193, 216
Simpson 122
Smith, (Chaplain), Colonel Ralph 180
Sinatra, Frank 166
Sixth, US Army Group 35
Skorzeny , Obersturmbannfuhrer Otto 24, 27, 40, 52, 53, 55, 56, 70, 71, 93, 94, 95, 99, 100, 101, 102, 103, 104, 124 134, 135, 140, 145, 149, 150, 151, 152, 153, 154, 155, 156, 165, 166, 167, 168, 171, 200, 201, 202, 218
Slovik, Margaret 59
Smith, Bedell 123, 126, 169
Sobolewski, Margaret 13
Sommer, Colonel Henry 84, 85, 87, 88, 109, 118, 119, 127, 128, 129, 215
Special, 50 Panzer Brigade 201
Speidel, General Hans 42
Spiegel, Der 101
SS, 1st 134
SS, 1st Battle Group Peiper 135
SS, 1st Panzer Division. 18
SS, 6th Panzer Army 55, 100, 104, 133, 164, 201
Stalin 27, 52, 95
Stars and Stripes 166, 170
Ste-Marie-aux-Mines. 191
Steiner, Madame 184, 188, 191
Strickler 140, 141
Strong, General Kenneth, 68, 69, 71, 151, 164
Summersby, Kay 39, 68, 120, 123, 125, 151
Swindle, Dwayne 12

T

Tankey, John 13, 16, 44, 45, 46, 61, 62, 66, 67
Thomas, Yeo 202
Tongres 155

U

US, 106th Infantry 163
US, 1st Army 135
US, 3rd Infantry Division 169, 172
US, 6th Army Group 178
US, 7th Armour 163

W

Wallendorf-Bollendorf 33

Washington, Post 11, 201
Wayne, Lt. Hurd 73
Weispfennig, Lieutenant 172
Wharton, General, Brigadier James E 64
Wilkow, Captain, 215
Wiltz 141, 144, 146, 184, 214
Winterbotham, Freddie 40
Woods, Captain Edward 87, 109, 110, 111, 141, 142, 214, 215

Z

Zygmont, Lt. Koziak 170